one way or another

ASIAN AMERICAN ART NOW

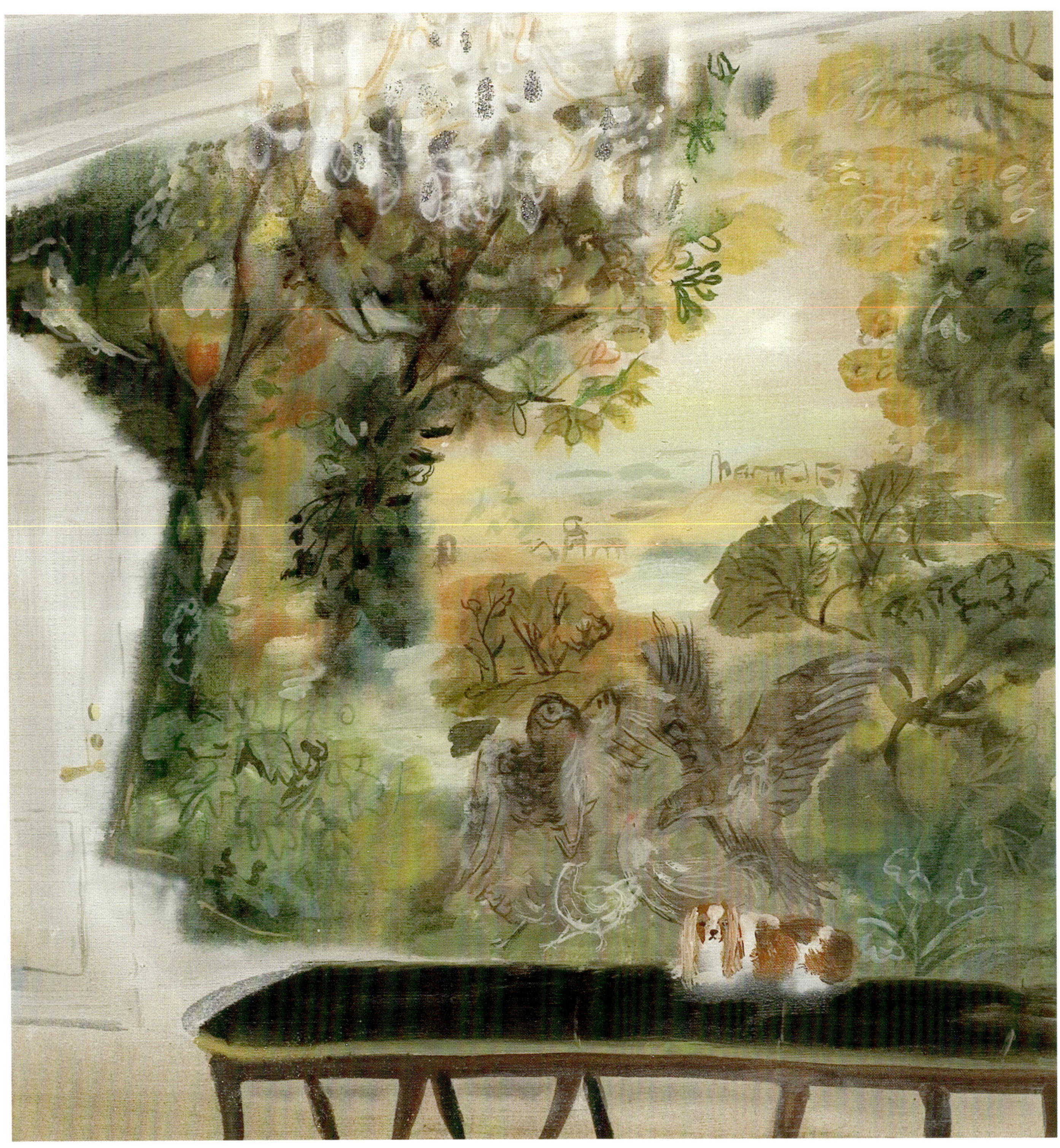

Mari Eastman, *Chelsea on Bench in front of Tapestry*, 2003. Acrylic, oil, glitter on canvas. 32 x 30 inches. Collection of Karyn Lovegrove and Peter Leak.

one way or another

ASIAN AMERICAN ART NOW

Edited by
Melissa Chiu
Karin Higa
Susette S. Min

With essays by
Margo Machida
Helen Zia

With contributions by
Atteqa Ali
Kóan Jeff Baysa
Aimee Chang
Doryun Chong
Tim Davis
Reena Jana
Miwako Tezuka
Christina Yang

Asia Society in association with
Yale University Press, New Haven and London

Published on the occasion of "One Way or Another: Asian American Art Now," an exhibition organized by the Asia Society, New York

Asia Society and Museum, New York
September 8–December 10, 2006

Blaffer Gallery, the Art Museum of the University of Houston
January 20–March 31, 2007

Berkeley Art Museum and Pacific Film Archive, University of California
September 19–December 23, 2007

Japanese American National Museum, Los Angeles
February 9–May 2, 2008

Published in the United States by
Asia Society
725 Park Avenue
New York, NY 10021

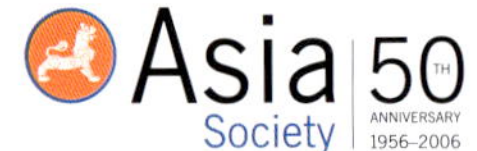

Distributed by
Yale University Press
P.O. Box 209040
302 Temple Street
New Haven, CT 06520-9040
www.yalebooks.com

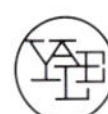

ISBN–10: 0–300–12059–1
ISBN–13: 978–0–300–12059–2

Library of Congress Control Number:
2006930702

Curators: Melissa Chiu, Karin Higa, Susette S. Min
Assistant Curator: Miwako Tezuka
Project Manager: Marion Kocot
Designer: Miko McGinty, assisted by Rita Jules
Copyeditor: Mary Chou
Printer: Friesens Corporation

The exhibition and publication are made possible with generous support from our lead sponsor Altria Group, Inc.

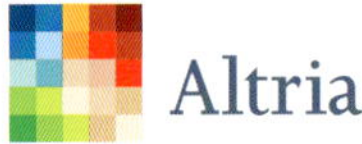

Additional support for the exhibition is provided by the W.L.S. Spencer Foundation, Nimoy Foundation, and Asia Society's Contemporary Art Council.

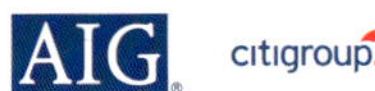

Cover illustration: Mika Tajima, *Grass Grows Forever in Every Possible Direction* (video still), 2004. Fabric, photo print, tape, amps, guitars, fluorescent lights, video projection, performance. Dimensions variable. Collection of the artist. Photograph by Mika Tajima, courtesy of the artist.

PRINTED IN CANADA

Table of Contents

PREFACE

Melissa Chiu

"One Way or Another: Asian American Art Now" occurs nearly forty years after the birth of an Asian American consciousness from the civil rights movement and a decade after the Asian American art movement of the early 1990s. Much has changed, and continues to change, for Asian American artists today. This exhibition was born from a desire to evaluate an Asian American sense of self in this new environment. It is not based on a treatise but instead centers on the work of seventeen artists living in New York, Los Angeles, Chicago, Atlanta, and the San Francisco Bay Area.

The exhibition is presented during Asia Society's fiftieth anniversary celebrations. Founded in 1956 to further the understanding of Asia in the United States, Asia Society has long provided a platform for the discussion and presentation of Asian American issues. Asia Society's first ever contemporary art exhibition, "Asia/America: Identities in Contemporary Asian American Art" in 1994 heralded a commitment to contemporary art as seen in major exhibitions organized by Asia Society over the past ten years. "One Way or Another: Asian American Art Now" is one part of this strategy to integrate living artists into Asia Society's programs and activities. This exhibition and accompanying book should be considered a part of the growing body of scholarship in the field of Asian and Asian American art history.

One of the main challenges in the initial phase of planning for the exhibition was determining how it should be curated. It became clear that a single voice might limit the scope of the project so a curatorial team was assembled with Karin Higa, Senior Curator of Art at the Japanese American National Museum in Los Angeles, Susette S. Min, Assistant Professor of Asian American Studies and Art History at the University of California, Davis, and myself. Much discussion at the outset of the project assessed the efficacy and potential contributions of such an exhibition. Susette Min's essay title in this book, "The Last Asian American Exhibition in the Whole Entire World," reflects some of these early discussions. I was surprised by how well we were able to work together, spending the greater part of a year meeting, seeing exhibitions, and visiting artists' studios. What came out of this process was a decision to focus on the work of artists born mostly in the late 1960s and 1970s in the United States, representative of a younger generation. Few if any of these artists participated in the Asian American art movement of the early 1990s. In contrast to an older generation of artists whose works largely drew substantial connections to Asia through a diasporic longing for a previous homeland, the artists in this exhibition rarely depict an overt connection to Asia; associations, however, do surface in different, sometimes subtle ways. To an extent, these artists have the freedom to create works that have multiple references depending on the social and political context in which they are viewed. The exhibition is not intended as a definitive presentation of Asian American art but rather, a continuing examination of what it might mean to be an Asian American artist.

The authors of this book establish a framework for seeing this generation as part of a larger cultural shift. Helen Zia's essay, "Asian American: An Evolving Consciousness," provides an account of how the relationship between the Asian American community and the state has been defined by immigration laws. She describes key "flashpoints" in this history from Vincent Chin's death to Margaret Cho's television show *All American Girl*. Margo Machida's essay, "Reframing Asian America," offers a comparative view between the circumstances around the exhibition she curated for Asia Society in 1994, "Asia/America: Identities in Contemporary Asian American Art," and the current exhibition, "One Way or Another: Asian American Art Now." Susette Min discusses the theoretical implications of multiculturalism today and its impact on Asian American art scholarship while Karin Higa writes on her involvement in the collective Godzilla and her experiences during the Asian American art movement. My own contribution to this book is a conversation between leading scholars, curators, and artists who articulated numerous issues through personal anecdotes. In addition, we commissioned brief entries on each artist by Atteqa Ali, Kóan Jeff Baysa, Aimee Chang, Doryun Chong, Tim Davis, Reena Jana, Miwako Tezuka, and Christine Yang.

My fellow curators, Karin Higa and Susette Min, deserve recognition for their unique vision and perspective, which contributed greatly to making the show happen with good humor and generosity. Thanks also to the artists whose works and individual expression are central to the exhibition; their enthusiastic participation in this project will be a great contribution to the study of art in times to come. I would also like to thank the lenders to the exhibition for their support.

In the museum, I would like to thank Marion Kocot, Assistant Director, for managing all aspects of the exhibition and especially the book production with unending patience; Miwako Tezuka, Assistant Curator, who oversaw the exhibition with great attention to detail and a commitment to the idea of the exhibition; Clare McGowan, Associate Registrar and Exhibitions Coordinator, who attended to all the challenges in the creation of new works; Clayton Vogel, Installation Coordinator, whose sensitive design of the exhibition and installation allowed the art works to shine; and Mary Chou's essential work on the images, copyright, and texts for the book. Also crucial to the project are Nancy Blume, Head of Museum Education Programs, who created education programs for the exhibition, and Hannah Pritchard, who has provided administrative assistance. Others at Asia Society who should be thanked for their support include Jamie Metzl, Executive Vice President; Rachel Cooper, and Linden Chubin's creation of public programs to accompany the exhibition; Elaine Merguerian and her team on publicity and marketing; and Todd Galitz and Julie Lang for their fundraising efforts.

"One Way or Another: Asian American Art Now" is an exhibition that will tour across the United States. I would like to acknowledge Terrie Sultan at the Blaffer Gallery, University of Houston, for expressing interest early in the development of the project. Kevin E. Consey, Director, and Constance Lewallen, Senior Curator for Exhibitions, at the Berkeley Art Museum and Pacific Film Archive, University of California as well as Irene Y. Hirano, President and Chief Executive Officer, and Karin Higa, Senior Curator of Art, at the Japanese American National Museum for their commitment and support of the exhibition. The exhibition will have a life beyond New York, in Houston, Berkeley, and Los Angeles.

The exhibition project is funded, in part, with major support from Altria Group. Additional support for the exhibition is provided by the W.L.S. Spencer Foundation and Nimoy Foundation. AIG is the lead global sponsor of Asia Society's fiftieth anniversary year. We also appreciate the support of Citigroup, a sponsor of Asia Society's fiftieth anniversary year.

INTRODUCTION

Melissa Chiu, Karin Higa, and Susette S. Min

"One Way or Another: Asian American Art Now" brings together seventeen artists from across the United States, who, for the most part, were either born in the country or grew up here during the 1970s. The title of the exhibition is drawn from the 1978 Blondie hit and reflects the increasingly visible influence of popular culture on their works, which are grounded as much in American culture as Asian culture. In fact, our discussions with artists and other leaders in the Asian American and arts communities revealed a greater multiplicity than ever before: multiple positions as well as multiple ways of describing an arts practice. It appears as if the momentum behind what appeared to be a unified and, at times, collective art movement in the 1990s has dissipated and been replaced by a greater emphasis on individual modes of working. The conception and organization of this exhibition illustrates such a shift. This exhibition is not conceived as an account of any single art movement or trend but instead, shows each artist's work as an individual response to various influences.

As curators, we were faced with an exciting, though at times daunting reality: the large number and wide range of engaging and exciting artists working throughout the United States. "One Way or Another" does not purport to be a survey of this dynamic proliferation—frankly such a goal would exceed the resources of any single exhibition. Rather, the exhibition aims to suggest the startling array of practices employed by Asian American artists today, working primarily in three locales: Los Angeles, New York, and San Francisco, with a smattering of artists from other areas. Aside from being major nexuses of art—with arts ecologies of schools, galleries, museums, and collectors—these regions also have significant populations of Asian Americans and the attendant resources serving these diverse communities.

Our process was simultaneously systematic and open-ended. We began by looking at hundreds of slides culled from various institutional resources, including the Bronx Museum of Art's slide file, which has a national range. We consulted colleagues throughout the country. Individually and in various configurations, we visited countless nonprofit venues, galleries, and museums to see work "in the flesh." In some cases, we were overt in our search, stating our purpose outright. Our greatest realization was also a source of disappointment: there are far too many strong and promising artists to include in a single exhibition. After an eighteen-month period of looking at art by Asian Americans, we can safely assert that the multiplicity of practices evidenced in "One Way or Another" represents a sample, albeit one we vigorously endorse, of the work being produced by Asian American artists today. This exhibition offers many opportunities to gain new complex understandings of Asian American art.

Thanks to all of the institutions and individuals who offered professional assistance, intellectual inspiration and valuable insights, especially, Russell Ferguson, Eungie Joo, Christine Y. Kim, Kristine Kim, Kris Kuramitsu, Elizabeth Smith, Julie Rodrigues Widholm, Eugenie Tsai, and Lydia Yee.

Most importantly, we thank the wonderful artists whose engaging works continue to enrich the field of Asian American art.

Melissa Chiu, Karin Higa, and Susette S. Min
Exhibition Curators

ASIAN AMERICAN: AN EVOLVING CONSCIOUSNESS

Helen Zia

There was once a time, not long ago, when "Asian Americans" did not exist. The very idea of Asians who could be American was inconceivable—indeed, repugnant—to politicians, pundits, and the public at large. This, in spite of Spanish chronicles from the early seventeenth century about established communities of Chinese in North America, or the Pacific migrations from Asia and Polynesia which anthropologists date back to many thousands of years. But since the reality of Pacific crossings from Asia and the Pacific Islands didn't match a master narrative invested in the Atlantic, the stories of those early Asian migrants have been largely ignored, even deliberately repressed, and rendered missing in history.

The inability to conceptualize "Asian Americans" continued until 1968, when young activists on the campuses at San Francisco State University and the University of California, Berkeley named themselves, proclaiming their existence to the world. They recognized that the act of defining themselves as Asian Americans was revolutionary, emblematic of the radical movement that sent young activists into Chinatowns, Little Tokyos, and other communities where they created storefront nonprofits and nongovernmental organizations—some remain today as established community institutions (fig. 1). It's no wonder that the first wave of Asian American art as part of that declaration was bold and brash, a conscious statement of self-determination intended to break through the years of imposed invisibility.

Since that historical proclamation of Pan-Asianness, much has been written on the limitations of lumping all the peoples and cultures of Asia in America into one clumsy category.

Some argue that the more natural or authentic affinity is through ethnicity, immigrant or refugee status, class, generation, language, or other cultural markings. Others reject this umbrella grouping altogether, on the grounds that this unwieldy combination is a modern device of political expediency.

There is merit to such critiques, but the lumping-together process began far before those Yellow Power activists, harking back to the horse-and-buggy days, when the only people granted full personhood were those who came from across the northern Atlantic Ocean. Those whose roots pointed toward the Pacific Ocean were simply "Orientals," "Asiatics," "Mongoloids," or worse. Even though their lives were centered on this continent, they could never attain "American" status when federal law prohibited anyone of Asian ancestry from becoming American.

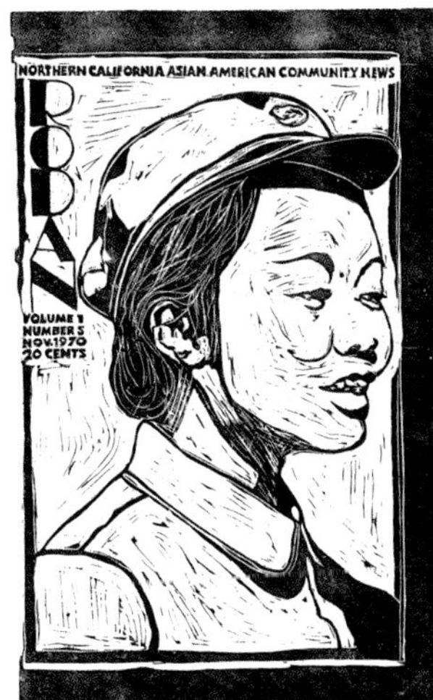

Fig. 1. Linoleum block print of Pat Sumi, one of the political leaders of the Asian American movement, by Saichi Kawahara, 14 x 11 inches. Printed on the cover of *Rodan*, an Asian American movement newspaper published in San Francisco, November 1970 issue.

A very few Asian immigrants managed to become U.S. citizens before the exclusion laws were enacted. Yet they continued to be viewed as perpetual foreigners and when the anti-Asian federal laws were enacted, they were "denaturalized"—stripped of their citizenships and denaturalized retroactively. Singled out in this way, "Orientals" became the first "illegal aliens" of the United States; mobs of white "real Americans" used violence to rid the United States of any Asians during that terrible "driving out" time. The population of Asians in the United States fell dramatically. Enfranchisement and participation in this democracy was inhibited until 1952, when the last of the nineteenth-century exclusion laws were finally repealed. Even in Hawaii, the Asian and Pacific Islander majority, which has had to contend with more than 100 years of genocide, colonial occupation, plantation economy, and exclusion had no access to political representation until 1959, when it received statehood.

—

Until the Asian American movement came roaring into the 1960s, Americans of Asian ancestry held a perpetual alien status for centuries, which relegated them to the fringes of society and subjected them to racist hate-mongering and threats of violence. To survive, some Asian Americans adopted the defensive posture of the colonized as a means of survival in a hostile environment, choosing the path of invisibility and not "making waves," hoping to stay under the radar of racism. Even today, some people believe that Asian peoples and cultures are *by nature* passive, docile, and apolitical—a notion easily countered by pointing to the rich history of vocal political resistance in Asia. Yet even in the presence of blatant racism, these early Asian Americans raised families, resisted their persecutors in the courts and on the streets, and created distinct communities, institutions, and cultures. They made lives in the United States in spite of being forced into the shadows by a society that nakedly and intentionally denied their full personhood.

When the various federal exclusion laws against immigrants from Asia were finally repealed, the 1952 U.S. Census reported only 500,000 Asian Americans living in the entire country—less than one-tenth of one percent of the American population. With most Asians and Pacific Islanders concentrated in urban ghettoes, ethnic enclaves, and the islands of Hawaii, they were virtually invisible in mainstream America. Then, beginning in the mid-1960s, a series of monumental events set in motion changes that altered the country—and transformed Asian America.

The first tectonic shift came with the passage of the Immigration and Nationality Act of 1965, which removed the race-based immigration restrictions that had kept Asian migration to a trickle even as European migrants came pouring in. The new law struck down the old policy of limiting immigrants from the "colored" countries to a hundred or fewer people per year. In contrast, the 1965 immigration policy stressed family reunification, with preference accorded to immediate relatives of current U.S. citizens. The motivation behind this approach was a direct result of the civil rights era, which exposed the bias of the old quota system and turned it into a source of international embarrassment for the United States. As Representative Philip Burton (D-CA) said in Congress in 1965, "Just as we sought to eliminate discrimination in our land through the Civil Rights Act, today we seek by phasing out the national origins quota system to eliminate discrimination in immigration to this nation composed of the descendants of immigrants."[1]

Yet no one, not even the law's advocates, anticipated the subsequent sea change; indeed, most tried to downplay any potential demographic impact. Senate Immigration Subcommittee Chair Edward Kennedy (D-MA) reasoned, "First, our cities will not be flooded with a million immigrants annually. . . . Secondly, the ethnic mix of this country will not be upset. . . . [The bill] will not inundate America with immigrants from any one country or area, or the most populated and deprived nations of Africa and Asia."[2] As he signed the bill at the foot of the Statue of Liberty, President Lyndon Johnson said, "This bill we sign today is not a revolutionary bill. It does not affect the lives of millions. It will not restructure the shape of our daily lives."[3]

When asked in 1965 about possible immigration from India, Secretary of State Dean Rusk said, "The present estimate, based upon the best information we can get, is that there might be, say, 8,000 immigrants from India in the next five years."[4] Senator Hiram Fong (D-HI), asked a similar question about an influx from Asians, replied, "Asians represent six-tenths of 1 percent of the population of the United States . . . The people from that part of the world will never reach 1 percent of the population . . . Our cultural pattern will never be changed as far as America is concerned."[5]

We can now look back in amazement at how massively wrong they were. In the first five years after the law's enactment, 27,859 Indian immigrants arrived and their numbers continued to increase, so that by 1993, immigrants from India totaled 558,980. In 1960, the census counted 877,934 Asian Americans; by 1970, the numbers had doubled to 1.4 million. By 1980 the numbers doubled again from the last census to 3.4 million—well beyond the one percent mark predicted by Senator Fong. In the 1990 census, there was another doubling to 7.2 million as Asian Americans were designated the fastest growing minority group. Today, Asian Americans and Pacific Islanders exceed 14 million, more than 4 percent of the U.S. population, a far cry from the days of invisibility, when the population was not even six-tenths of one percent.

The stunning population growth did not all flow from the 1965 immigration act. The end of the U.S. war in Vietnam in 1973 brought nearly 1 million refugees from Vietnam. Continued turmoil and warfare in the region turned Cambodians, Lao, Hmong, Mien, and others into refugees as well. Congress passed the Indochina Migration and Refugee Assistance Act of 1975 and then the Refugee Act of 1980, adopting the broader United Nations definition of refugee status and creating a separate admissions policy for refugees. Another law, the Amerasian Homecoming Act of 1987, brought about 100,000 Amerasian children—the offspring of American GIs—and their Southeast Asian mothers to the United States. All told, more than one million Southeast Asians came to United States after 1975. After the Tienanmen Square crackdown in China, tens of thousands of Chinese political refugees were admitted. In addition, the numbers of international adoptions from Korea continued to grow, with more than 100,000 children adopted since the end of the Korean War in 1954. These events are part of the global amalgam that forms the collective experience of the post-1965 generations.

—

It is impossible to overstate the impact that the combined influx of the new immigrants and refugees had on the nation as a whole and Asian Americans in particular. The shift from 877,934 in 1960 to over 14 million today has been a transformation of immense magnitude. At first the changes were subtle, almost imperceptible. Many of the new Asian Americans were absorbed into the vast suburban landscape, especially those professionals with the advanced degrees and skills preferred by the new immigration policies, while the resettlement policies governing the refugees emphasized dispersal throughout the United States, often to rural communities or poor urban neighborhoods.

Perhaps the first visible signs of change were the restaurants, shops, and signage of the new immigrants: chaat and pho, sushi and kimchee, pad thai and lumpia, nail parlors, donut shops, gas stations, motels. For example, in 1971, a tiny Chinese restaurant simply named "A Kitchen" opened at a gas station in the New Jersey hinterlands. The fact that it shunned chop suey fare and instead served a far less familiar Beijing-style cuisine created such a stir that the *New York Times* reported on it and droves of New Yorkers made the long trek to Princeton to stand in line for one of the thirty-two seats. The impact on other Chinese Americans, who came from far and wide to have an authentic down-home restaurant meal, not altered for *lofan* tastes, was electrifying. Few of those diners in search of a novel cuisine could have imagined they were witnesses to the demographic revolution in progress.

Less benign flashpoints were inevitable when refugees and immigrants unfamiliar with U.S. culture, language, or people located or were placed in monochromatic communities where Asian Americans of any stripe were rare sightings. A report by the Massachusetts Attorney General's Civil Rights Division in 1983 noted numerous racially motivated assaults against Southeast Asian refugees; "Often, [they] cannot even walk along the public streets without being physically attacked and threatened because of their race or national origin."[6]

Just as the civil rights movement gave rise to such bold legislation as the Immigration and Nationality Act of 1965, so it inspired the Yellow Power activists who gave Asian Americans a name. The convergence of these developments—the blossoming of an Asian American consciousness, the building of an Asian American infrastructure, and the tremendous growth of an increasingly diverse population—set the stage for the dynamic formation of new communities, organizations, institutions, and cultural forms to meet the needs of the post-1965 migrants. Among them were visionary artists, poets, filmmakers, writers, dancers, actors, musicians, and others in every medium who, through creative expression, translated the profound metamorphosis that enveloped our communities.

In New York, the Basement Workshop opened on East Broadway in the early 1970s, providing a locus for artists and their political expression through magazines, newspapers, poster art, and murals. Asian CineVision, Asian American Arts Alliance, Pan Asian Repertory Theatre, and other institutions all sprang from this tremendous activist energy. A similar cultural revolution took hold in Los Angeles, San Francisco, Seattle, Philadelphia, Minneapolis, and Honolulu—wherever the Asian American spark found creative voices waiting to ignite.

It is not surprising that so much of that art was outspoken, politically daring, and in-your-face direct for anyone who might not get the message that "We're Asian, we're here, get used to it!" After centuries of having no name or other accoutrements of humanity, Asian Americans were finally claiming ourselves, and there was no reason to make the declaration quietly.

Indeed, there were those in the "mainstream" of the United States who either could not comprehend or flat out rejected the notion of an Asian American people—such as the white autoworkers who beat Vincent Chin to death in 1982 and the judge who freed them with a sentence of probation. Even the Michigan American Civil Liberties Union (ACLU) and the local National Lawyers Guild defended the judge's actions; they reasoned that Asian Americans are not entitled to protection by civil rights laws because, firstly, Asians weren't in the United States when these laws were drafted in the 1860s (wrong!), and secondly, we do not experience racism or discrimination. The director of civil rights for the United Auto Workers union even told a group of Asian American community activists that if Vincent Chin had been Japanese instead of Chinese, he would have deserved to be killed.[7]

Asian American artists of multiple media captured the story of Vincent Chin through songs, poetry, plays, sculpture, paintings, poster art, T-shirts, performance art, films, and dance. Singer/performer Charlie Chin, singer/law professor Chris Iijima, playwright Cherylene Lee, artist Nancy Hom, documentary filmmakers Christine Choy and Renee Tajima-Peña, composer and pianist Jon Jang, as well as Latina sculptor Consuelo Echeverria and T-shirt designer Blacklava—these are but a few of the noted artists who have created works on this single incident (fig. 2). Their subject, by its very nature, is overtly political and intended to wake people up to the possibility of Americans of Asian descent.

Even as the dynamic evolution of Asian American communities intensified in the decades following the Asian American movement and the Immigration and Nationality Act of 1965, these enormous changes remained largely invisible in popular, mainstream culture. Instead, "yellowface" portrayals by white actors unconvincingly disguised as Asians continued to be common fare on TV programs like *Kung Fu* or Broadway hits like *Miss Saigon*. Except for works by Asian American playwrights like David Henry Hwang and Philip Kan Gotanda, real Asian actors were still forced to perform such demeaning roles as Long Duk Dong (Gedde Watanabe) or obedient, sexless sidekicks like Kato (Bruce Lee) and Mrs. Livingstone (Miyoshi Umeki).

Even national headlines about Asian Americans in the 1990s—rare and noteworthy as they are—seem distant now: the burning of Koreatown in Los Angeles, the campaign finance inquisitions on Asian Americans, the hunt for China spies, the first appointment of an Asian American to a president's cabinet—or Margaret Cho's *All American Girl*, the first TV show featuring Asian Americans. Anything happening before 1985—let alone before 1965—may as well be ancient history to those born after the immigration revolution began.

These days, with a population of 14 million and growing, the post-1965 generations of Asian Americans have grown up with a confidence in themselves that comes with the increased numbers and visibility unknown to previous generations. Within their families and communities, they have proudly maintained their Asian language, customs, and culture, without the level of fear of discrimination or shame that existed in the past. Many have lived in neighborhoods, communities, even entire suburbs, centered around the many diverse Asian American cultures—with access to community service and advocacy organizations, with in-language, culturally-specific media, retail districts, and shopping malls. Communications with and travel to Asia take place much more easily and less expensively now than in previous decades, adding to the sense of a global, transnational society. While Asian American role models in popular mass culture remain abysmally few, at least they exist—from astronauts and cabinet officers to world-class athletes and award-winning performers and artists. In other words, for post-1965 generations, the social attitude is significantly more visible and affirmative to their Asian Americanness.

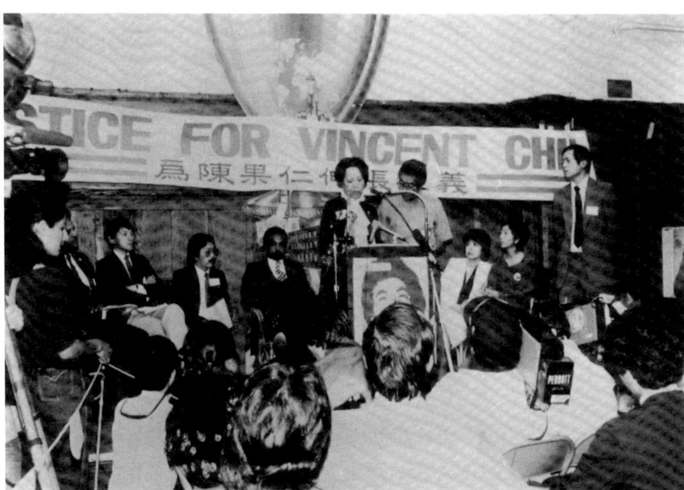

Fig. 2. Christine Choy and Renee Tajima, *Who Killed Vincent Chin?*, 1988. Color video. 82 minutes.

Such broad strokes require some big caveats; they are meant only to show the qualitative leap Asian Americans have made in our own self-awareness. Our existence is still largely unrecognized by diehards who cannot see beyond the Eurocentric master narrative of America or the white-black paradigm of race or those who adopt the post-9/11 fundamentalism of the "good" and "real" American versus the "evil" foreigner. Pointing out the transformational changes and advances does not validate the myth of the model minority, the dominant stereotype of Asian Americans to emerge from the post-1965 era. The notion that Asian Americans are the "good" and successful minority that never complains (and has nothing to complain about), unlike the "bad minorities," has done great harm and injustice to our communities. For example, the Asian Americans and Pacific Islanders in Philanthropy reports that a miniscule 0.4 percent of philanthropic support goes to Asian American communities; it is likely that funding to Asian American arts follows a similar pattern.

The impact of the model minority stereotype on Asian American self-worth is two pronged: first, there is the expectation that Asian Americans are bound to succeed and outperform other groups, especially in the sciences, technology, engineering, math, and business. Asian Americans who are not good at math or otherwise not inclined toward such subjects (artists and writers, for example) find little support or encouragement. Asian American college students often end up with double or even triple majors—molecular biology to satisfy the parents, the arts to nurture themselves. Second, there is the anxiety and stress that accompanies the fear of not living up to the considerable expectations of family and society; for example, the alarming rates of depression and suicide by Asian Americans frequently go undetected and untreated because, after all, the "model minority" has no problems. To be an Asian American in the arts is so obviously and deliciously subversive, undermining both external stereotypes and internalized expectations.

—

When I lecture on such topics, I am often asked this question: If Asian Americans must live with a stereotype, isn't it better to be the model minority than the evil enemy "gook" invader or other noxious types? My reply is, no, it is not better. Our humanity extends far beyond one or two simplistic cartoon characters that ultimately lead to the same invisible and emasculated status in society. The quantum leap for Asian Americans will be to break out of such one-dimensional chains and to allow ourselves to breathe, stretch, and grow into any dimension we choose to define for ourselves; this is infinitely preferable than being forced to choose from one or two stereotypes. Rather, more expression of every kind is the antidote to the invisibility and silencing of the times before 1965.

This, I believe, is where the post-1965 generations are today in this long march towards an Asian American critical mass: the door has opened into a broad landscape of ever-increasing possibilities to express the full range of our being. The long march is, of course, far from over, especially in the face of the anti-Muslim, anti-immigrant repression that has fallen so heavily on Arab and South Asian Americans. It is a reminder that the 1965 immigration revolution was born out of the civil rights movement—a connection that is not always understood by the newer generations of immigrants and refugees who came as a result of that great struggle. It matters little whether today's Asian Americans make overt reference to this richly textured past or not, whether they wave the banner of AZN pride or decide to take some other path. Together, they are creating the space for the multitude of stories that have brought us to this point.

There is no turning back as the next generations of Asian American artists step forward to show the myriad ways of declaring themselves in their work and revealing new facets in the personhood of Asian Americans. Such is the opportunity before Asian American artists today—to express themselves in whatever creative forms they choose. As they add their marks to the rich textures and tapestries of society, we all stand to gain and revel in the freshness of their visions.

Helen Zia is the author of *Asian American Dreams: The Emergence of an American People* (FSG: 2000) and coauthor of *My Country Versus Me* (Hyperion: 2002).

1. *Congressional Record*, August 25, 1965, 21783.
2. U.S. Senate Committee on the Judiciary, Subcommittee on Immigration and Naturalization Washington, D.C., February 10, 1965, 1–3.
3. Lyndon B. Johnson, *Public Papers of the Presidents of the United States*, U.S. Government Printing Office, Washington, D.C., 1966, 1037–40.
4. U.S. Senate, Subcommittee on Immigration and Naturalization of the Committee on the Judiciary, Washington D.C., February 10, 1965, 65.
5. Ibid., 71, 119.
6. Attorney General's Civil Rights Division. *Report on Incidents of Anti-Asian Violence* (Boston: Office of the Attorney General, 1983).
7. Author's notes of meeting with Joe Davis, Director of Civil Rights Division, United Auto Workers, May 1983.

REFRAMING ASIAN AMERICA

Margo Machida

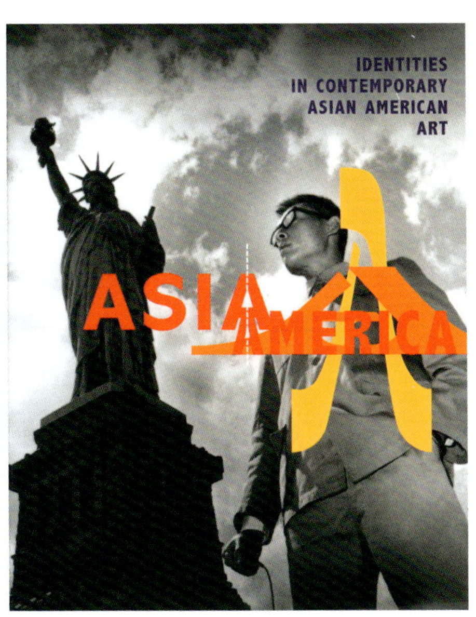

Fig. 3. Cover of exhibition catalogue, *Asia/America: Identities in Contemporary Asian Art*, 1994.

The sensibilities and predilections of every generation of artists and curators are shaped by the conditions, concerns, and conflicts of their times. In an evolving and still relatively nascent area like Asian American art, the narratives provided by contemporary exhibitions have an especially powerful impact on the ways in which that art is subsequently understood, and this in turn shapes the evolution of how artists and curators conceive of their own practices. "One Way or Another: Asian American Art Now" speaks to significant shifts that have occurred in the intellectual and ideological ground of Asian American art and cultural criticism since the early 1990s, when I organized "Asia/America: Identities in Contemporary Asian American Art" for Asia Society Galleries (fig. 3). With the far-reaching impact of critical theory, and feminist and postcolonial discourse on the intellectual climate, scholars, curators, and artists alike are increasingly self-conscious about the potential analytical and ideological pitfalls associated with projects that foreground race, ethnicity, and other markers of identity as frameworks in which to situate visual art and its producers. As they interrogate and challenge the premises upon which artists and their work are gathered together under collective rubrics like "Asian American art," they build on what is now a well established and highly elaborated body of critique surrounding the construction of identity, "othering," and the politics of representation.

Despite the considerable breadth and diversity of Asian American artistic production—in which visual artists, like their non-Asian contemporaries, have long produced work in every medium, genre, style, and subject matter—the subject of identity has nonetheless come to be closely associated with art and exhibitions produced in the 1980s and early 1990s, following the emergence of multiculturalism and identity politics as prominent issues in the American art world. By contrast, younger critics and scholars point to a generational shift that has taken place in the interim, contending that for those born since the late 1960s and 1970s, a host of other critical issues and artistic questions have assumed greater significance. Even for those artists who are concerned with questions of identity, their approaches are seen to be significantly different and often more oblique, rather than directly confrontational.

To signal a perceived rupture with the past, some commentators invoke "post-identitarian" or "post-ethnic" rhetorics. While this approach allows for a strong sense of dramatic contrast, it could equally be argued that many of the countervailing and often contradictory impulses on display in exhibitions like "One Way or Another" were already evident in the daring and inventive art produced by Asian Americans throughout the 1990s. Indeed, as the concerns and visualizing strategies of younger artists owe a great debt to their predecessors, there is considerable merit in considering today's complex currents in terms of a continuum of Asian American discourse in the arts—thereby recognizing what has always been a heterogeneous and unruly conversation marked by tension and contrary assertions. Whatever one's conviction, it is noteworthy that the often-contested theme of identity/identification remains a marker against which change continues to be measured—suggesting the lingering impact of these debates in shaping successive generations' concerns and reactions.

"Asia/America" was the first major exhibition of contemporary Asian American art mounted by Asia Society in 1994, under the leadership of then-Director of the Galleries (and now President of the Society) Vishakha N. Desai, herself a first-generation Indian American. Given that its prior focus had been on traditional Asian art and antiquities, this project represented an ambitious and risky departure for the institution. It signaled a desire to inaugurate a closer level of engagement with Asian American communities, and was accompanied by public programming in its two-year tour across the nation. During extensive early discussions, many thematic possibilities were considered, including a multigenerational exhibition. However, given the Society's longstanding involvement with Asia, and the profound effects that expanding globalization and the new post-1965 migration were having on the domestic Asian communities, in the end it was agreed that a project concentrating on contemporary Asian-born artists who lived and worked in the United States would provide a suitable premise for this first effort.

As a New York-based Japanese American independent curator and scholar, my research and writing during the 1970s and 1980s was primarily shaped by the intellectual and political matrix of cultural activism, ethnic studies, and U.S. multiculturalism. Taking part in the emerging Asian American community arts movement, I shared in my generation of activists' belief that the visual arts were a potent means by which formerly marginalized communities could document and project their histories and lived experiences into the civic realm, in their pursuit of collective recognition and social justice. Many of the early leaders of that movement were American-born second and third generation East Asians who found commonalities in being raised in this country, and often in struggling with institutionalized discrimination, racism, and ethnic stereotyping. At the time I was invited to submit an exhibition proposal to Asia Society, however, the expanding presence of foreign-born Asian artists and intellectuals (including a major wave from mainland China) was increasingly transforming the American art world and Asian American arts communities. Their concerns were being keenly felt by artists, scholars, and cultural activists alike, spurring the U.S.-born to respond to the changing domestic situation by finding fresh ways to engage with the newly arrived. Seeking to gauge the effects of this sweeping development, as it played out in individual expressive endeavors, the trajectory of "Asia/America" followed my efforts to stimulate open-ended dialogue with these foreign-born artists.

As a counterpart to "Asia/America," "One Way or Another" marks consequential developments that have taken place since the nineties—a period when growing numbers of cultural institutions and university art galleries mounted exhibitions of Asian American art[1]—while also providing an opportunity to develop a more relational understanding that allows not only for the recognition of differences but also for delineating important points of continuity in the concerns of different generations of artists gathered together under the aegis of "Asian American art" (however defined). Like historical and generational "book ends," both exhibitions allow us to fruitfully examine various strategies of representation and intervention, clusters of themes, and subjecthoods-in-formation emerging from the Asian American social and cultural landscape. The twenty artists in "Asia/America" were born between 1936 and 1965, and primarily came to the United States as teenagers or young adults. Most arrived within two decades of 1965, following changes in restrictive federal laws that opened this nation's doors wide to new Asian immigration. By contrast, the seventeen foreign- and U.S.-born artists featured in "One Way or Another," born between 1966 and 1980, came of age in this country amid the dramatic transformations of the post-'65 era, and, as the curators assert, primarily view themselves as American. Whereas the civil rights movement and major military conflicts in the twentieth century involving Asian nations and the United States (including World War II, the Korean War, and the Vietnam War) are within the living memories (and in some cases, personal experience) of a number of the artists in "Asia/America," for the younger artists such pivotal domestic and overseas events are comparatively distant from their immediate lives.

Incorporating a range of work, "Asia/America" showcased various strategies of self and collective representation that drew on multiple cultural and historical sources as well as different media, styles, and artistic precedents by twenty artists of East, Southeast, and South Asian descent. Through the lens of crosscultural identification and identity formation, "Asia/America" sought to shed light on how larger processes of global movement and interchange play out in the expressive transactions of artists who have used their work to negotiate their complex positionings as Asians living in the West, and their passages between societies. Seeking to foreground the ways in which artists conceive of their engagement with this society through specific works, the readings were based on my oral interviews and thus reflect the issues that each artist chose to bring forward in discussing her or his own work at the time. Influenced by the unconventional thematic model offered in Lucy Lippard's groundbreaking work, *Mixed Blessings: New Art in a Multicultural America* (1990), "Asia/America" was organized under four broad themes—Traversing, Situating, Speaking To and Of Asia, and East/West Interaction—each intended to delineate different processes by which artists engaged with this society, with their cultures of origin, and with sites of passage and settlement. A foundational premise of the research and selections behind the exhibition was that identities are fluid, multivalent, and continually being re-imagined through the symbolic interventions of individual artists.

While there were a number of group shows featuring Asian American artists during the 1980s and 1990s that also touched on subjects like migration, diaspora, identity, gender, and this nation's often troubled engagement with Asia and Asians, it appears in retrospect that the mounting of this thematic exhibition in a prestigious, New York-based venue (accompanied by an extensive catalogue) provided a degree of national visibility and sustained attention that ultimately made it canonical by default. Although never intended to assert that identity is the sole optic through which art is to be viewed, or to function as a definitive survey, "Asia/America" initially attracted and continues to draw acclaim and criticism for its particular framing of Asian American art during the early nineties. Reactions to the exhibition as it traveled across the nation were strongly polarized, both within and outside the Asian American arts communities. Among the many positive responses was a review noting that, "the work . . . doesn't emphasize identity politics in the national context so much as what [the] curator . . . refers to as a 'transnational cultural terrain.' [It] probes not the issue of race, but the cultural self, the layering of psychic trajectories that follows the geographic wanderings, which are a fact of life for increasing numbers of non-Westerners."[2] Conversely some Asian American viewers found that they had little in common with the artists in the show and rejected it for not enfolding a wider range of Asian nationalities, or for not speaking directly to the issues and circumstances of the American-born. More commonly, "Asia/America" was criticized for being exoticizing; for foregrounding sociology and politics at the expense of aesthetics; for interfering with audience responses by using explanatory wall labels; for dwelling on wrongs and mistreatment; for conflating the experiences of Asians with very different origins; and for emphasizing ethnic and racial difference as the primary basis of identity.

Yet with multiculturalism and identity-based art already being contested in many quarters of the mainstream art world and the academy, the mixed reception attending the appearance of "Asia/America" in 1994 was not surprising. Indeed, controversy had also surrounded "Black Male: Representations of Masculinity in Contemporary American Art" and "Bad Girls"—two other shows revolving around identity that were mounted in the same year by New York museums.[3] It followed a pattern already set by 1990, with the contentious response to "The Decade Show: Frameworks of Identity in the 1980s" and the overwhelmingly negative reaction to the 1993 Whitney Biennial, which featured political art and artists of color.[4] As with "Asia/America," there were viewers who certainly found validation for their own experiences in the art, even as such exhibitions were decried for being of marginal interest to mainstream audiences, for perpetuating stereotypes and rhetorics of victimization, and for endorsing negative views of American society or Western culture. Throughout, significant questions were raised over whether the language and social agendas of identity politics are meaningful in framing cultural production or instead delimit discourse and force artists into racialized or ideologically driven straitjackets.

Although Asian Americans during the 1980s were already expressing misgivings about the perceived limitations of having contemporary art labeled as ethnic-specific, this critical turn is best captured by the late art historian Alice Yang. She argues that curatorial practices which frame Asian American identities as a negation of, or as a corrective to, mainstream norms and stereotypes

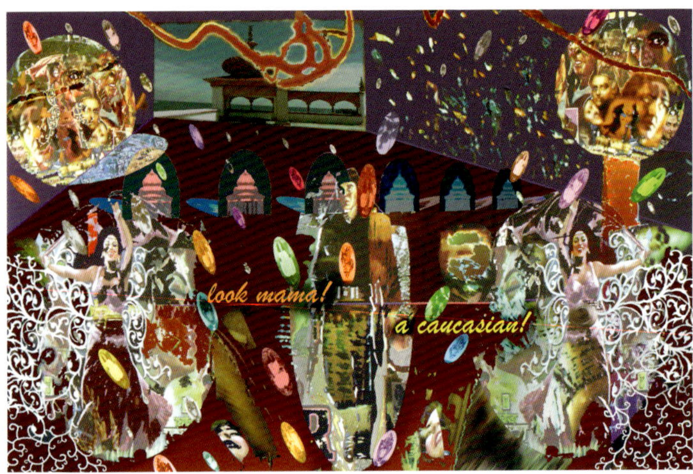

Fig. 4. Allan deSouza, *Mama India* (from the *Coconut Chutney* series), 1996. C-print. 26 x 38 inches.

tend to simply "reinscribe difference in the effort to circumvent it."[5] Yang asserts instead that the task is to shift the emphasis to reveal the multiple concerns that shape artistic practices, whether configured along axes of nationality, culture, religion, class, sexuality, or other points of affiliation. More recently, video artist Paul Pfeiffer has drawn a parallel between identity politics and consumer culture, likening the foregrounding of (group) identity to a type of commodification in which artists are encouraged to sell themselves by "act[ing] as ambassadors of their identities."[6] Amid such critiques are also temporizing voices. Despite his own ambivalence about terms like "Asian American art," artist and cultural critic Allan deSouza notes that although it would be expedient to claim that such a designation has "outlived its usefulness… there are questions unanswered, exclusionary practices left intact, and vistas yet to explore that still require some kind of model or platform from which they can be at least addressed even if not resolved"[7] (fig. 4). Rather than attempting to "pass as unnamed"[8] by abjuring any status other than that of the universalized "artist," deSouza asserts that declarations of hybridity and multivalency can provide a strategic means of asserting the various investments and identifications claimed by Asian American artists.

The impact of such shifts in critical awareness and efforts to reframe Asian American cultural production through both artistic and curatorial practices could already be seen in 1990s exhibitions like "The Curio Shop" (1993) and "Uncommon Traits: Re/Locating Asia" (1997–98). "Uncommon Traits" brought together Asian artists from North American diasporas—Americans and Canadians—under the umbrella of transmigration and shared transcultural circumstances,[9] while "The Curio Shop" explored the ways in which commodification, economic exchange, and local tourism in Asian urban communities in the United States have served to reinforce distorted and static notions of cultural authenticity.[10] Along similar lines, in the color photographic print *Mama India* (1996) from the *Coconut Chutney* series, Allan deSouza combines gaudy inserts from Hindi film posters with nineteenth-century ethnographic portraits of native types and images of the Taj Mahal Casino in Atlantic City to suggest the ways that European Orientalist visions of India are overtly celebrated and commodified in American popular culture.

A number of Asian American artists, including the photographer Pipo Nguyen-duy and filmmaker and photographer Marlon Fuentes, sought to directly link questions of social and personal identification to the mechanisms and systems of representation by which Asians and Asian cultures are known in the West. Both subversively reworked Western conventions: Pipo by inserting his own image into scenarios derived from classical European paintings and photographs of the nineteenth century American West, and Fuentes through textual and filmic fabrications such as *Bontoc Eulogy* (1996), a fictitious ethnographic documentary about the Philippines told from the perspective of an Igorot tribesman placed on display at the 1904 St. Louis World's Fair. Conversely, connections to an ethnic heritage can also be self-consciously constructed through the use of stereotypic sources. In the *Untitled (flip side)* series (1995), for example, American-born photographer Mimi Young fixes her attention on miniature ceramic figurines purchased by tourists from Chinatown souvenir shops. Others, like Byron Kim and Paul Pfeiffer, took different routes: Kim through the indirect referencing of diverse human skin tones in the large-scale geometric grids of paintings like *Synecdoche* (1992), and Pfeiffer by digitally removing the figures of African American boxers from historic footage of famous matches in the *The Long Count* (2000–01), thereby allowing elements beyond race and ethnicity (the audience, the ring, ambient noise, etc.) to come forward in the video and reshape interpretations of such events (fig. 5).

Moves to stake out fresh positions for an emergent generation of Asian American artists can be seen in a number of recent exhibitions. Among them are two multimedia projects: Centre A in Vancouver's "Charlie Don't Surf: 4 Vietnamese American Artists" (2005) and "Pirated: a post asian perspective" (2005) at San Francisco's Kearny Street Workshop. Viet Le, the curator of "Charlie Don't Surf," reflects that for younger Vietnamese like himself, the difficult years of war and its aftermath are often little more than an imaginative reconstruction devised chiefly through traces from film, video, and television images, alongside poignant family photographs and stories.[11] Nevertheless the show's re-articulations of that legacy provide a locus for fresh and provocative imaginings by successive generations of artists. Taking global and cultural piracy as their theme, the curators of "Pirated" address how material and symbolic goods are continually appropriated and manipulated by "global elites," ranging from European colonialists to the World Trade Organization and the World Bank. Their invocation of "post Asian" echoes rhetorics of "post-black" art, while simultaneously seeking to solidly situate the exhibition in an Asian American landscape.[12]

It goes without saying that all exhibition practice entails a selective framing whose organizing principles and end results emerge from a highly collaborative editing process involving the individual curator(s)—each with her or his own sensibilities, intellectual investments, and professional trajectories—and mediated by competing demands and interests, foremost among them the needs and expectations of a specific arts venue. Moreover, with Asians continually crossing and recrossing multiple boundaries—political, social, intellectual, metaphorical—no single master narrative, critical paradigm, or dominant discourse can truly be said to characterize and encapsulate the panorama of Asian American cultural production. Every Asian American exhibition, therefore, is inevitably a partial view of a particular time and place that provides a selective cross-section of that larger body of work. Provided that the substantial critical dissatisfaction with 1980s-style conceptions of identity and identity politics already evident prior to "Asia/America" is acknowledged, there is value in framing the present artistic climate through a "now/then" paradigm premised on recognizing an accelerated

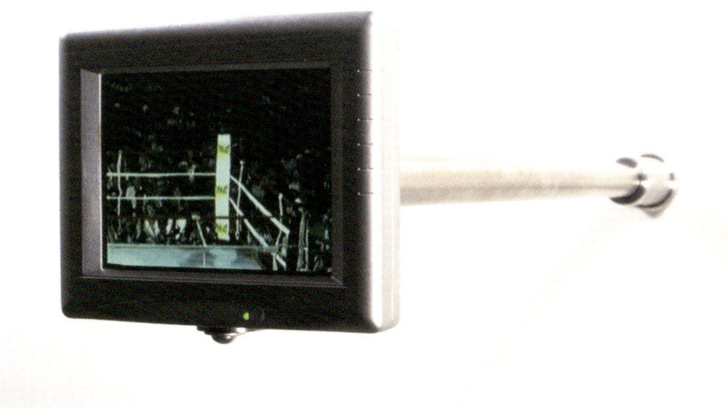

Fig. 5. Paul Pfeiffer, *The Long Count (Rumble in the Jungle)*, 2001. Digital video loop, LCD monitor, DVD player, and metal armature. 6 x 7 x 60 inches. Edition of 6, AP of 1.

shift in the questions, sensibilities, and expressions of a younger generation toward a sense of being in an open-ended, "post-identity" world. Conversely, what may distinguish many in the current generation of artists is not necessarily a thorough rejection of earlier Asian American discourse, but the degree to which the concerns and efforts of their predecessors—alongside a grab bag of other cultural and life-based personal choices—have been thoroughly integrated into their intellectual, emotive, and aesthetic repertoires and are therefore being manifested in less overt, even offhand ways. Nevertheless, critical discourse continues to shift. Currently some are raising the concept of a new "post post-identity" politics intended to test the critical limits of both identity politics and the strategic disavowal of identity and the refusal to be named.

While "Asia/America" foregrounded art that was mainly engaged with matters of identity and identification emerging from migratory experience, "One Way or Another" draws out certain distinctions between the attitudes and production of one generation and the next by selecting work that points away from or complicates such issues. Yet despite significant differences in orientation and curatorial methods (the present show was organized by a three-member team), these exhibitions share kindred features. Both have been originated by Asia Society, which remains strongly associated with Asia rather than being regarded as a museum of American art. While "One Way or Another" also includes artists of mixed heritages, both shows group artists together by Asian ethnicities, and enfold them in the rubric of "Asian American art." Indeed in order to take part in these exhibitions, artists must consent to being identified within an Asian-specific context.

Gathering varied works under common themes helps to focus attention around important moments in the ongoing evolution of the Asian American cultural imagination. By acting as a public locus of identification, exhibitions like "One Way or Another" and "Asia/America" allow for the formation of new lines of affiliation and spaces of transmission around which people may come together. Such projects, moreover, also point to the fact that grouping artists together based on shared perceptions of ethnicity, culture, or "Asian American-ness" does not necessarily contradict a critical recognition of internal diversity. Indeed, as philosopher José Medina has observed, drawing upon Wittgenstein's metaphor of familial resemblance, although members of a family may share certain traits, there are also significant variations among them. Since, as he maintains, "identity is bound up with difference," it follows that "all identity categories are intrinsically heterogeneous and necessarily unstable."[13] Accordingly, one may speak of collectivities without necessarily positing a totalizing homogeneity among individuals or their particular concerns.

A work of art involves a communicative act that projects its maker's ideas, beliefs, and experiences into the sphere of the social imaginary, where these images become part of a shared body of information through which we constitute our understandings of the present historical moment, our positions within it, and our relations to one another. Seen in dialogic and processual terms, the presence of art in the social realm opens communicative spaces that offer fresh and often unpredictable opportunities for making linkages with other peoples, events, and subjectivities, while also suggesting the vista of constructive possibilities waiting to be explored. In light of the spirited responses generated by "Asia/America" over the last dozen years, "One Way or Another" will undoubtedly contribute appreciably to this maturing conversation.

Margo Machida is Associate Professor of Art History and Asian American Studies at the University of Connecticut at Storrs, and Visiting Scholar in New York University's Asian/Pacific/American Studies Program.

1. Exhibitions during the 1990s include: "The View from Within: Japanese American Art from the Internment Camps, 1942–1945" (1992), "Relocations and Revisions: The Japanese American Internment Reconsidered" (1992), "Across the Pacific: Contemporary Korean and Korean American Art" (1993), "They Painted From Their Hearts: Pioneer Asian American Artists" (1994), "Picturing Asia America: Communities, Culture, Difference" (1994), "With New Eyes: Toward an Asian American Art History in the West" (1995), "Memories of Overdevelopment: Philippine Diaspora in Contemporary Art" (1996), "Uncommon Traits: Re/locating Asia" (1997–98), "Out of India: Contemporary Art of the South Asian Diaspora" (1997), and "At Home & Abroad: 20 Contemporary Filipino Artists" (1998). Each offers a different mode of framing Asian American artistic production, whether its orientation was historical, ethnic-specific, regional, transnational, or some combination of approaches.

2. Suni Chen, "Us Others in the Global Village," *Colors* (Minneapolis: Four Colors Productions Inc.) 4, no. 4 (July–August 1995), 54.

3. "Black Male: Representations of Masculinity in Contemporary American Art," 1994–95, Whitney Museum of American Art, New York, New York; "Bad Girls," 1994, New Museum of Contemporary Art, New York, New York.

4. "The Decade Show: Frameworks of Identity in the 1980s," 1990, co-organized by and presented with the Museum of Contemporary Hispanic Art, the New Museum of Contemporary Art, and the Studio Museum in Harlem; "1993 Whitney Biennial," Whitney Museum of American Art, New York, New York.

5. Alice Yang, "Asian American Exhibitions Reconsidered," in *Why Asia? Contemporary Asian and Asian American Art*, eds. Jonathan Hay and Mimi Young (New York: New York University Press, 1998), 97.

6. Paul Pfeiffer, "Paul Pfeiffer and John Baldessari in Conversation," in *Paul Pfeiffer* (Chicago: Museum of Contemporary Art, Chicago, 2003), 33.

7. Allan deSouza, "Name Calling," in *Tradeshow: New Currents in Recent Asian American Art* (Shanghai: c2 Gallery at the Pottery Workshop Shanghai, 2003), 2.

8. Ibid.

9. "Uncommon Traits: Re/Locating Asia" was a three-part exhibition organized for CEPA Gallery in Buffalo, New York running consecutively from September 13, 1997–March 28, 1998. It was co-curated by Marilyn Jung, Monica Chau, and Margo Machida.

10. "The Curio Shop" was collaboratively organized by members of the New York-based Godzilla: Asian American Art Network, and presented at Artists Space from February 18–April 3, 1993.

11. See Viet Le, "How Come Charlie Don't Surf?" in *Charlie Don't Surf: 4 Vietnamese American Artists* (Vancouver: Vancouver International Centre for Contemporary Asian Art, 2005), 7–12.

12. Samantha Chanse, telephone conversation with the author, January 10, 2006. "Pirated: a post asian perspective" was on view at Kearny Street Workshop from May 5–29, 2005.

13. José Medina, "Identity trouble: Disidentification and the problem of difference," *Philosophy & Social Criticism*, 29, no. 6 (2003), 657.

ORIGIN MYTHS: A SHORT AND INCOMPLETE HISTORY OF GODZILLA

Karin Higa

What was Godzilla? From 1990 until the middle of the decade, a shifting configuration of individuals committed to a broad notion of "Asian American artists" gathered under that name in New York. From a dozen people, it grew exponentially, even spawning offspring elsewhere. The underlying intent was simple but it had a catalytic effect: artists, writers, and curators with shared interests could band together, harness their intellectual and social networks, challenge each other, and take action to support art by Asian Americans.

My own association with Godzilla was short and intense, but because I was there at the beginning—not at its birth but early enough—I'm granted some measure of credibility as an OG (fig. 6). For a year or so, I was one of Godzilla's loyal partisans—not one of its leaders or visionaries, but a fervent participant. After I moved to Los Angeles to work with the newly formed Japanese American National Museum, I witnessed how Godzilla grew and flourished while its activities took on a near-mythic status among Asian Americans in the visual arts. Godzilla was proof that Asian American artists could be a force with an irreverent tone that counteracted an art world version of the model minority myth of Zen-inspired artists and venerable traditions. But by the middle of the 1990s, the changing social context necessitated different ways of conceptualizing the display and interpretation of art by Asian Americans. The proliferation of "identity-based" work developed into a conventionalized language, triggering a backlash, which unfortunately lumped divergent and distinct practices under a simplistic rubric. The early thinkers pursued other projects. There wasn't necessarily an official end to Godzilla. It just slowly petered out.

Looking back after more than fifteen years, I see how Godzilla—at least in its early incarnations—was even more radical in its concept of an Asian American arts practice than I understood at the time. The flimsy and scientifically unsupported notion of race may make any race-based alliance suspect, but Godzilla's loose structure, openness to diverse formal and conceptual artistic practices, and nonjudgemental stance to varying approaches of Asian American identity accommodated critique at the same time it strategically accepted notions of race as a pragmatic organizing principle. It was three artists—Ken Chu, Bing Lee, and Margo Machida—who met in July 1990 with the idea to form some kind of alliance to address the state of contemporary Asian American visual artists.[1] They understood that power within the field of culture aligned along

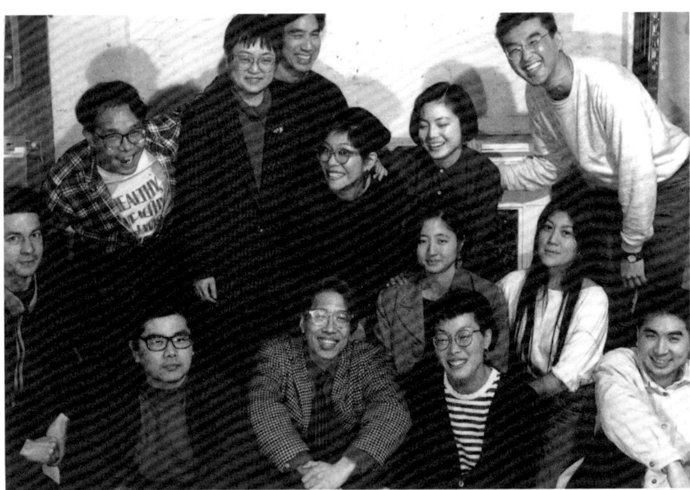

Fig. 6. Members of Godzilla; Standing left to right Arlan Huang, Margo Machida, Charles Yuen, Helen Oji, Janet Lin, Ken Chu; seated left to right: Colin Lee, Byron Kim, Bing Lee, Karin Higa, Eugenie Tsai, Tomie Arai, Garson Yu. Not pictured: Yong Soon Min, Mei-Lin Liu, Stefanie Mar.

axes of privilege where making art was only one part of the equation. Access to dialogue, venues for display, and engaged critical response were essential components of an arts ecology. The absence of any one part halted the cycle.

The politics of art rather than the making of art was therefore a central concern of the original organizers. The minutes taken from the first meeting at Margo's studio are revealing. Aside from their astute analysis of cultural race politics, that there were minutes at all suggests a seriousness of intent from the outset. Many of the things they discussed at the first meeting are still relevant today. They talked about the need for a library or archive that systematically collected material on Asian American artists, the wish for informed critics, the definitions of "Asian" versus "Asian American," an interest in ways of working outside of "majority" culture, and the need for institutional support—an Asian American art museum—to not only validate Asian American artists, but also to allow them to work outside of a de facto quota system operative among mainstream art institutions. Asian American artists had grown tired of being invited to participate in activities in May—Asian/Pacific American Heritage Month.

The interest in forming a museum no doubt derived from "The Decade Show: Frameworks of Identity in the 1980s," a messy and unprecedented three-part exhibition in 1990 coorganized by the Museum of Contemporary Hispanic Art, the New Museum of Contemporary Art, and the Studio Museum in Harlem that explicitly foregrounded explorations of race and identity in contemporary art, though at those early Godzilla meetings there were debates about the feasibility and ultimate desirability of duplicating conventional institutional structures. Two books were influential. Lucy Lippard's *Mixed Blessings: New Art in a Multicultural America*, a panoramic exploration of artists throughout the country, was staggering in the sheer breath and diversity of artists it documented. Lippard's role as an influential critic, whose ability to see and assess major moments in art as they were forming, validated an interest in artists of color at the same time criticism of the book showed how dismissive mainstream culture could be. In an approach quite distinct from Lippard's, the anthology *Out There: Marginalization and Contemporary Culture*, edited by Russell Ferguson, Martha Gever, Trinh T. Minh-Ha, and Cornel West with images selected by Felix Gonzalez-Torres, assessed cultural marginalization by examining underlying institutional and theoretical frameworks of difference through the various lenses of race, gender, sexual preference, and class. Yet a prevailing attitude is perhaps best summarized by a 1991 remark by Helen Frankenthaler. In reference to the National Endowment for the Arts's funding recipients, according to the *New York Times*, Frankenthaler "questioned whether the demand for cultural diversity and social consciousness in grant giving was subverting the criteria for artistic excellence"[2]—the implication being that cultural diversity and artistic excellence were mutually exclusive.

By the third meeting in September 1990, when I joined, the group had grown to include Tomie Arai, Mo Bahc, Arlan Huang, Byron Kim, Stefani Mar, and Yong Soon Min. Shortly thereafter, we decided on several things including the name Godzilla. Was it too "camp?" Would its Japanese origins inadvertently signal a predominance of one ethnicity rather than the pan-Asian American coalition we intended? Would we get in trouble for using a presumably copyrighted name? In the end, the monster's origins seemed the perfect metaphor.[3] After all, Godzilla wasn't even the monster's real name, but rather an anglicization of *Gojira*. His reemergence from the depths of the Pacific was tied to postwar American atomic intervention in the region. His celluloid existence was filled with Asian masses whose English words didn't match their lip movements and the primary vehicle for his dissemination was the mass medium of American TV. Nothing about Godzilla was authentically Asian. He was the ultimate hybrid monster.

A spirit of adventure, self-reliance, and collectivity characterized Godzilla's incarnation. Membership was conferred upon anyone who showed up. In the early months, the meetings were small, consisting of a dozen or so of us who met in the studios, apartments, or workplaces of whoever volunteered. While the organizational structure—such as it was—was flat, the unofficial leaders were Ken and Margo. It was pretty much agreed that Ken was the tallest Chinese American man anyone had ever met. His height, effusive intelligence, and goofy enthusiasm became an inspiring force. Margo brought an organizational rigor and seriousness to the group that helped maintain its focus. Both had the vision, the organizational savvy, and dogged optimism to channel divergent perspectives into a cohesive group. We didn't have uniform opinions about art and what forms it should take, but we did share an openness to engaged dialogue about art by Asian Americans.

Some of the more formative experiences for me were the small gatherings where Godzilla-ites and invited out-of-towners would make informal slide presentations about their work followed by discussion. It took little in the way of resources to organize but enacted the theory that we could learn by looking, thinking, and talking about Asian American artists. Allan deSouza, who then lived in London and had founded Panchayat, a group for South Asian and other artists of color in Britain, was one of the early visitors and provided an international perspective over a potluck dinner at Helen Oji's loft. This was later followed by visits from David Medalla and Mel Chin, though by this time the number of people that constituted Godzilla took us from private homes to borrowed public spaces in New York City like the Clocktower Gallery, Artists Space, and the Chinatown History Museum (now called the Museum of Chinese in the Americas). Panel discussions broadened the conversation. Pamela Lee, Eugenie Tsai, and Alice Yang talked about curatorial practice in a session moderated by Tomie Arai, who along with Kerri Sakamoto later organized a discussion on notions of "quality" and "Asian American aesthetic."[4]

One of the first public actions of Godzilla was to publish a newsletter "to establish a dynamic forum that will foster information exchange, mutual support, documentation, and networking among the expanding numbers of Asian American visual artists all across the United States."[5] The first edition was published in March 1991, with a design by artists Charles Yuen and Garson Yu. Each of us pitched in $40 to cover printing and mailing costs. Although a modest four pages, including listings of exhibitions, regional news, and short pieces on critical issues in the art world, the newsletter explicitly telegraphed a diverse approach to what constituted Asian American arts. While the Asian American community arts movements of the 1960s and 1970s were recognized as significant antecedents, what distinguished Godzilla's approach was its ecumenical approach to Asian American identity.[6]

In our current age of instant communication and the broad dissemination of information through electronic formats, it may be difficult to fathom how the initial printed newsletter could make such a radical impact, but it did. It was tangible evidence of the existence of Asian American artists and linked seemingly unconnected activities under a single rubric. The power of the printed word became even more apparent after Robert Atkins wrote a mere eight lines about it in his "Scene & Heard" column in *The Village Voice*,[7] which generated considerable buzz and gave Godzilla currency as something official. (In a sign of how much times have changed, it also included Ken's home phone number for those seeking more information.)

Atkins's column asked the question, "What if there are no Asian American artists in the Whitney Biennial?" Although the 1991 exhibition had yet to open, the artist list showed no Asian American painters, sculptors, or photographers, though Martin Wong was included in the installation by artist collective Group Material. After the exhibition opened, a working group consisting of Bryon Kim, Margo Machida, Yong Soon Min, Paul Pfeiffer, and Eugenie Tsai drafted a letter to the new Whitney Museum of American Art director, David Ross. It excoriated the Whitney for its conspicuous absence of Asian American visual artists: "We feel the Biennial fails to live up to its intention, as stated in the official brochure, of providing 'a framework for better understanding the diverse creative vitality that characterizes the art of this period.'"[8] In the fall, Ross invited a small group of us to meet with him. While at a basic level we talked of inclusivity and representation, our larger argument was more nuanced. Curators and museum professionals make

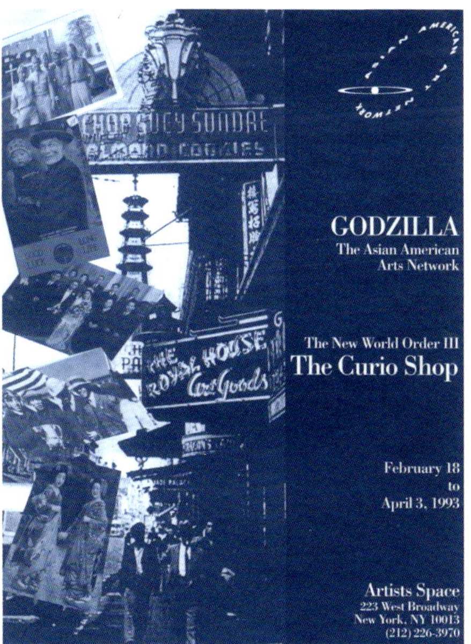

Fig. 7. Cover of exhibition brochure for "The New World Order III: The Curio Shop," February 18 to April 3, 1993, Artists Space, New York. Designed by Carol Sun, member of Godzilla.

value judgments that are based on spheres of knowledge. What if those spheres are limited because of race? Ross sympathetically and succinctly observed in our meeting that, "People tend to order what's on the menu." We proposed to expand the choices. We presented specific educational initiatives which included submitting slides of Asian American artists, organizing studio visits, and coordinating roundtable discussions. For many of us, the Whitney action was symbolic and strategic. It was not about a specific number of Asian American artists on an exhibition checklist; it was about unmasking the institutional and theoretical frameworks that limited what and how people could see.

There is nothing like controversy to generate interest. The June 1991 issue of *Art in America* covered our Whitney challenge in a small notice, "Guerrilla Girls Move Over?" The Godzilla meetings became large and heady affairs, attendance at which had a certain cachet. The newsletters, which came out irregularly from 1991 to 1993, grew in the number of pages and the ambition of content, due in part to the increased editorial involvement of Eugenie Tsai and Kerri Sakamoto. The early 1992 issue weighed in at 12 pages and featured extended reviews, expanded listings and regional news, and idiosyncratic musings like Abe Yoshida's, "Marcel Duchamp on Asian American Art," a half-page compilation of Duchamp's writings that *could* be about Asian American art.[9] In the same issue, Paul Pfeiffer's perspectives on "Out in the 90s: Contemporary Perspectives on Gay and Lesbian Art,"[10] a symposium at the Whitney Museum that included Ken Chu as one of the panelists, perceptively explored the intersections of sexuality, race, gender, class, and age, complicating a simple notion of Asian American identity.

In 1993, at the invitation of curator Connie Butler, Godzilla organized a major exhibition at Artists Space titled "The Curio Shop," coordinated by Godzilla-ite Skowmon Hastanan (figs. 7–9). The choice of the curio shop as an organizing framework for an exhibition of Asian American artists organized by Asian American artists contains several reversals. The curio shop in an Asian American context brings to mind Chinatowns, where non-Chinese can buy kitschy representations of supposedly authentic Chinese culture. But who's playing whom? The consumer with the buying power or the seller who plays with stereotype to move goods? Godzilla, as the organizer of the exhibition, seems to call attention to and implicate itself in the various and complex transactions between object and consumer, cultural producer and cultural performer.

The 1993 Whitney Biennial, now referred to as the "political" biennial, explored the issue of race head-on, beginning with Daniel J. Martinez's admission tags with single words that added up to the infamous statement, "I can't imagine ever wanting to be white." It also featured a number of Asian American artists. The next year,

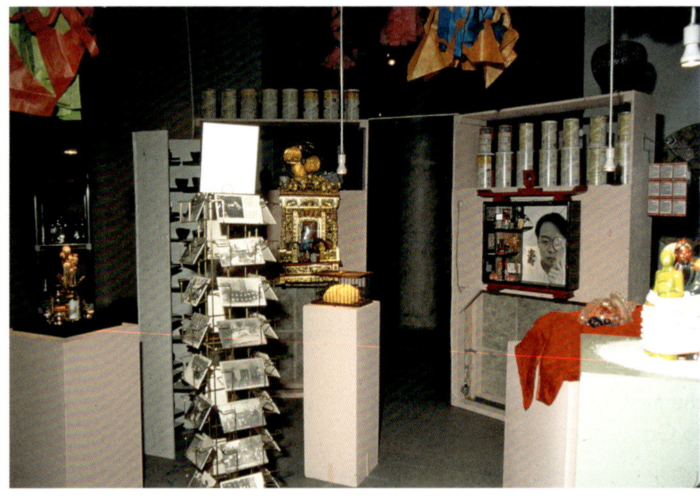

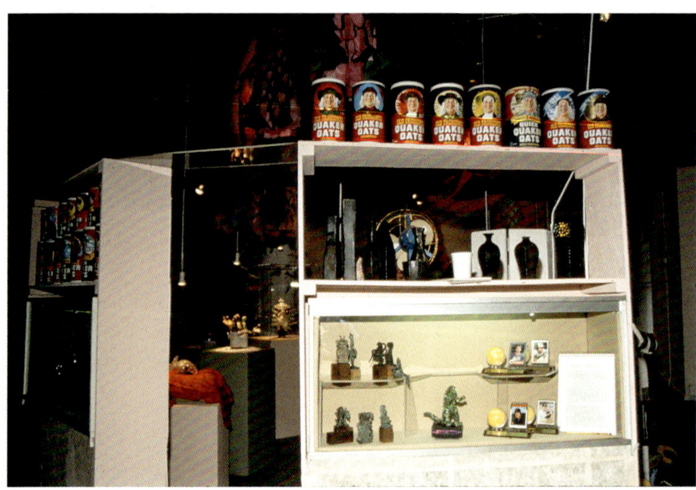

Figs. 8 and 9. Installation view of "The Curio Shop," organized in 1993 by Godzilla at Artists Space, New York.

in an unprecedented move, Asia Society held its first exhibition of contemporary Asian and Asian American art. Organized by Margo Machida, it focused on artists who were immigrants and their negotiation of identity as expressed in the narrative of their art. Two major institutions—one of American art, the other of Asian art—were foregrounding Asian American artists. Museums hired or expanded the responsibilities of Asian American curators: Eugenie Tsai at the Whitney, Alice Yang at the New Museum, and Lydia Yee at the Bronx Museum of the Arts. The Japanese American National Museum, a cultural history museum founded and run by Japanese Americans presented another paradigm of art and community. Before this period, it was commonplace for museums to have no Asian Americans on staff or no Asian American artists in their exhibition programs. For credible institutions today, this is inconceivable—a lasting impact of Godzilla.

Clearly, the context that propelled Godzilla had changed by the mid-1990s. At the same time, Godzilla seemed to change too, morphing from its earlier incarnations into a set of increasingly fixed positions. From both within the group and without, Godzilla and "Asian American art" came to signify a specific type of artistic practice rather than a set of artistic interrogations. "Identity-based" art took on a codified language and mode of exposition that Asian American artists were increasingly expected to manifest rather than the multifarious approach to Asian American identity and art central to Godzilla's origins.

In a 1992 Godzilla newsletter, Byron Kim obliquely addressed the burden of representation for an Asian American artist. As an abstract painter obsessed with the paintings of Ad Reinhardt and Brice Marden Byron wrote, "I'd like to make some large paintings exactly like Brice Marden's Grove Group. And I mean exactly like his. "These paintings would respond directly to those who ask me, 'Why are you making abstract paintings?' The 'you' meaning Asian-American-artist, artist-of-color, artist-with-something to say. Of course, my intention would be to make this line of questioning the inevitable content of the painting."[11] In a double critique, Byron challenged the implied assumptions in the query "why abstract paintings?" at the same time he hints at the expansive possibilities for complex content in the language of abstraction.

For me, "One Way or Another: Asian American Art Now" begins where early Godzilla left off. It takes a heterogeneous approach to artistic practice that defies the notion that there is such a thing as "Asian American art," at least one with a shared and cohesive set of formal or conceptual characteristics. Instead, there are Asian American artists from many different places who make different kinds of art. Yet the scientifically suspect notion of race remains a factor in the American experience. In a 2003 conversation with Eve Oishi, Patty Chang underscores the specificity that her race gives to her work when she appears; regardless of the other content in the video, Chang states, "I'm always doing an Asian woman."[12] What "Asian woman" or Asian American signifies today is what "One Way or Another" proposes to question.

Karin Higa is Senior Curator of Art at the Japanese American National Museum in Los Angeles.

1. Meeting Summary, July 25, 1990. From the personal archives of the author.
2. Cited in Byron Kim, "NEA Chief Reserves Denial of Grant to Mel Chin," *Godzilla* 1, no. 1 (spring 1991), 2.
3. Other names considered included "East West Works" and "Project for Asian Pacific American Art." Meeting Summary, September 14, 1990.
4. "Notions of the 'Q' Factor," *Godzilla* 2, no. 1 (summer 1992), 2.
5. "Open Letter to Our Readers," *Godzilla* 1, no. 1 (spring 1991), 1.
6. The section on regional news included reports of Vishakha Desai's recent appointment as Director of Asia Society Galleries, the Asian Pacific Islander participation at the AIDS Coalition to Unleash Power (ACT UP) benefit auction, Mayumi Tsutakawa's position with the King County (Seattle) Arts Commission.
7. Robert Atkins, "Scene & Heard," *The Village Voice*, April 2, 1991, 82.
8. The full letter and a summary of the events were published in *Godzilla* 1, no. 2 (winter 1991), 1–2.
9. Abe Yoshida, "Marcel Duchamp on Asian American Art," *Godzilla* 2, no. 1 (summer 1992), 6.
10. Paul Pfeiffer, "Out in the 90s," *Godzilla* 2, no. 1 (summer 1992), 4.
11. Byron Kim, "An Attempt at Dogma," *Godzilla* 2, no. 1 (summer 1992), 8.
12. Cited in Russell Ferguson, *Patty Chang: Shangri-La* (Los Angeles: Hammer Museum, 2004), 17.

A CONVERSATION ON TODAY'S ASIAN AMERICA

Melissa Chiu

This transcript records a conversation between Professor John [Jack] Kuo Wei Tchen, Associate Professor in the Gallatin School of Individualized Study and Director of the Asian/Pacific/American Studies Program at New York University; Lydia Yee, Senior Curator at the Bronx Museum of the Arts; and artists Laurel Nakadate and Patty Chang. The rationale for bringing these four speakers together was to assess questions and issues pertinent to working in the visual arts today, with specific attention on recent developments in the field of Asian American art. Asian American determination has a history dating back to the civil rights movement of the 1950s and 1960s yet any discussion of Asian American art today must acknowledge questions on the efficacy of a separate field of enquiry from American art. These questions come nearly a decade after the height of discussions on Asian American art, when artists were vocal about their visibility in the community as individuals and collectives, exhibitions on Asian American art were numerous, and museums and galleries showed the work of Asian American artists with greater regularity. One of the motivations behind this conversation is to set these questions in the context of issues on community, cultural memory, and art history that remain unattended and less discussed today than in the early 1990s. What is the current state of play for Asian American art and artists? The conversation below recognizes the very different political, social, and cultural climate today and provides an introduction to how leading thinkers within the community view these changes and how their respective work in the academy, museum, and individual arts practice responds to these shifts.

Melissa Chiu When we staged the exhibition, "Asia/America: Identities in Contemporary Asian American Art," in 1994 at Asia Society the debates surrounding the exhibition and discussion of work focused on identity politics. The exhibition occurred the year following the Whitney Biennial that focused on identity and multiculturalism and included the Asian American art collective, Godzilla. Our exhibition scheduled for September this year looks at a new generation of artists and how their approaches toward making art may or may not have changed from their predecessors in the early 1990s. We have focused mostly on artists who were born in the 1970s in order to get a clear sense of another generation since most of these artists would not have been exhibiting at that time. They are from the generation that has grown up in very different circumstances from their predecessors in the "Asia/America" show. Most artists were also born in the United States, which makes a clear break with the artists in the "Asia/America" show whose works were about issues of migration, diaspora, and dislocation. What we find with this selection of works from seventeen artists is a difficulty in categorizing the types of works they might produce. One of the criticisms of the "Asia/America" show was that the biographical details of the artists too heavily prescribed an interpretation of the artwork. What we wanted to suggest with this exhibition is that there are multiple ways that an artist might engage with being Asian or for that matter, being American. The exhibition is intended as a way of taking stock of what is going on today with the exhibition "Asia/America" forming both the backdrop and counterpoint. You have all been brought together for the different perspectives that you represent including scholarship and the academy, the museum, and practicing artists. Why don't we start with your perceptions of where and how we think things have changed from the early 1990s?

Lydia Yee The question for a lot of artists today is not so closely connected with identity and the immigrant experience. The list for your current exhibition is arguably a broader, more diverse group. Their works might not reflect their identity in any way. I also notice from a lot of the bios of younger artists today that you often can't tell their identity—on their list of exhibitions there are no Asian American or artists-of-color group shows. That said, I still think there is a need to make exhibitions that address the concerns of artists of color. The art world today is in many ways less conscious about the issue of diversity than in the 1990s; for example, the 1993 Whitney Biennial included many artists of color but the current Biennial has a small number.

There is a change in terms of how artists are positioning themselves; they don't have to say their work is tied to their identity and this frees their work to be read in different ways.

Lydia Yee

MC What can we deduce from this though? Does this mean things have gotten worse?

LY I think that race is and isn't an issue. If curators want to be colorblind and say that they don't think about these issues that's all fine and well but if you look at the checklists for a lot of big shows now they still include predominantly white male artists. The diversity may come in other areas such as where the artists live, but there is still a need to support artists of color and to find mechanisms to get their work out there.

MC From what you are saying there are two changes within this past decade. On the one hand it is how artists are positioning themselves and on the other hand the institutions have reverted back to the days before the focus on multiculturalism.

LY Yes, there is a change in terms of how artists are positioning themselves; they don't have to say their work is tied to their identity and this frees their work to be read in different ways. On the other hand, if you are not vigilant you could end up with a show of all white males. So we have to make sure that a diversity of perspectives is part of any exhibition.

MC Often in exhibitions it comes down to the curatorial vision but most importantly it comes down to the curators because they select the artists. Perhaps it is of greater importance to have curators who are from different backgrounds. Jack, are you seeing this happen in the academy as well? Is it a case that the institutional frameworks have not changed at all but the individual's response has?

Jack Tchen The demographics have changed things. We have more people who have been here longer so as a consequence things have changed. Just speaking for myself, my sixteen-year-old daughter is dealing with a range of issues that are different from what we saw emerge from the "Asia/America" show in 1994. The intensity and awareness was greater back then and with the culture wars there was a greater attention toward racialization, gender, and sexuality. It is not to say that immigration is any less now. As an historian I tend to think of a larger cycle. Just to be crude, at the moment of the nation's founding at the end of the eighteenth century, overtures towards Asia were seen in terms of trade through the lens of British and Dutch colonialism and other kinds of attitudes. Places like China and India were seen as wealthy court cultures that the elite here wanted to trade with, emulate, and gain favor with.
In the twentieth century, exclusion and marginalization was at its height. In 1924, the immigration laws clamped down on an idea of being 100 percent American. Now at the beginning of the twenty-first century we see China, Japan, and India in a very different light. These are the big cycles and within these big cycles a certain kind of envy or fear can emerge. It makes a difference in terms of where you are in the cycle as to how the art world or the art institution reacts and does or does not want to pay attention to Asian artists. I feel like institutions and artists are caught between these

shifts and what is possible and exciting at one moment might be rejected at another. To see these bigger cycles helps us avoid a sense of linear progression—an automatic march towards diversity. I don't think this is what has happened in this country. Foreign policy, for example, has been very subjective in the past, and has affected Asian Americans and immigration laws.

MC Patty, can you speak about your own experiences and your approaches? Your earlier works were about your family and I wonder what impact a sense of community—whether it be Asian American or not—has had on your work?

Patty Chang I guess I want to begin by saying that I started making work for myself at about the time of the "Asia/America" show so I feel like I matured at that time. I got all the benefits of it, but then I could go on to explore it in my own way which then dealt with being a physical performer. In the beginning, race and gender were a big part of my work. The focus on identity politics when I first came on the scene helped me to think through these issues and allowed me to use personal issues or ideas that came from my growing up in suburban white California. I guess this sense of difference was important to my work. You could describe it as two communities that had an impact on my work: my own Chinese family within the white middle-class suburb of California.

MC Do you think this had anything to do with you wanting to use your body in a performative fashion in your early works?

PC Yes, it might have had something to do with it. It was a process of working through the tension between these two communities butting up against one another in my mind.

MC Laurel, I have heard you speak about being much more comfortable in the Midwest than in New York when you plan your performance videos, especially with older men (fig. 10). Can you talk about this sense of community?

Laurel Nakadate I grew up in central Iowa. I trust midwesterners more, or perhaps I understand them better. I feel like I can trust my instincts and not worry so much about getting into trouble. I also think it is important that I make work in the Midwest because it is the place where I grew up and started to figure out my identity and how I fit in the world. The East Coast is more of a playground for me. In 1994 I was 18 years old and a senior in high school. I vaguely remember seeing the catalogue from the "Asia/America" exhibition and thinking "is being an Asian American artist to make

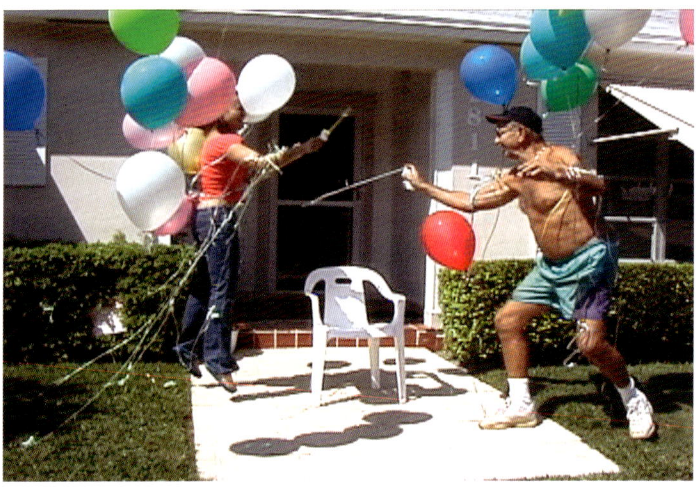

Fig. 10. Laurel Nakadate, *Untitled* (video still from *We Are All Made of Stars*), 2003. Video. 17 minutes, 20 seconds. Collection of the artist.

works about being Asian?" It was confusing to me. My dad is an American literature professor so I didn't grow up thinking I am Asian and I should be doing work about Asia. When I got to college my professors really pushed me to make work about being Asian but I kept on thinking, "I was born in Texas! What does that mean?" I am fourth generation American. My mother is white and my father Japanese. When I grew up that's who I was. It was not about being one or another. I don't see that the work I make is anything specifically about being Japanese but I do think that the more and more things I see, the more they can be related back. One example is the portraits I was making with different men I met on the street. At first I thought it was about girlishness and going out and finding lives to try on but then I remembered finding out that my great-grandmother was a war bride. These women had photos taken of them before they left—a photograph of them with the strange men they had just married. I then realized that these were the same kind of pictures that I was making. It struck me that I was making these pictures that I had never seen. But I didn't go into the project thinking that I would make these photos about being an Asian American woman.

JT It's really interesting to hear this. My daughter is half Chinese American and half Jewish so it's a little different. I grew up in the Midwest, born in Madison, Wisconsin. But I am wondering if those portraits are mere coincidence or if there is a trace?

LN I think it might be a trace. I am sure I heard my dad talk about these photos because he did a lot of family interviews for his own research. I am sure I must have overheard a conversation about them because the coincidence would be too much.

JT I grew up in the suburbs of Chicago. On the one hand it was comfortable and convenient but on the other hand it was very alienating. I remember my mother telling me stories about missing her home. She was part of another generation and I was the one born here. When I took my daughter to Shanghai, Hong Kong, and Beijing this past summer she was very curious but it is not the same relationship that I have to China. I don't talk about China that much—I talk about Asian Americans—so I am curious as to what traces she has received. Often there is a longing. Your father, for example, is sansei, so there might be unresolved issues with his parents or with the first generation that somehow has been carried through.

LN Absolutely—my dad doesn't speak Japanese. He spent his first year in an internment camp and did not learn to speak Japanese but his younger siblings, his two sisters, do speak Japanese because they were not in the camp and able to take lessons. He has a lot of resentment about that and it is the one thing that eats at him. I know I wish I spoke Japanese. I never had an opportunity to in Iowa. The strange thing is that my grandmother taught Japanese and ikebana and I didn't have her there to teach me these things. All the Asian Americans I have met of my generation are angry about not having learned these things.

My mother is white and my father Japanese. When I grew up that's who I was. It was not about being one or another.

Laurel Nakadate

MC There is a sense that knowing the culture where you came from or at least having access to it through language does arm you against feeling lost. If people say you are not American, even though English is your first and only language, then what do you have to fall back on? I always think that it might make it easier for some Asian Americans if they have some sense of an Asian language or culture so that they have choices.

LY Now with the world being so much smaller there are more opportunities to speak different languages. I also grew up in the Midwest and there were few chances to speak another language. The world has really changed. You hear so many different languages around the city.

MC Something that occurs to me also, right now, is the dissipation of collectivity, compared to the 1990s when artists were more willing to come together as a group. I tend to see more artists wanting to work as individuals. For example, Godzilla which was a collective succeeded by Godzookie, which did not operate in the same collective way. There is a sense of artists coming together but not in the same politically engaged way.

LY The art world has become very individualistic. A lot of it has to do with the market and the demands to find the next hot young artist. And of course you can't bring your whole posse to the dinner after the opening.

MC So you've seen this as well.

LY Yes, unless you are functioning as a collective, which is a very different way of working. There is so much pressure on the individual artist to perform. The artist's personal identity is tied up with his or her work. It is harder for art institutions, museums, galleries, and magazines to deal with and market the notion of a collective identity.

JT For me it raises an interesting question. If the first and second generations still have very strong connections to mutual obligations to family then I am curious about the tension between making the choice to be an artist with those sorts of obligations. And of course, negotiating the art world system and larger society, how people make choices or how they code switch according to the context.

MC Patty and Laurel, it would be good to hear from you about what it meant to make the decision to be an artist. And I say this in the context of Jack's comments which play into the idea of the model minority: that you shouldn't be an artist but a doctor or engineer to make your parents happy.

LN I was lucky because my father took the bullet for me. My grandfather was a doctor and wanted my father to be a doctor but he became an English literature professor. When I came along, my father said that as long as I was happy he was fine. There was never a problem.

LY But I bet your parents said you should get a Master's degree so you can get a teaching job on the side . . . (general laughter)

MC Perhaps it is also a generational issue here. The first generation arrives, works really hard and settles, the second generation has to get an education and become a professional while the third generation has a lot more freedom.

PC My parents came over as immigrants but they became professionals so maybe they jumped a generation for me. There was a half pressure for me to do something with my life. But perhaps because they straddled the two there were more options for me. I was just thinking though, out of my generation of cousins there are a lot who are in the arts, either writers or studying art and architecture. Maybe that's my family though . . .

MC Let's return to an idea of community. What was your sense of a community, whether it is Asian American or not?

LY For me, the professional and personal have been intertwined. I was fortunate to work at the New Museum in the early 1990s with people like Alice Yang. "The Decade Show"[1] had just happened so there was a culture about supporting the artist and a lot of my early professional and personal contacts came from that context. It was a support system, a network, a place for dialogue. I don't know where artists are getting that kind of sustenance today.

PC I don't really feel like I have ever officially been part of any community. I guess when I came to New York and started doing performance work I was involved in a downtown performance and film community. Maybe because I was immersed in it; there are only so many communities you can be involved in.

MC What are your thoughts on this, Jack? I remember at one of the symposia I attended at NYU last year, one of your students very proudly announced that the problem with the Asian American community was that there were not enough popular culture role models and what the Asian American community really needed was some films like the Godfather, in its portrayal of the Italian American community. Is this what you hear from your students and a younger generation?

PC But what about Bruce Lee?

MC I don't think this young man had even been born when Bruce Lee was at his height!

JT That student is trying to find male figures to identify with through his film work. It is true for a lot of my students now. The male students are really dealing with the absence of Asian men in the media so they are interested in creating their own heroic, masculine figures. I do identify with this generation even though I am a fair bit older. I was the first one in my family born here but also subject to midwestern suburban life in the 1950s and 1960s. I have been to suburbia, survived it, and left it, never to return. I feel that this life is one that some elements in society want us to return to today. There is a political battle going on right now that is not necessarily a march toward progress but a return to an earlier period that these people romanticize as being better for them.

MC What about this idea of role models? Who do you think they are for this generation?

JT I think the world is much smaller today. Younger people are drawing on film stars and pop stars more easily than before. A lot of my students are on top of Canto pop and things like that.

My relationship with China, which is where my parents were from, was formed through my mother talking to me about the place she left in 1949.

Patty Chang

MC But that's a change, isn't it? The role models are based in Asia, rather than in the U.S. The rise of Asia is on many people's minds today. The increased affluence and the emergence of a youth culture in places like Japan and Korea has had an enormous influence.

JT There is a process of going back and forth but I would say that this younger generation remains quite Americanized. They have more choices today than they once did. One source of frustration is representation in the media and I have seen some get quite upset by comments of various politicians circulated in the media since this is often where role models are identified.

LY New media has also shaped communities in new ways. There may have been more face-to-face contact before but now there are people we know whom we have never met.

PC When you started to talk about a network this is the first thing that came to mind. Networks have changed with the Internet, such as Friendster and those things, where you can start a community of people that you might never meet. It is about making connections.

LY It's about a contingent sense of a community—how you position yourself based on those one-to-one relationships within a larger group and how they are constantly shifting.

MC Another idea that comes from this is the potential for misrepresentation, to create new identities for yourself. This also strikes me as playing into your work, Laurel, because you have this community of people you interact with to produce your works. In fact you probably couldn't do what you do without these people.

LN You mean the different men I work with?

MC Yes, exactly.

LN I was trying to think if I have a network and who that would be made up of, beyond my peer group of MFA graduates. It is probably the men I meet and the other men they introduce me to. They don't always work out but sometimes you meet great people.

MC How do you maintain these relationships?

LN By telephone . . .

MC How would you describe the relationship?

LN I would say I have a relationship with three or four of them in New Haven who I see four times a year and then talk to them on the phone just as often. This year I got Christmas cards from some of them and it made me realize that they are really thinking about me.

MC So they know where you live?

LN Yeah (laughter) but I was very touched by this. You could see the shaky handwriting which was very endearing.

JT Is there a play between trust and wariness? Part of my family's experience is about that. Not knowing who to trust or who you can rely on, and that kind of thing.

LN Part of it is circling one another, figuring out where we stand and what the power dynamic is. The feeling of not knowing what is going to happen next and that each person is equally responsible for this.

MC I wanted to talk about the relationship between Asian Americans and Asia because we have seen much greater attention on Asia today than ever before and some in the Asian American community see it to the detriment of a focus on Asian American issues here. What are your thoughts on this? Maybe we should start with you, Patty, since one of your most recent works was titled *Shangri-La* and involved you spending time in China (fig. 11). Was this an idea of going back?

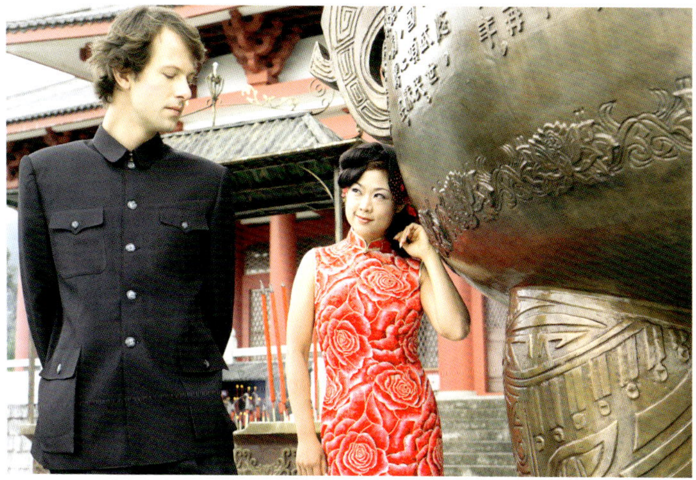

Fig. 11. Patty Chang, *Shangri-La* (Wedding), 2005. C-print. 11 x 16 inches. Edition of 5.

PC It was like going back, but it was not anywhere that I had ever been. My relationship with China, which is where my parents were from, was formed through my mother talking to me about the place she left in 1949. Her idea of China was frozen at this time. What I learned about it was not anything realistic. It was never going to be anything she said it was. Starting from the idea of going back to China, but also going to Shangri-La, a land that exists and does not exist was very appealing. It is a real place but it is based on an idea generated from outside China. Shangri-La is located in a small town in Yunnan province near the Tibetan border. The back story on this is that Shangri-La was based on James Hilton's classic book *Lost Horizon* but there is also a Chinese relationship where the place was reported during the Cultural Revolution as a utopia. There is knowledge of what Shangri-La might be. One town in the province began to call itself by this name, and then others followed in order to attract tourists. Then the government intervened to determine one place that was officially called Shangri-La. I went there for a few months. I was really viewed as a foreigner because they weren't sure if I was Han Chinese or not. This is a place where 30 percent of the population is a minority and they are opposed to the Han majority. It didn't make sense to them that I was Chinese American.

MC What about you Jack? You have some of the most direct contact with a student body. There is a trend for many Asian students to study here and then return to Asia, although the greatest impact is possibly the return of these students to Asia. There has not been a lot of work done on the impact of this influx of students on the Asian American community.

JT Well there is a much more mobile population than ever before which is tied to class and resources. It is an interesting time. How people use that cultural capital in one place or another varies on the possibilities or limits of that place. Some of those folks are committed to space building projects where they are trying to create platforms for communities and others are concerned with individual success. What I am finding is that there is less of a need to be Chinese or nationalistic, as was the case for my parents, but a desire to have more connections to people who share a commitment to politics or certain ways of working. For example, it might be a group of Filipinos who are doing a certain type of work or Hawaiians and Puerto Ricans who are doing another sort of work. We recently did some work with Reyum in Phnom Penh[2] and I think that the connections with what we do at the A/P/A in New York are closer than any idea of ethnicity (figs. 12, 13). There are now new possibilities to find networks of people who are not caught up in nationalistic ideas of identity but are interested in shared beliefs and practices.

What I am finding is that there is less of a need to be Chinese or nationalistic, as was the case for my parents, but a desire to have more connections to people who share a commitment to politics or certain ways of working.

Jack Tchen

MC Lydia, on a curatorial level, what do you think this focus on Asia means for Asian American artists?

LY It's a tricky thing because Asian American artists are not always seen as being Asian in Asia. And though the art world is increasingly international, I know a number of artists who have decided to move back to China because they are somehow seen as being more authentically Chinese and curators prefer to travel to Beijing, instead of going to Brooklyn, to do studio visits with Chinese artists. But I do think that artists of Asian descent have an opportunity to position themselves differently now. There is much more of an openness than ten years ago.

LN I went to Japan for the first time in 2005 and I did not feel the love. I am sure most of it was because I do not speak Japanese and that it was very difficult to navigate my way around and communicate. When Patty was talking about Shangri-La I felt like I had a similar experience in Japan, a place I had never been but somehow had a connection to. I wandered around by myself and stayed in love hotels.

MC It occurs to me that what we can say about the current state of things is that there is not the same sense of momentum towards defining a movement that we saw in the early 1990s but now we have a much more varied and by that, harder to characterize, community of Asian Americans. It's not something we talk about as a community anymore. We all have our own interests.

JT It is about recognizing the changing nature of our students for example. But at the same time, I am someone who believes in the idea of movements and social change.

MC So what are we in the midst of today? The non-movement?

JT It's not necessarily an Asian American movement but rather other movements. When I was recently in Hawaii I was observing some of the sovereignty questions and the complicated relationship that Asian Hawaiians have to indigenous Hawaiians and the shifting categories of how they identify themselves. That's an ongoing hotspot that is relevant to me and to a sense of being Asian American. I see it happening in different places, mostly outside of New York. My daughter is an artist and is not so much thinking about art as a collective enterprise, which is what characterized some earlier artists. She's thinking of art as a career. A lot depends on these issues as well and whether a movement can be built and sustained. I am fairly optimistic. I don't want things to get so bad just so a movement can develop. I see lots of awareness and efforts to do things.

LN I don't know how connected this is but lately I have seen the emergence of a whole generation of people coming together who are half Asian and half American. I know U.C. Berkeley has a huge half Asian club and Friendster has a group of half Asians. In some ways I have been sucked into this identity rather than an Asian American identity. It is like a third community out there.

MC I think that we will see this emerge as an important element to an Asian American community because there are other issues involved. In fact, I had originally wanted to write an essay on this subject but there are not enough artists yet who you could identify in this way. I do think that as this community matures we will see more artists.

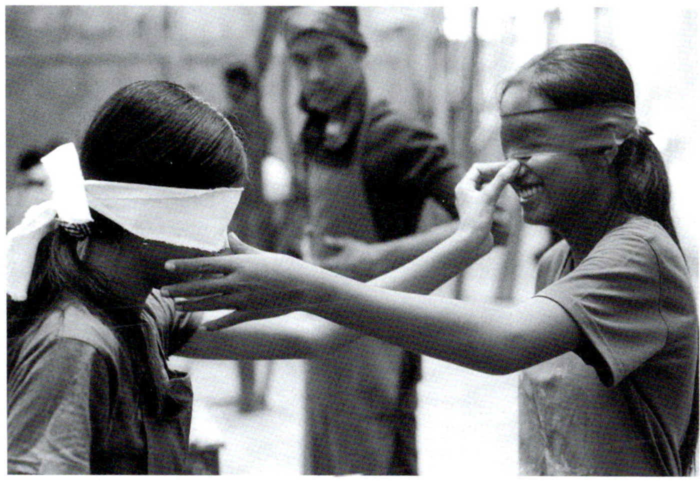

Fig. 12. Reyum Art School students sculpting each other's faces out of clay, June 2004. Reyum Art School Courtyard, Phnom Penh, Cambodia.

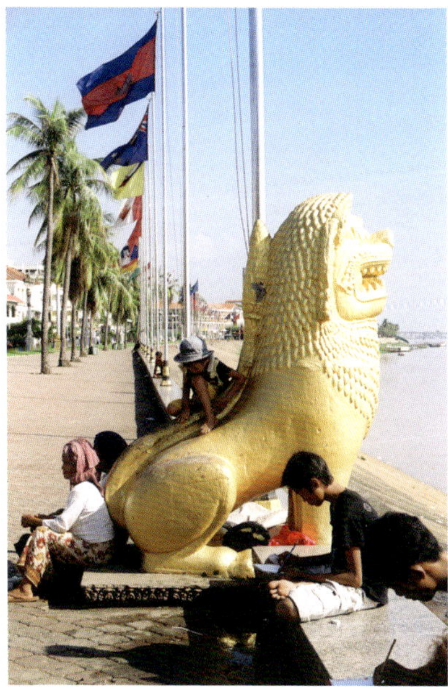

Fig. 13. Reyum Art School students drawing on the bank of the Tonle Sap River, July 2004. Phnom Penh, Cambodia.

JT In a more metaphorical sense, a lot of us are "halfies," a name used by one of my students. We may not appear to be but we really are. We should come out of the closet and admit this because we are caught between our parents thinking that we are never speaking the language well enough and our children thinking that we should teach them but we can't. In fact I am just as much a "halfie" as my daughter even though she doesn't see it that way.

LY In another ten years from now, maybe there'll be a "halfie" show!

MC I think this is a good place to end, on a prediction for the future. Thank you for contributing to this conversation.

Recorded Monday, February 27, 2006 in New York.

Melissa Chiu is Director and Curator of Contemporary Asian Art at the Asia Society Museum in New York City.

1. "The Decade Show: Frameworks of Identity in the 1980s," 1990, co-organized by and presented with the Museum of Contemporary Hispanic Art, the New Museum of Contemporary Art, and the Studio Museum in Harlem.
2. The Reyum Institute of Arts and Culture in Phnom Penh was founded in 1998 to promote traditional and contemporary Cambodian arts and culture (www.reyum.org).

THE LAST ASIAN AMERICAN EXHIBITION IN THE WHOLE ENTIRE WORLD

Susette S. Min

Blocks of bright red and green color in *Peking Inn, Memphis, Tennessee* (2004–05), transform the façade of a former roadside haunt into a place that is at once desolate and comfortingly familiar (fig. 14). Situated along cross-country and interstate highways, in between gas stations and fast food franchises, the architectural and cultural presence of Chinese restaurants has become a ubiquitous sight in the American landscape. These restaurants are an Asian American phenomenon that Indigo Som, the photographer of *Peking Inn*, describes as "the most pervasive manifestation of Chinese American presence in this country."[1] Som's road trip through the South is quintessentially American; a journey of alienation and loneliness interspersed with rare moments of joy, like the one shared with Taft Wong, a youth from Greenville, Mississippi. Som writes that it is while standing on the bank of the Mississippi with Taft that ". . . I get my sweetest glimpse of the essential beauty in that slowness."[2] It's not clear which slowness she is referring to—that of the river or of life—but keeping in mind her larger project, perhaps the "that" can be apprehended as an encounter with a person whom Som does not have much in common with, but experiences simply as a kind of being-with.

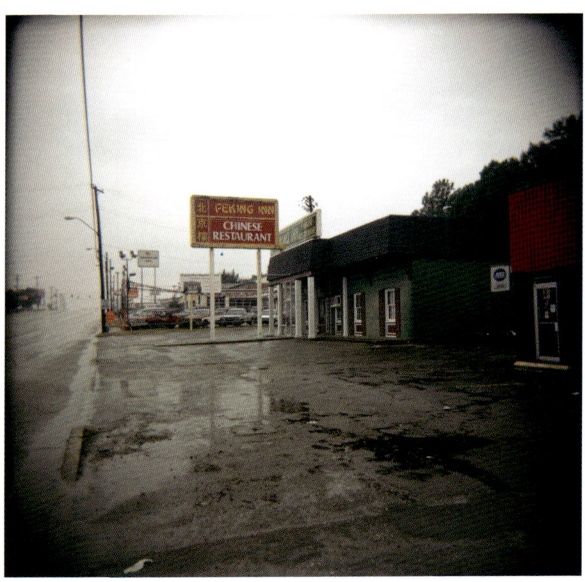

Fig. 14. Indigo Som, *Peking Inn, Memphis, Tennessee* (from the series *Mostly Mississippi: Chinese Restaurants of the South*), 2004–05. Digital pigment print. 34 x 34 inches.

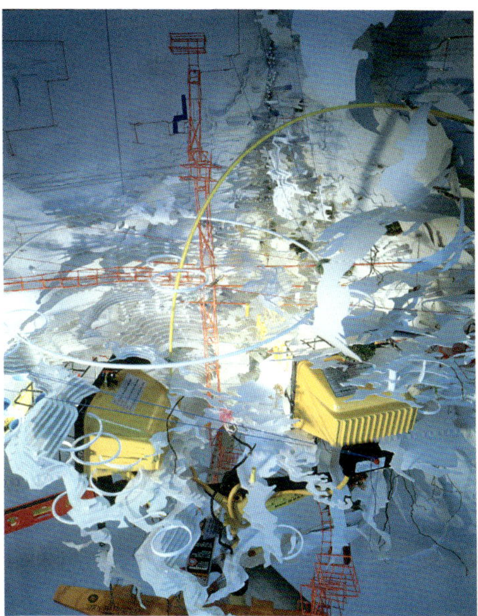

Fig. 15. Sarah Sze, *Hidden Relief*, 2001. Mixed media. 168 x 60 x 12 inches. Collection of Nancy and Stanley Singer, New York. Installation view at the Asia Society, New York.

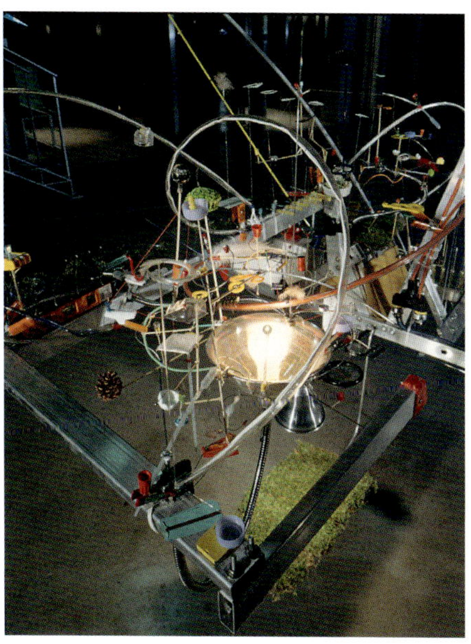

Fig. 16. Sarah Sze, *Everything that Rises Must Converge*, 1999. Mixed media. Dimensions variable. Collection of Fondation Cartier pour l'art Contemporain. Installation view at Fondation Cartier pour l'art Contemporain.

Nikki Lee, Do-Ho Suh, Paul Pfeiffer, Sarah Sze, and Rirkrit Tiravanija share unlikely artistic affinities, but all prominently belong to the contemporary art scene or art world (a nexus made up of art historians, gallerists, artists, curators, dealers, collectors, administrators, and art historians) (figs. 15, 16). Their works are frequently cited as examples in relation to art historical criticism on matters ranging from site-specificity to relational aesthetics. They are described as either "American" or cosmopolitan, or simply addressed as "artists." The high visibility of these Asian American artists within mainstream art venues inflects the need for exhibitions organized around Asian American identity and raises the following questions: If "One Way or Another" was the last specifically Asian American exhibition in the entire world, what might that mean? Would it mean that the era called multiculturalism is over? Would it mean that the art world has finally reached an understanding of "difference?" The idea of the Asian American artist transcending the specificities of his or her race and being treated with the same consideration as other artists whose work is supposedly evaluated by a universal set of criteria in a post-identity world, is not only premature, but a misguided ideal. Were this truly a post-multicultural world could we really see Asian American art with fresh and untainted eyes?

There is a desire, a wish to sidestep the sour effects of multiculturalism. To unmoor art from race is alluring. The desire to go beyond identity politics has been articulated since the early 1990s, but it has yet to happen. What follows are some thoughts on the critical labor of organizing exhibitions around identity; the phenomenon of identity-based survey exhibitions; and how "One Way or Another" fits in with these kinds of multicultural survey exhibitions. These thoughts are presented as an exercise that highlights the urgency, shortcomings, and possibilities of this model of curating.

Emerging out of the Asian American Movement, the naming or categorizing of art as Asian American began as a historical and sociopolitical project to challenge racial oppression, secure parity of representation, and represent the specificities and contributions of the Asian American experience. This project gained critical mass as it became visible on the national scene in the late 1980s through the mid-1990s with a series of exhibitions including "The Decade Show: Frameworks of Identity in the 1980s," "1993 Whitney Biennial,"

Fig. 17. Byron Kim, *Mom*, 1991. Oil and wax on canvas. 50 x 40 inches. Collection of the artist.

"The Curio Shop," and "Asia/America: Identities in Asian American Art,"[3] during a period that is now being referred to as the "multicultural" years.[4]

As a response to the Reagan-Bush years of the 1980s, which turned back some of the gains from the social movements of the 1960s, multiculturalism became the umbrella term under which various modes of discourse and culture highlighted the systemic discrimination by cultural institutions against women, artists of color, and queer artists. As a political force and strategy, multiculturalism mobilized those who were underrepresented to expose, confront, and unsettle structures and networks of power.

Art history will mark multiculturalism and identity politics as major influences on art and curatorial practice in the early 1990s, because it was during this time that a flurry of exhibitions focused on different aspects of the interlocking forces of race, sexuality, and gender, specifically, introducing to the art world as well as to the larger public a number of issues and artists previously excluded from major institutions and highly visible galleries.[5] For a very brief moment in time, multiculturalism became a meaningful category of analysis to explain the exclusion of artists of color as well as a motivation to interpret works of art beyond a prescriptive formalism.

The underside of exposing so many "new" artists whose work had never been seen led inevitably to the sustained acceptance of only a few Asian American artists into mainstream art venues and discourses. For some, this recognition came with a toll, as it not only foreclosed readings of the work aside from those focusing on race, but also required the artist to become a spokesperson or surrogate representative for an entire racial or ethnic community. For example, in the case of Byron Kim, whose monochromatic paintings (in particular portraits of his friends and family that cleverly alluded to the impossibility of rendering skin color) brought him to national attention, the aftermath was stifling (fig. 17). Despite attempts at presenting different kinds of artwork over the years, Kim described in his own words in 2003 that the 1990s chapter of his career was finally closed: "It is only recently that I don't think of myself as the skin-painting guy. So it has taken all this time, ten years, to get to that point."[6]

For others, the spotlight on race as the sole determining factor in considering Asian American art fixed that art within a representational economy, understood as a transparent portal into the social realities of the Asian American experience, and racialized it to such a degree that the category itself has provoked in many, but especially in Asian American artists, a range of public and private sentiments—from ambivalence to disenchantment to disavowal. Since the mid-1990s, some Asian American artists have felt the need to evade the dogged shadow of the label; for others, if this were the last Asian American exhibition on earth, their reaction I am sure would spell relief.

Many of the artists in "One Way or Another" have for the most part bypassed such preoccupations of identity to focus on their individual projects in which they have at their disposal, a wide array of art historical practices, popular cultural references, and local influences. What characterizes much of their art, as distinguished from its predecessors in the 1990s, is a *freedom* to pick, choose, manipulate, and reinvent different kinds of languages and issues, both formal and political. For example, Kaz Oshiro's trompe l'oeil reproductions of amplifiers, trashbins, and domestic objects constructed out of canvas and paint, evoke a kitschy nostalgia that on the one hand engages a sustained conversation about painting in relation to pop art and photo realism, and on the other hand, presents an allegory of commodified objects that come alive and bear witness to a certain time and place (fig. 18, 19). The requirements and expectations placed on work such as Oshiro's as "Asian American" do not have to be ideological. The impulse to critically examine or comment on U.S. imperialism, for example, remains a sustained pursuit in some Asian American artwork such as the poignant portraits of fallen American soldiers by Binh Danh, Mike Arcega's intricate over-the-top sculptural remnants of the Spanish occupation of the Philippines, the pointed satiric wasli paintings of Muslim-Western relations by Saira Wasim and by other artists not in the exhibition, including Paul Chan's work with the political action group Downtown for Democracy and An-My Lê's photographs of Iraq and Aghanistan-bound troops training in a remote outpost in the California desert (fig. 20). The manifold artistic approaches, formal aspects, and focal interests of the artists in "One Way or Another" underscore the idiosyncratic landscape of Asian American art. Its indebtedness to a certain kind of multiculturalism which "endorsed racially based identities and antiessentialism at the same time" has enabled these artists to cultivate their art practice unimpeded.[7]

In contrast to the institutionalization of Asian American literature where, for example, one can go to a Barnes and Noble and see a section (well, a shelf or two) reserved for books about Asian America, Asian American art lacks the uniformity implied by an Asian American shelf, and this is both its strength and its weakness. Asian American art remains a nascent field, understudied even within the field of Asian American Studies. Its paradox consists in its lack of coherency, and more often than not, the lack of easily recognizable visual markers that identify it as Asian American. On the one hand, the survey exhibition seems to be the ideal mode in which to curate such a multivisual grouping in a capacious way. On the other hand, a survey exhibition seems to connote a beginning, an introduction. Despite the consistent programming and contributions of such venues as the Asian American Arts Centre in New York City's Chinatown (which most recently presented "DETAINED," a 2006 exhibition that focused on the impact of 9/11 on Asian Americans) and major exhibitions such as "Asia/America" and now "One Way or Another," there is a familiar kind of scenario that develops and is reproduced in and through identity-based survey exhibitions.

Initially promoted as a protest and contestable response against exclusion from major art institutions, such exhibitions as "One Way or Another" and "Asia/America" are historically necessary as a way to present work that otherwise may be difficult to see, especially in a market-driven art economy. The value of these exhibitions in introducing a set of exciting, emerging artists is important curatorially and institutionally, but such an emphasis on the new and emerging has the potential also to foreclose and undermine the forward movement of an emancipative politics. In other words, focusing on the new gives the impression of trying to start over again and

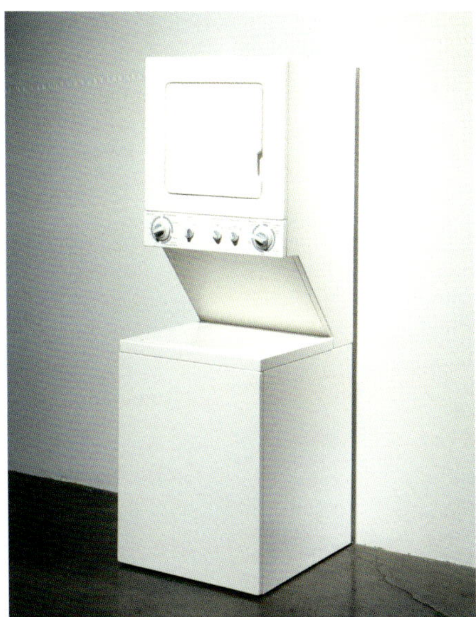

Fig. 18. Kaz Oshiro, *Combo Washer/Dryer #1*, 2005. Acrylic and bondo on stretched canvas. 71½ x 24 x 26½ inches. Private collection of Diana Zlotnick, Los Angeles.

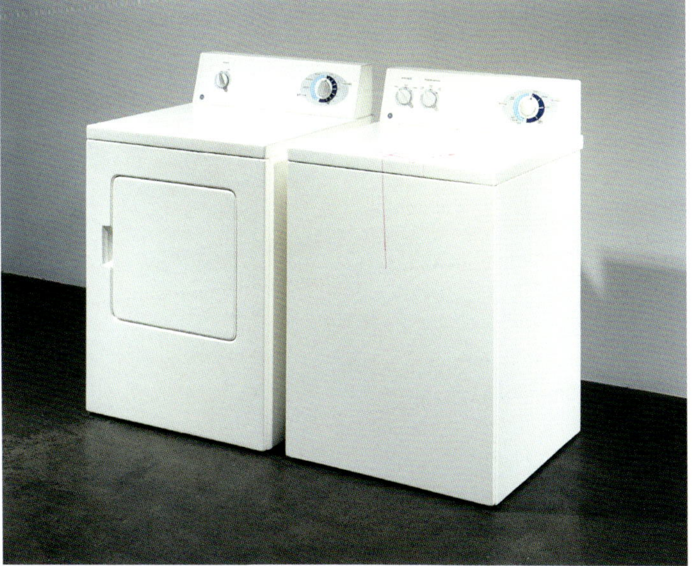

Fig. 19. Kaz Oshiro, *Washer/Dryer #2*, 2005. Acrylic and bondo on stretched canvas, 2-part. Dryer: 43 x 27 x 28 inches; Washer: 43 x 27⅛ x 28¼ inches. Collection of Nora Eccles Harrison Museum, Logan, Utah.

recalls Kobena Mercer's salient comment about a similar sense of urgency surrounding exhibitions with work created by black artists in Great Britain during the 1980s: ". . . expectations [like these] would not arise in a situation where such [exhibitions] could be taken for granted and normalized. But . . . because they are not—because our access to such spaces is rationalized by the effects of racism . . . and, what is worse, because there is no continuity of context, we seem to be constantly reinventing the wheel when it comes to black arts criticism."[8]

At the end of the day, multiculturalism was less about a comprehensive analysis of race and racism and more about a question of belonging, diverting deep analysis about race and racism into debates of political correctness and common core values. In the art world, multiculturalism became a Band-Aid solution, retrofitted to what Avery Gordon has called "diversity management": a phenomenon where diversity does not subvert the status quo, "does not demand assimilation quite as we have known it, nor does it require undifferentiated social control."[9] Rather, the management of racial and gender differences for example requires recognition of an institution's encouragement and practice of diversity and inclusion within the work environment. Race is among many interlocking factors of difference (class, gender, sexuality), multiple positionalities (transnational affiliations), relations of power, and historical formations and conditions (national origins, U.S. interventions) that impact the subject formation, the subjectivity, and the marginalization of artists of color. This resonant version or strain of multiculturalism, as reductive or liberal pluralism, levels out difference. It also creates an environment of tolerance in the ambiguous, double-edged sense that it promotes a taken-for-granted attitude that such issues of difference were never significant, but just a "trend" that has now fallen out of fashion.

Race matters. Collection acquisition, critical reviews, exhibition programming, dissertations, and course syllabi serve as barometers to measure how far we've come. Still today Asian American representation is not commensurate with the number of recent acquisitions in permanent collections of major museums, or in the curatorial selections of highly visible exhibitions that range from the Whitney Biennial to major retrospectives to thematic exhibitions on conceptual art, the end of painting, and so forth. This is not simply a numbers game. Through a supposed objective institutional policy of neutrality and color-blindness, compounded by a market-driven art world, a neo-conservative turn in national politics, and a complacent sensibility in society (not an exhaustive list by all means), the status quo has remained the same. Consistent with this notion of a flexible management strategy, the performative call of multiculturalism imposes an ideological limit, contains and compartmentalizes questions about

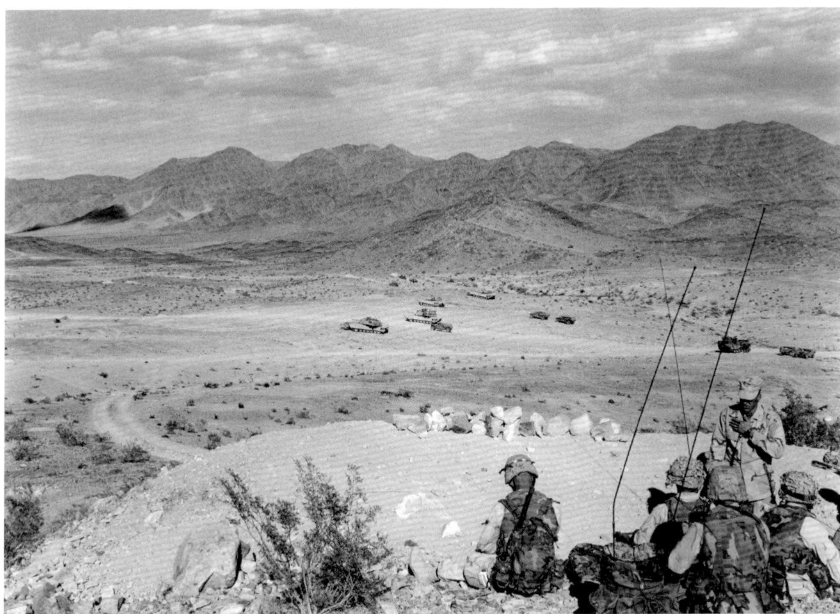

Fig. 20. An-My Lê, *29 Palms: Captain Folsom*, 2003–04. Gelatin silver print. 26 x 37½ inches. Edition of 5.

race and identity to be raised and dealt with by only those who are marginalized, as if to say, "it's their problem and not ours."

Representation matters. Indeed, "One Way or Another" has the potential, within the framework of identity politics, to serve as a catalyst to bring these unresolved issues of the 1990s—race and multiculturalism—to the foreground beyond the intellectual and cultural circles of those who remain marginalized. Yet the works selected in the exhibition do not address these issues directly, let alone confrontationally. In order to move forward, the pronoun "we" needs to be addressed, to bridge the growing disjunction between this collective need and the approaches by which to meet it.

Despite the overdetermination and homogenization of difference, I agree with Kandice Chuh when she says that we continue "to mobilize and deploy the term 'Asian American' in light and in spite of contemporary critiques of its limitations."[10] Underlying the field of Asian American Studies lies a necessary commitment to envisioning and promoting Asian American art not as an antidote leading to social justice, but as a way to shift the frame of reference through which the disavowed or obscured experiences and contributions of Asian Americans to the history and culture of the United States can be recognized and made visible. Yet a large number of Asian American artists, including many of those selected for "One Way or Another," do not identify as Asian American. In contrast to the resurgent interest in collective social practices which includes democraticizing art through outreach programs, communicating information about political issues, or serving as a clearinghouse or support-service for fellow artists (for example, the collective Instant Coffee, based in Vancouver), there is little to no activism or collaborative effort committed to creating a critical space for Asian American artists, as there was, for example, with the 1990s Asian American arts organization, Godzilla.[11] Globalization, the changing demographics of Asian America, and the market interest in Asia, especially in Asian pop culture, have triggered a paradigm shift within Asian American Studies. Asian American Studies has always been invested in the transnational as a result of U.S. global expansion. But now there is an overwhelming pressure to see the Asian American experience through a diasporic lens rather than from a cultural national perspective; the goals of "claiming America" and of being recognized as "American" are no longer priorities as they once were.

This breach from a still ongoing political project cannot be explained by a mere generational divide or a simple dichotomy between aesthetics and politics. The multiple demands on Asian American art, constituted out of a politics of representation compounded by individual circumstances make this disjunction much more complicated and messy. On one hand, recognition by the nation-state, the art establishment, and the market are all forms of legitimization "which we cannot not want."[12] On the other hand, the need to build a critical mass of politically engaged artists seems crucial, especially post-9/11. But as Margo Machida warns, "It is important for the group [in this case Godzilla] not to be restricted to 'a singular idea of community' or to be vested in any one agenda."[13]

It is more important as ever to curate identity-based exhibitions. At the same time the current curatorial frameworks of such exhibitions delimit the ways to deeply examine or push forward a politics of representation. In other words, it is important to think about what part of this curatorial framework or strategy is outmoded and how, for example, identity-based exhibitions invariably serve ad hoc as an effective strategy, a regulatory mechanism for promoting difference so long as the parameters and values remain the same. Ten years ago, scholars from Gayatri Spivak to Jose Muñoz underscored the shortcomings of using identity as a framework. No matter how much emphasis is placed on difference, the use of identity as an organizing trope ultimately collapses into a communal uniformity and sameness-in-difference. But such practices are not easy to let go, and to do so seems counterproductive, even irresponsible, in this day and age, when resources and cultural capital are increasingly inaccessible and unequally distributed.

The number of Asian American artists producing and presenting visually compelling work today affirms the variants of multiculturalism and identity politics from the 1990s. But at the same time, the current version of multiculturalism is a thinly veiled strategy of assimilation that impinges to different degrees on the creative license of Asian American artists, imparting a strange practice of freedom. It is not the work that needs to "change" or move in certain directions (although some current work that purports to be politically edgy is so nuanced that the message is at times indiscernible). We (curators in this case) need to think about a different framework or perhaps a place outside the exhibition and institutional space as we know it. Rather than question our belonging to some canon or nation, perhaps we need to ask ourselves "what it means to be in common"—a question posed by philosopher Jean-Luc Nancy in his salient text *The Inoperative Community*.[14]

How can we build a community of singularities where affiliations, attachments, and bonds are unmarked, absent any shared value (of citizenship, say) or experience (for example of oppression)? Such thinking seems curatorially counterintuitive especially when it is generally understood that exhibitions—whether major retrospectives or thematic explorations—have some kind of common thread or narrative running through each selected work that underlies the curatorial premise, thus holding an exhibition together. At the same time, the most interesting exhibitions—those that are fraught with visually disparate works, uncomfortable or unanticipated viewing situations, and/or a true reliance on the contingent nature and multiple factors that activate an exhibition space—highlight the potential to transgress the "boundedness" of an identity-based framework in order to rethink this community of not belonging. The task of curating such an exhibition is not an easy one, nor perhaps even possible, but we can begin, at least for this exhibition, with Jean Shin's installation *Unraveling* (2006) which literally does "unravel" the presumed distinctions and boundaries of what constitutes the Asian American community. Known for her colorful installations made up of refabricated everyday objects collected from members of her various communities, Shin's *Unraveling* begins with the exhibition curators' donated sweaters, and their friends' and colleagues' sweaters, exposing a diverse network of people from all walks of life not utterly contingent or determined by chance. Shin's *Unraveling* juxtaposed with Mika Tajima's multi-sensory installation, evokes an ambivalent and intriguing visual manifestation of this alternative community. Informed by variant minimalist art practices and discourses, Tajima's use of repetition in her performances (a mix of live music with sample remixes) and mirrored sculptures complicates both minimalism's prohibition against subjectivity and the inability of identity politics to address difference.

The young artists in "One Way or Another" are very conscious of their audience and of what is at stake in their art making. They are savvy and poised and some are armed with a wry sense of humor, as in Anna Sew Hoy's *Haiku* (2005) (fig. 21). A two-toned yellowish-gray and jade-colored boulder made of polyurethane-based foam sits anchored to a tinted and colored mirror, the dimensions of which are slightly larger than the rock. Into the jade-green boulder, whose surface is flat and slightly tilted, Sew Hoy has inserted an array of knives including steak knives and cleavers. The composition of the knives, the Styrofoam, and the mirror is a clever take on the strictures of haiku and possibly, identity; the rock serves as a warning, perhaps, concerning the danger and impossibility of trying to discover a whole self. In a similar vein, the video performances of Laurel Nakadate and Patty Chang highlight through humor, self-exposure, and some discomfort the underlying absurdity and anxiety of their own or others' desires and projections of the other. They let loose in a way that reminds us of what art can offer: an open-ended imagining of another place, or being in someone else's place.

In a previous essay on Asian Canadian artist Jin-Me Yoon, I explored how through art, one could summon a politics of empathy and community, a mutual accommodation of difference, of caring about the other and the self that cut through indifference and ignorance especially when one was still entangled with issues of being unrecognized and marginalized. The title "The Last Asian American Exhibition in the Whole Entire World" derives from the title of a play by Suzan-Lori Parks.[15] Many of her early plays are wonderfully wicked riffs on the politics of representation. She sums up best in her own words the quagmire in which African Americans find themselves caught, a paradox that corresponds well with what I have been trying to articulate partially:

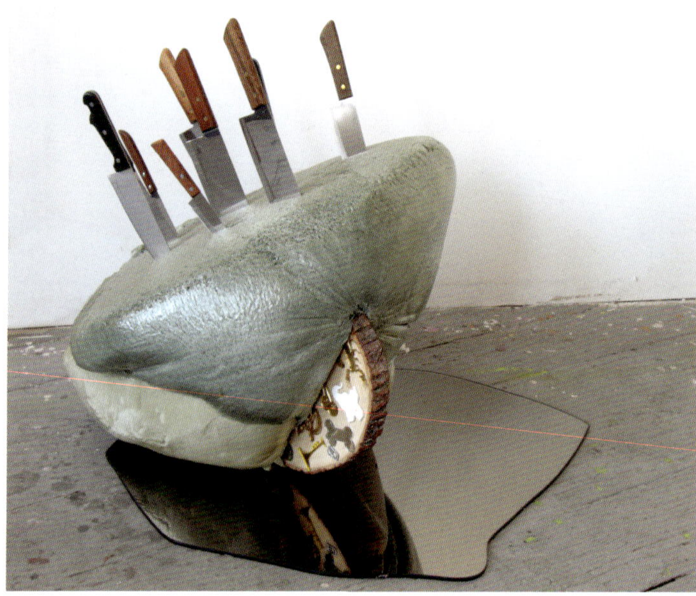

Fig. 21. Anna Sew Hoy, *Haiku*, 2006. Polyurethane foam, mirror, knives, wood, plastic. Approx. 36 x 36 x 36 inches. Collection of the artist.

> We have for so long been an 'oppressed' people, but are Black people only blue? . . . There are many ways of defining blackness . . . The Klan does not always have to be outside the door for Black people to have lives worthy of dramatic literature . . . As there is no single 'Black Experience,' there is no single 'Black Aesthetic' and there is no one way to write or think or feel or dream or interpret or be interpreted. As African-Americans we should recognize this insidious essentialism for what it is: a fucked-up trap to reduce us to only one way of being. We should endeavor to show the world and ourselves our beautiful and powerful infinite variety.[16]

In *The Death of the Last Black Man in the Whole Entire World*, the play's protagonist, Black Man With Watermelon, is "caught between the periphery and the center, caught between being written out of History yet trapped within the metaphoric parentheses of the stereotype that transcends (linear) Time as History."[17] Using a strategy of repetition and revision as a foil to being entangled in the fray, Parks uses a refrain about writing history in which a character named Yes and Greens Black-Eyed Peas Cornbread repeats throughout the play: "You should write that down and you should hide it under a rock."[18] And then towards the end of the play, he admonishes, "You will write it down because if you don't write it down then we will come along and tell the future that we did not exist."[19]

"One Way or Another" is underwritten in part by many different kinds of politics and investments. This essay may serve as a short history, a cautionary tale (not a coda) about an exhibition that exemplifies a future-yet-to-come. At the same time, the selected works by an exciting array of artists demand a willing attentiveness that calls for nothing short of a complete presentness of experience.

Susette S. Min is Assistant Professor of Asian American Studies and Art History at the University of California, Davis. Formerly, she was a curator at The Drawing Center in New York City.

1. Indigo Som, "Introduction to Chinese Restaurant Project," 2002, http://www.well.com/user/indigo/crpintro.html.
2. Indigo Som, "The River Itself," *Mostly Mississippi: Chinese Restaurants of the South* (San Francisco: Chinese Historical Society of America, 2005), 4.
3. "The Decade Show: Frameworks of Identity in the 1980s," 1990, co-organized by and presented with the Museum of Contemporary Hispanic Art, the New Museum of Contemporary Art, and the Studio Museum in Harlem; "1993 Whitney Biennial," Whitney Museum of American Art, New York; "The Curio Shop," 1993, organized by Godzilla at Artists Space, New York; "Asia/America: Identities in Asian American Art," 1994, Asia Society, New York.
4. This essay engages a number of interlocutors and is an attempt to extend conversations already pushed forward by the likes of Alice Yang, Kandice Chuh, Kobena Mercer, Luis Camnitzer, Margo Machida, Elaine Kim, Holland Cotter, and Olu Oguibe among others.
5. Other forces that shaped the formation and emergence of Asian American art include the theoretical discourses of poststructuralism, feminism, and postcolonialism, but my focus for this essay is primarily on multiculturalism and its affects on Asian American art from a curatorial perspective.
6. Constance M. Lewallen, "Generosity: A Conversation with Byron Kim, Janine Antoni, and Glenn Ligon," *Threshold: Byron Kim 1990–2004* (Berkeley: University of California, Berkeley Art Museum and Pacific Film Archive, 2004), 49.
7. Avery Gordon and Christopher Newfield, "Multiculturalism's Unfinished Business," *Mapping Multiculturalism* (Minneapolis: University of Minnesota Press, 1996), 104.
8. Kobena Mercer, "Black Art and the Burden of Representation," *Welcome to the Jungle* (New York: Routledge, 1994), 235–6.
9. Avery Gordon, "The Work of Corporate Culture: Diversity Management" *Social Text* no. 44 (autumn–winter 1995), 3. See also *Mapping Multiculturalism*, eds. Avery Gordon and Christopher Newfield (Minneapolis: University of Minnesota Press, 1996).
10. Kandice Chuh, *Imagine Otherwise: On Asian Americanist Critique* (Durham: Duke University Press, 2003), x.
11. The Asian American Arts Centre in New York City's Chinatown run by Robert Lee and Asian American Arts Alliance are notable exceptions.
12. Gayatri Spivak, "Bonding in Difference: Interview with Alfred Arteaga," *The Spivak Reader: Selected Works of Gayatri Chakravorty Spivak*, eds. Donna Landry and Gerald MacLean (New York: Routledge, 1996), 28. See also Kandice Chuh, "Nikkei Internment: Determined Identities/Undecidable Meanings," *Imagine Otherwise: On Asian Americanist Critique* (Durham: Duke University Press, 2003) 75, 150.
13. Quoted in Alice Yang, "Godzilla: The Anarchistic Lizard," *Why Asia? Contemporary Asian and Asian American Art* (New York: New York University Press, 1998), 92.
14. Jean-Luc Nancy, *The Inoperative Community* (Minneapolis: University of Minnesota Press, 1991), x.
15. The title of the essay also recalls *Screen*'s "The Last 'Special Issue' on Race" edited by Kobena Mercer and Isaac Julien which featured their seminal essay "De Margin and De Centre." Special thanks to literary scholar Cynthia Tolentino for bringing this to my attention.
16. Suzan-Lori Parks, "An Equation for Black People Onstage," *The America Play, and Other Works* (New York: Theatre Communications Group, 1995), 19–22.
17. Louise Bernard, "The musicality of language: redefining history in Suzan-Lori Parks's *The Death of the Last Black Man in the Whole Entire World*," *African American Review* (winter 1997), http://72.14.203.104/search?q=cache:S1QzKeVhdQsJ:www.findarticles.com/p/articles/mi_m2838/is_n4_v31/ai_20425714+death+of+last+black+man+suzan+lori+parks+what+is+it+about&hl=en&gl=us&ct=clnk&cd=6.
18. Suzan-Lori Parks, *The Death of the Last Black Man in the Whole Entire World*, in *The America Play, and Other Works* (New York: Theatre Communications Group, 1995), 104.
19. Ibid., 130–31.

ARTISTS

Michael Arcega by Kóan Jeff Baysa
Xavier Cha by Tim Davis
Patty Chang by Miwako Tezuka
Binh Danh by Aimee Chang
Mari Eastman by Aimee Chang
Ala Ebtekar by Aimee Chang
Chitra Ganesh by Christina Yang
Glenn Kaino by Doryun Chong
Geraldine Lau by Kóan Jeff Baysa
Jiha Moon by Reena Jana
Laurel Nakadate by Christina Yang
Kaz Oshiro by Miwako Tezuka
Anna Sew Hoy by Reena Jana
Jean Shin by Miwako Tezuka
Indigo Som by Miwako Tezuka
Mika Tajima by Reena Jana
Saira Wasim by Atteqa Ali

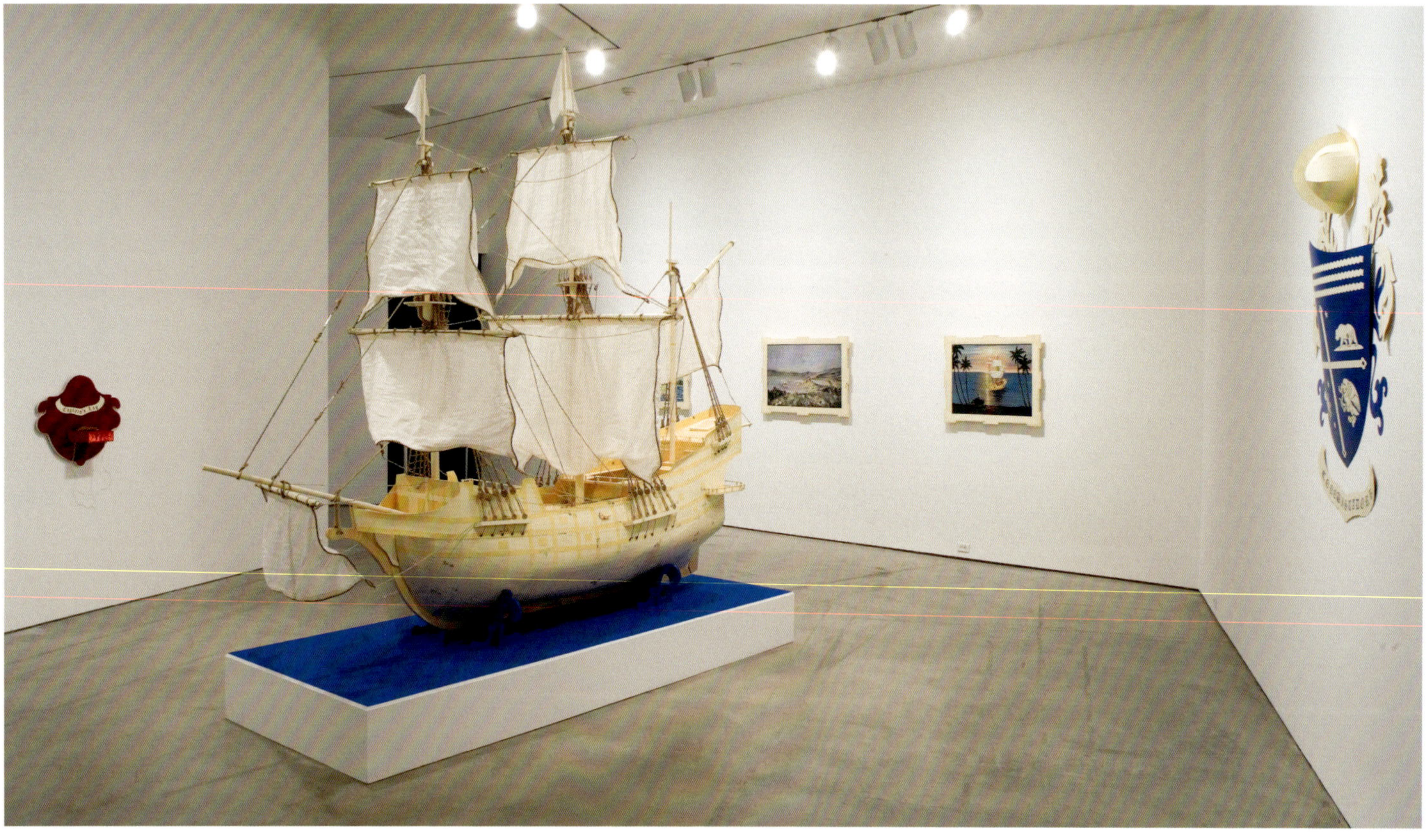

Michael Arcega, *El Conquistadork*, 2004. Manila folders, rope, wood, nylon, glue, fiberglass, foam, epoxy resin, metal. 120 x 157 x 60 inches. Installation view at Museum of Contemporary Art, San Diego, 2005. Below: Michael Arcega, *El Conquistadork* (detail).

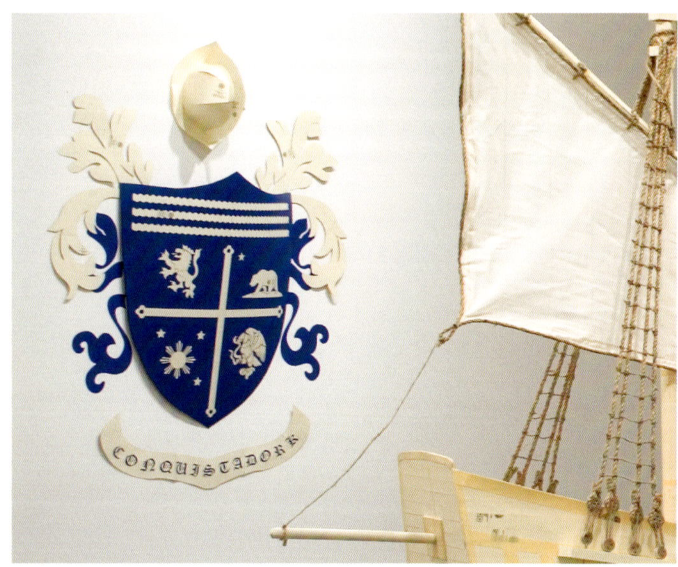

MICHAEL ARCEGA

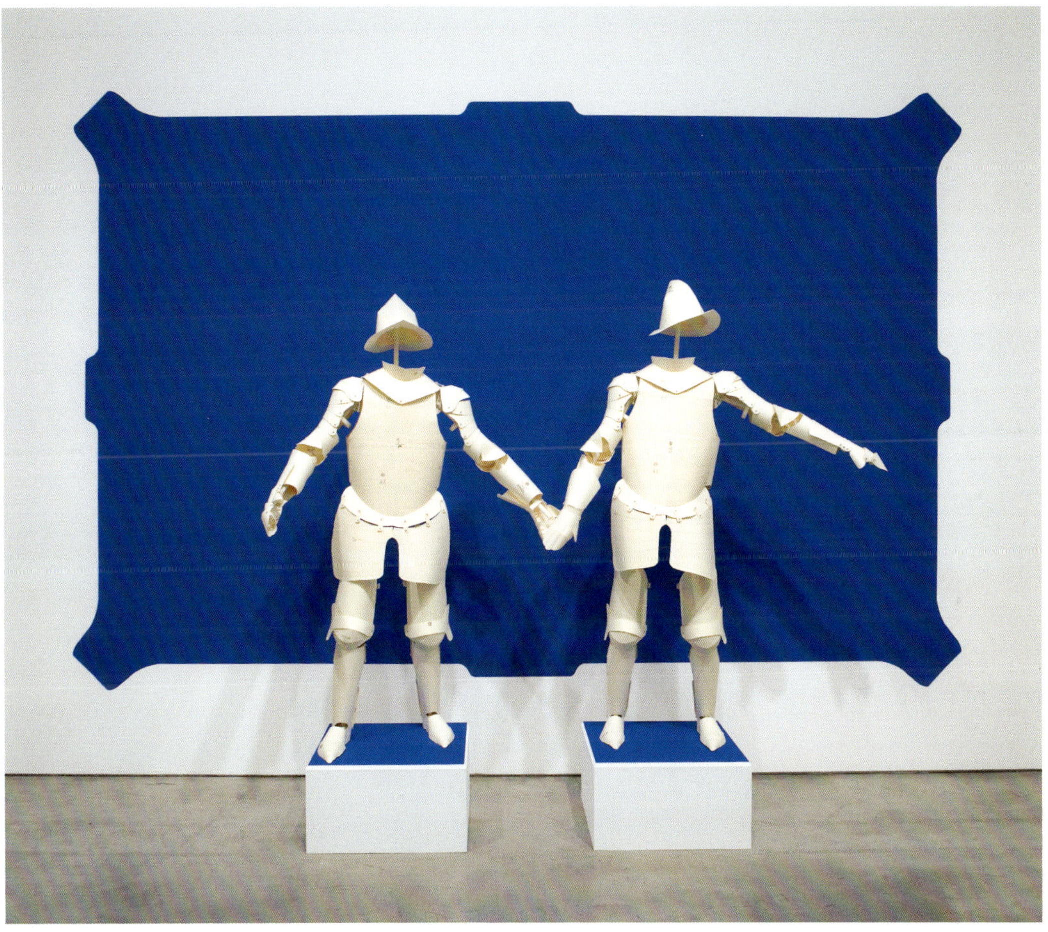

Michael Arcega, *El Conquistadorkes*, 2004. Manila folders, glue, acrylic hardware. 72 x 18 x 24 inches each. Installation view at Museum of Contemporary Art, San Diego, 2005.

Michael Arcega was born in the Manila suburb of Quezon City in 1973, moved to Los Angeles at the age of 10, and currently lives in San Francisco. A brilliant satirist and conceptualist working in all media, Arcega deftly interprets current political events in parody, visual puns, and his favorite modus operandi, the double entendre.

Arcega's reflections on nature's phenomenon, hurricane Katrina, and her disastrous effects on an unnaturally compromised ecosystem, compounded by tragicomic Federal Emergency Management Agency (FEMA) fumblings, are gathered in *Eternal Salivation* (2006), a ship held aloft by a pedestal of crates. The canted vessel harbors a surprising and startling interior: rows of various dried animal meats in a contemporary retelling of salvation from disaster. The parallel false tenors of spiritual and physical salvation are explored as futile "carrots"—always held beyond easy reach and used by both church and state as a means of controlling the allegedly "damned." Some "natural" disasters like landslides and flooding are caused by man's

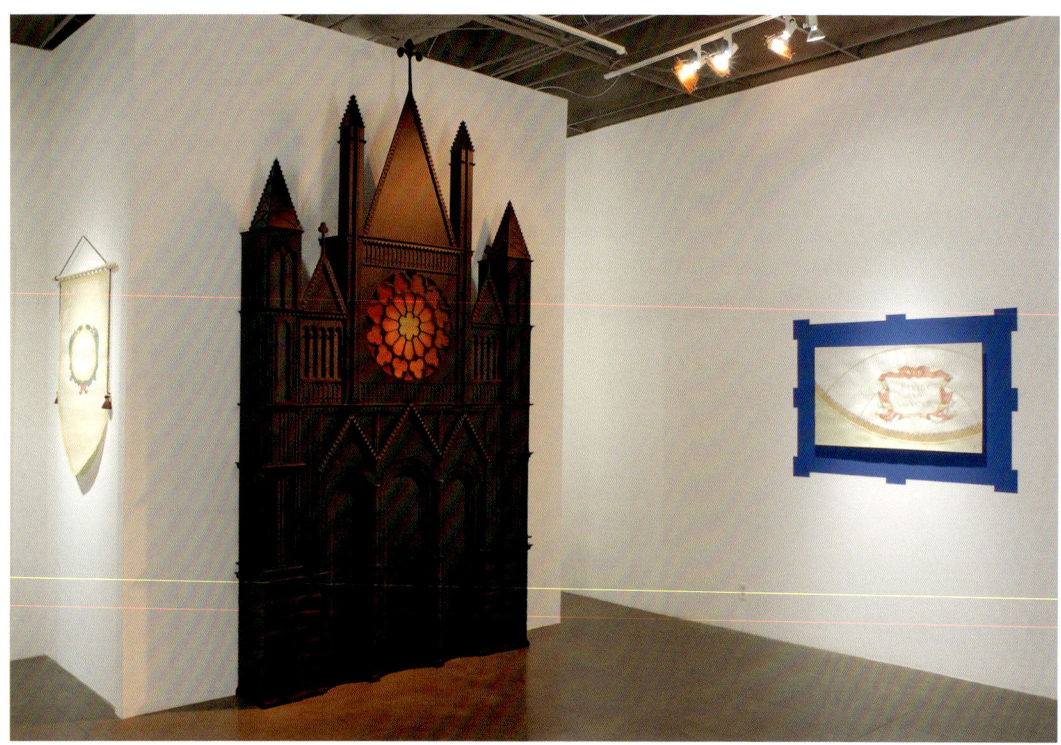

Michael Arcega, *In Gaud We Trust*, 2006. Petroleum-based plastic (PVC), acrylic, mixed media. 144 x 75 x 13 inches. Installation view at Heather Marx Gallery, San Francisco.

monetary and political greed and stupidity, factors that also foster terrorism and invoke nuclear winters. Arcega states, "I like the aesthetic of the 50s nuclear family/Norman Rockwell-value-meets-Gilligan's Island scenario. A cheerful display in the context of global turmoil."[1]

The common Tagalog saying, *bahala na* (literally "come what may") in the Philippines invokes the ancient supreme god Bathala, and affirms trust in divine wisdom. The ability to reframe an unfortunate circumstance as an absurdity does not trivialize it but rather defuses it, and is consonant with dark Filipino humor, a variation of optimism that renown painter Manuel Ocampo, who was also born in Quezon City, says is unrecognized and deeply misinterpreted in his own work.[2] It is an adaptive mechanism to calamity in a country that has been successively ravaged by the Spanish, Americans, poverty, insurgency, martial law, corruption, and destructive natural events like the volcanic eruption of Mount Pinatubo in 1991. Profit-driven collusion with the government allowed deforestation, leading to the most recent landslide tragedy in Southern Leyte province that devastated entire villages.

Arcega tackles such issues with typical black humor and abandon. Another nautical reference is found in *El Conquistadork* (2004), an installation that was part of his 2005 solo show at the Museum of Contemporary Art San Diego. The artist constructed a 13-foot long replica of a Spanish galleon from Manila folders with riggings of Manila hemp. Launched with a beer bottle in Tomales Bay, northern California, it references the incidental discovery of San Francisco Bay by a Spanish galleon taking plunder between Mexico and the Philippines. In an oblique reference to one country's plundering of another for (black) gold, a writer quipped, "That's just what Arcega does . . . leading us to wonder just how many other quests that appear gallant on paper turn out to be perilous follies once launched (Iraq, anyone?)."[3] His humor shows some teeth as he lampoons historical and current theaters of military conflict, affirming, "I get off on the idea of emasculating a powerful symbol like the conquistador, the conqueror of continents."[4] Similarly, with typical Arcega acerbic wit, *Eternal Salvation* is sharply critical of both church and state in a darkly delicious vein.

KJB

1. Michael Arcega, telephone conversation with author, January 9, 1999.
2. Ibid.

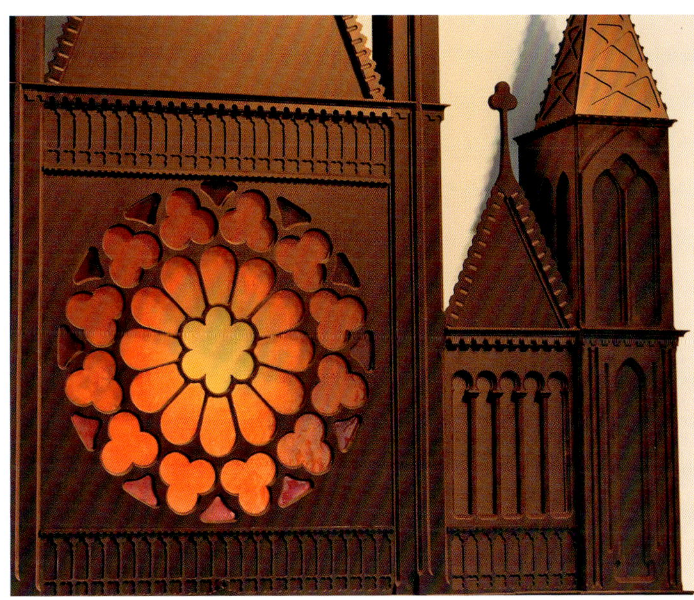

Michael Arcega, *In Gaud We Trust* (detail).

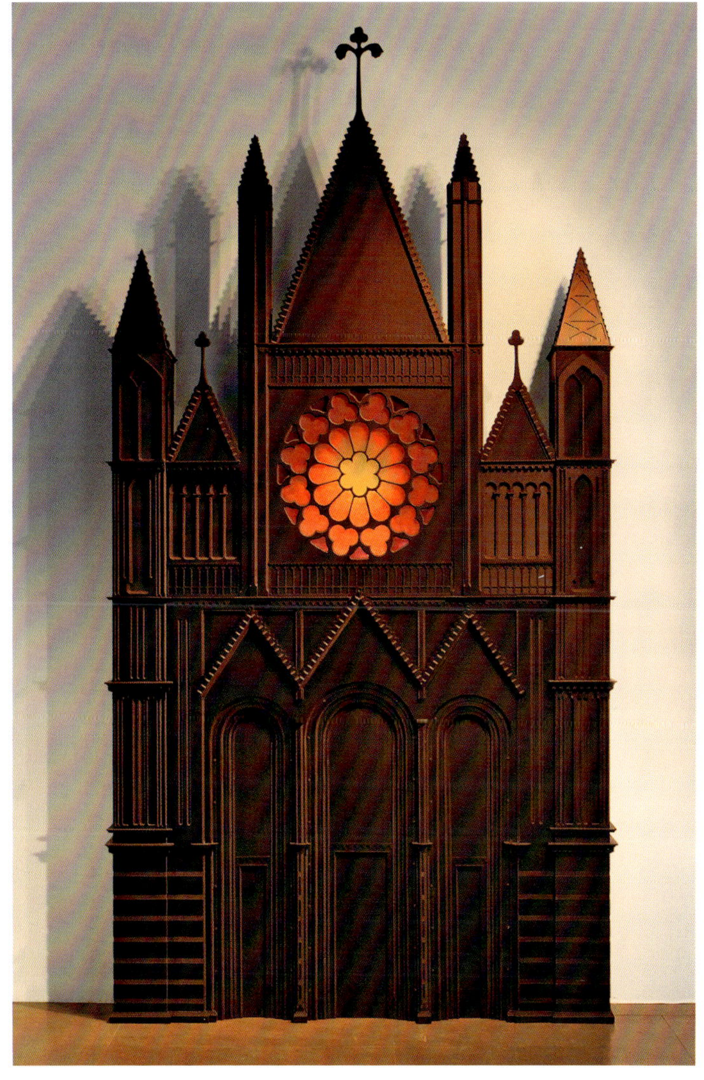

Michael Arcega, *In Gaud We Trust*, 2006. Petroleum-based plastic (PVC), acrylic, mixed media. 144 x 75 x 13 inches. Installation view at Heather Marx Gallery, San Francisco.

3. Reyhan Harmanci, "Bilingual Vision," *San Francisco Chronicle*, February 16, 2006, http://www.sfgate.com/cgi-bin/article.cgi?f=/c/a/2006/02/16/NSGT7H62Q11.DTL&hw=arcega&sn=001&sc=1000.
4. Matt Palmquist, "Dog Bites," *SF Weekly*, March 31, 2004, http://www.sfweekly.com/issues/2004-03-31/news/dogbites.html

MICHAEL ARCEGA

Born in 1973, Manila, the Philippines; Lives and works in San Francisco, California

EDUCATION: 1998, Bachelor of Fine Arts, San Francisco Art Institute, California; **SOLO EXHIBITIONS:** 2002, "Plein Hair," Leefahsalung at the New Chinatown Barbershop, Los Angeles, California; 2000, "Objects and Installation," Bucheon Gallery, San Francisco, California; **GROUP EXHIBITIONS:** 2005, "Big Deal," Yerba Buena Center for the Arts, San Francisco, California; 2004, "California Dreamin'," Heather Marx Gallery, San Francisco, California; 2002, "APAture 2002," SomArts Cultural Center, San Francisco, California, "Census 2000: Asian Pacific Islander Americans," Pro Arts Gallery, Oakland, California; **AWARD:** 2005, Artist in residence, Headlands Center for the Arts, Sausalito, California

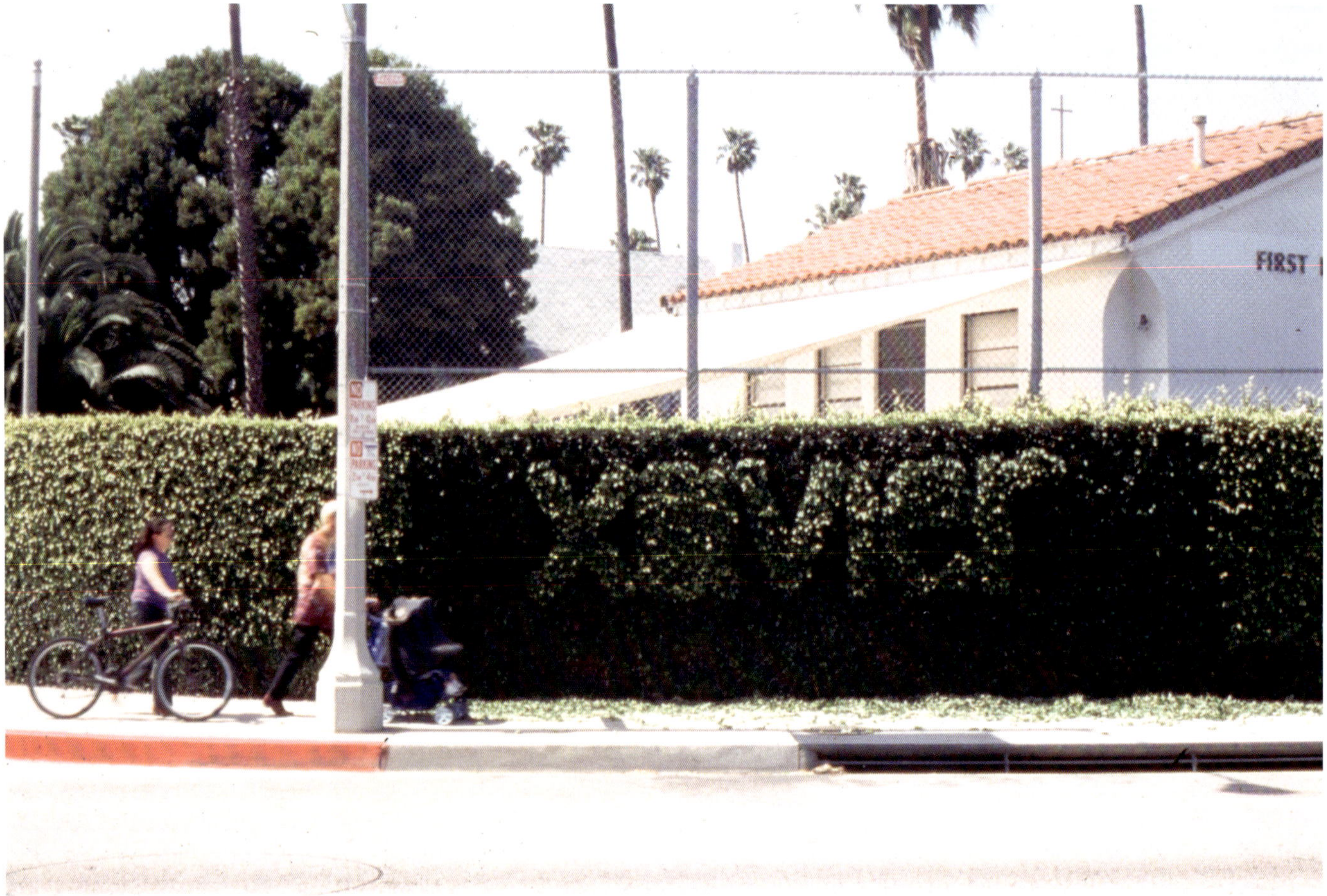

Xavier Cha, *Topiary Tags* (video still, one of twenty), 2004. Digital video. Approx. 48 x 192 inches.

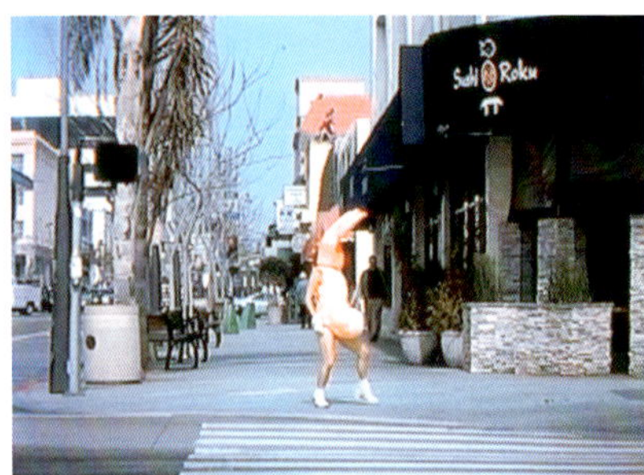

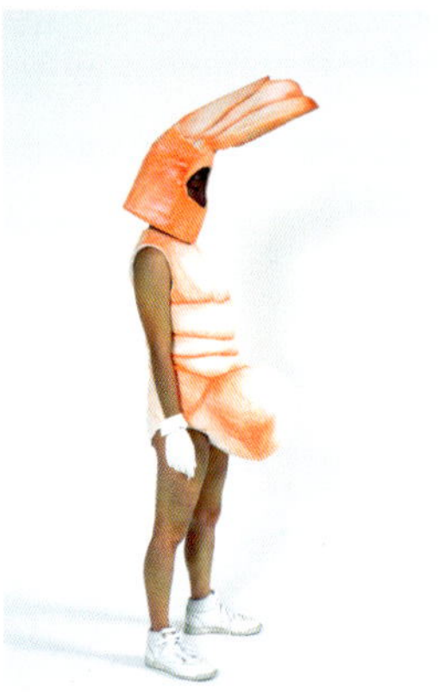

Above: Xavier Cha, *Shrimp* (video still from the *Human Advertisement Series*), 2004. Digital video. 1 minute 15 seconds. Right: Xavier Cha, *Shrimp* (poster from the *Human Advertisement Series*), 2004. Digital C-print. 24 x 18 inches.

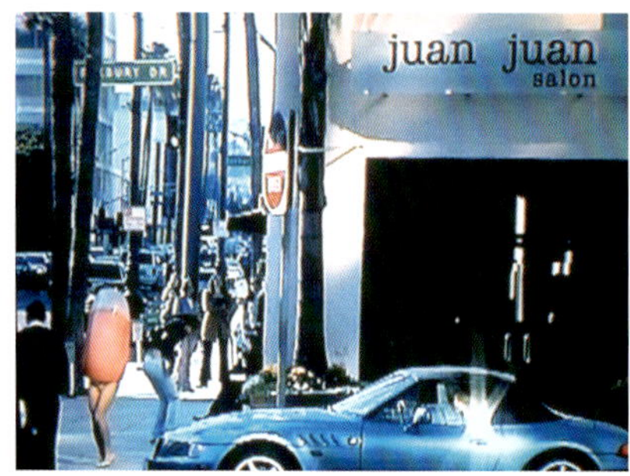

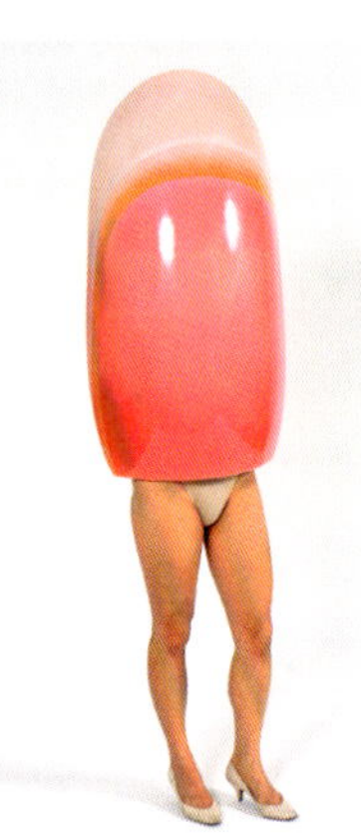

Above: Xavier Cha, *Juan Juan Salon* (video still from the *Human Advertisement Series*), 2004. Digital video. 1 minute 15 seconds. Right: Xavier Cha, *Nail* (poster from the *Human Advertisement Series*), 2004. Digital C-print. 24 x 18 inches.

XAVIER CHA

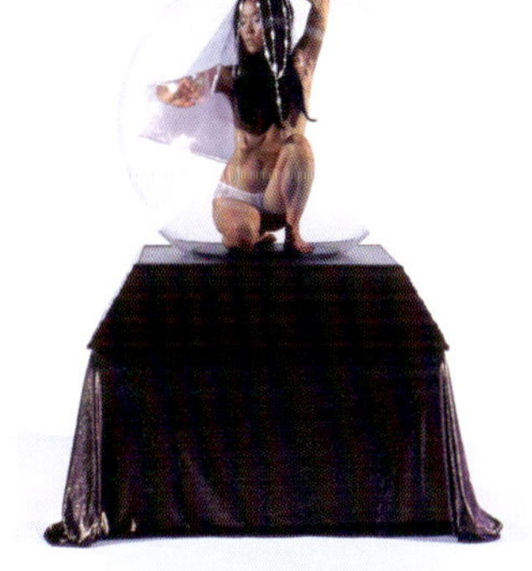

Xavier Cha, *Crystal Ball* (poster from the *Human Advertisement Series*), 2004. Digital C-print. 24 x 18 inches.

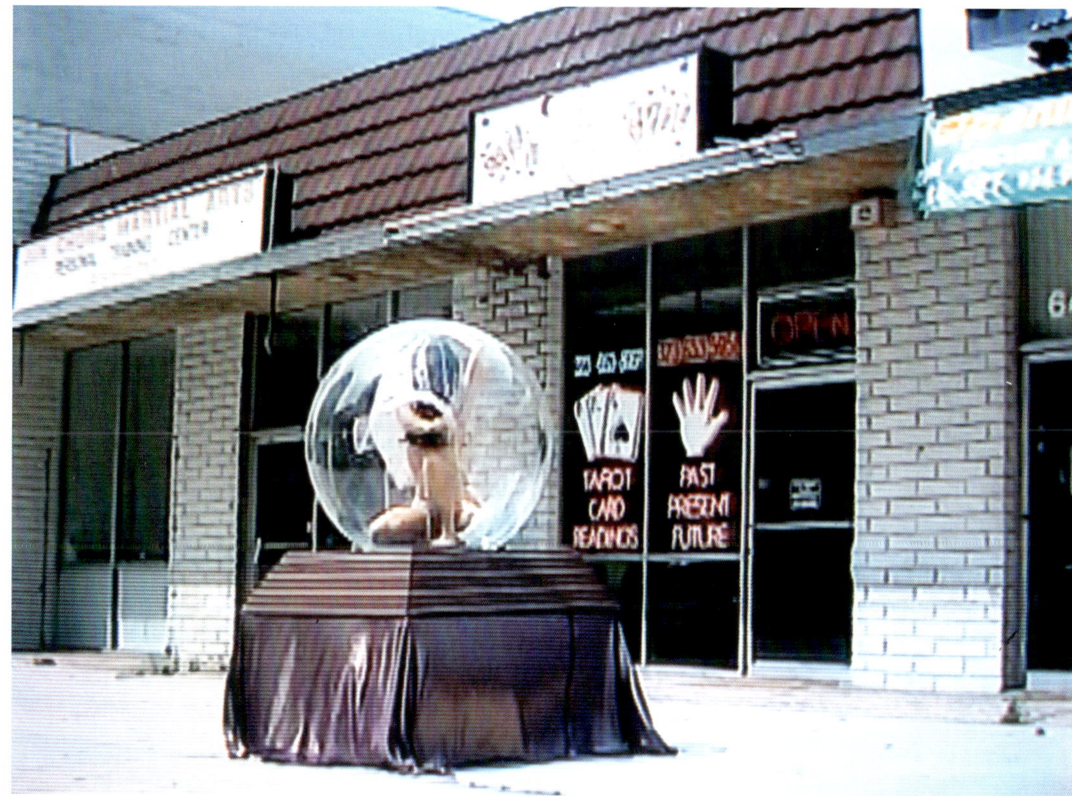

Xavier Cha, *Crystal Ball* (video still from the *Human Advertisement Series*), 2004. Digital video. 1 minute 15 seconds.

There is a great deal of what former Bush spokesman Ari Fleischer, (referring to the Valerie Plame case) called "kerfuffle" in the current art world about collectivity. With the art community feeling like over-tired, sugared-out trick-or-treaters coming home from the commercial Gallerias of Chelsea, curators are touting collectivity as a refreshing renewal of the Alternative. The trouble is, most of the work of these collectives fits comfortably in the gallery context, looking a lot like slightly scruffy drawing, painting, sculpture, and photography. The mainstream surge of the commercial seems capable of washing away the most willful of marginalized positions.

Xavier Cha is an antidote to this contagious gift-shopping of the collective. All her work has added doubt and distraction to our assumed distinctions between individual and collective, public and private. In *Topiary Tags* (2003) she incised enormous "XAVIERs" into Los Angeles hedgerows. The hedge is the public face of a private place, and a graffiti tag is the privatization of public space.

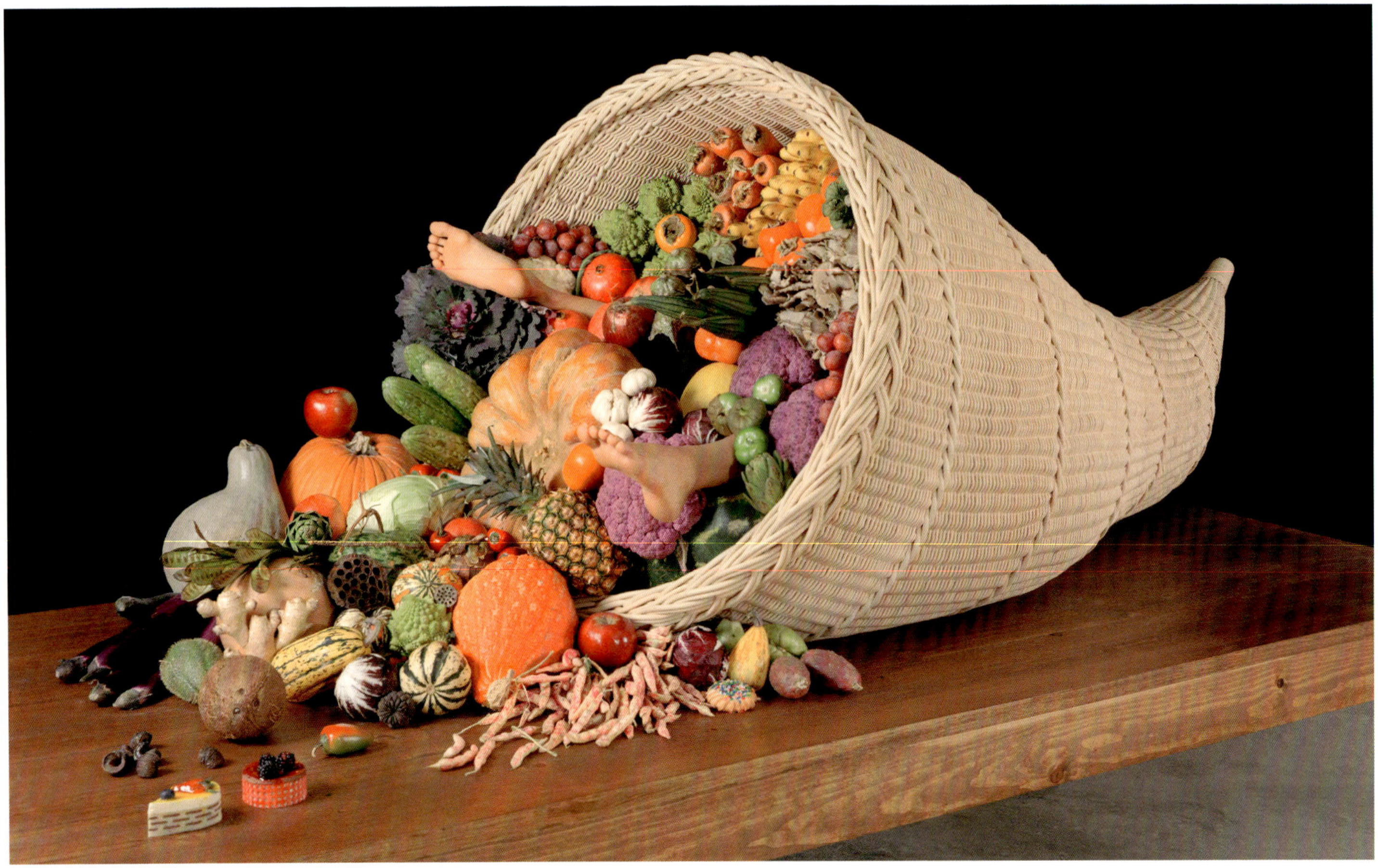

Xavier Cha, *Horn of Plenty* (part 1 of *Holiday Cruise!*), 2006. Wood, wicker, fresh produce, artist. 108 x 48 x 84 inches. Collection of Dean Valentine.

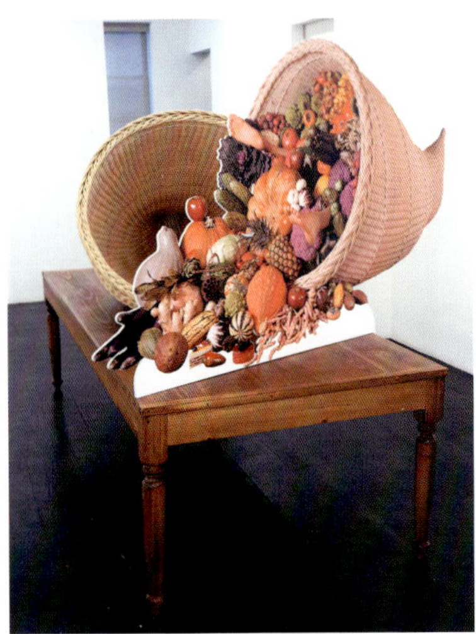

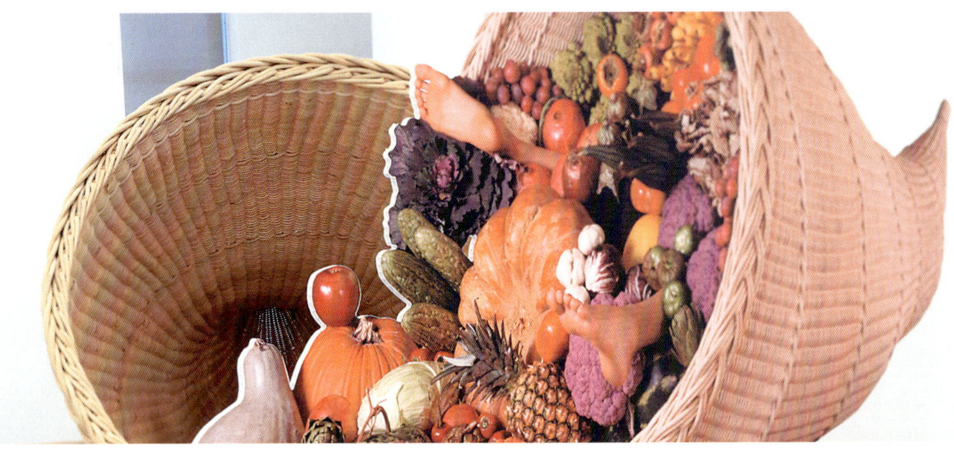

Left and above: Xavier Cha. Installation view: Xavier Cha, *Holiday Cruise!*, April 15–May 13, 2006, Taxter & Spengemann, New York.

P.D. James wrote, "There is more violence in an English hedgerow than in the meanest streets of a great city,"[1] and while James was talking about the harshness of nature, Cha's glamorous vandalism emphasized the scarring violence of exclusivity and the absurdity of a wall made of leaves.

In "Holiday Cruise!," her 2006 show at Taxter and Spengemann Gallery in New York, she created and inhabited three distinct, complex, gaudy, elaborate personae—Cornucopia, Cornrow Hairbraid, and Polyhedra—and invited performers to share the gallery with her. A spectrum of performances stretched out over the month, from the savvy to the naïve: covens, satyrs, opera singers doing Offenbach, strippers, astrologists, fashion designers, sensitive songwriters. The gallery became a place where every crackpot with an extroverted streak, and societies of varying degrees of secrecy, could hold their coming out parties. Collectivity could have easily broken out. But Cha's characters stayed willfully outside the collective fray, like Greek caryatids holding up the roof at the Diyonisia. Cornucopia lay in an enormous effulgent horn of plenty. Polyhedra stood undetectably still in an inscrutable high priestess costume that felt fought over by Matthew Barney and Buckminster Fuller. No riots ensued, but eddies curled off the Mainstream into corners of the gallery usually reserved for facelifts and critics. Nothing collective could touch Cha. She was, after all, a work of art.

The artist as audience isn't a new idea. In recent years Sophie Calle laid in bed all night atop the Eiffel Tower listening to bedtime stories and Marina Abramovic stared out at observers for twelve

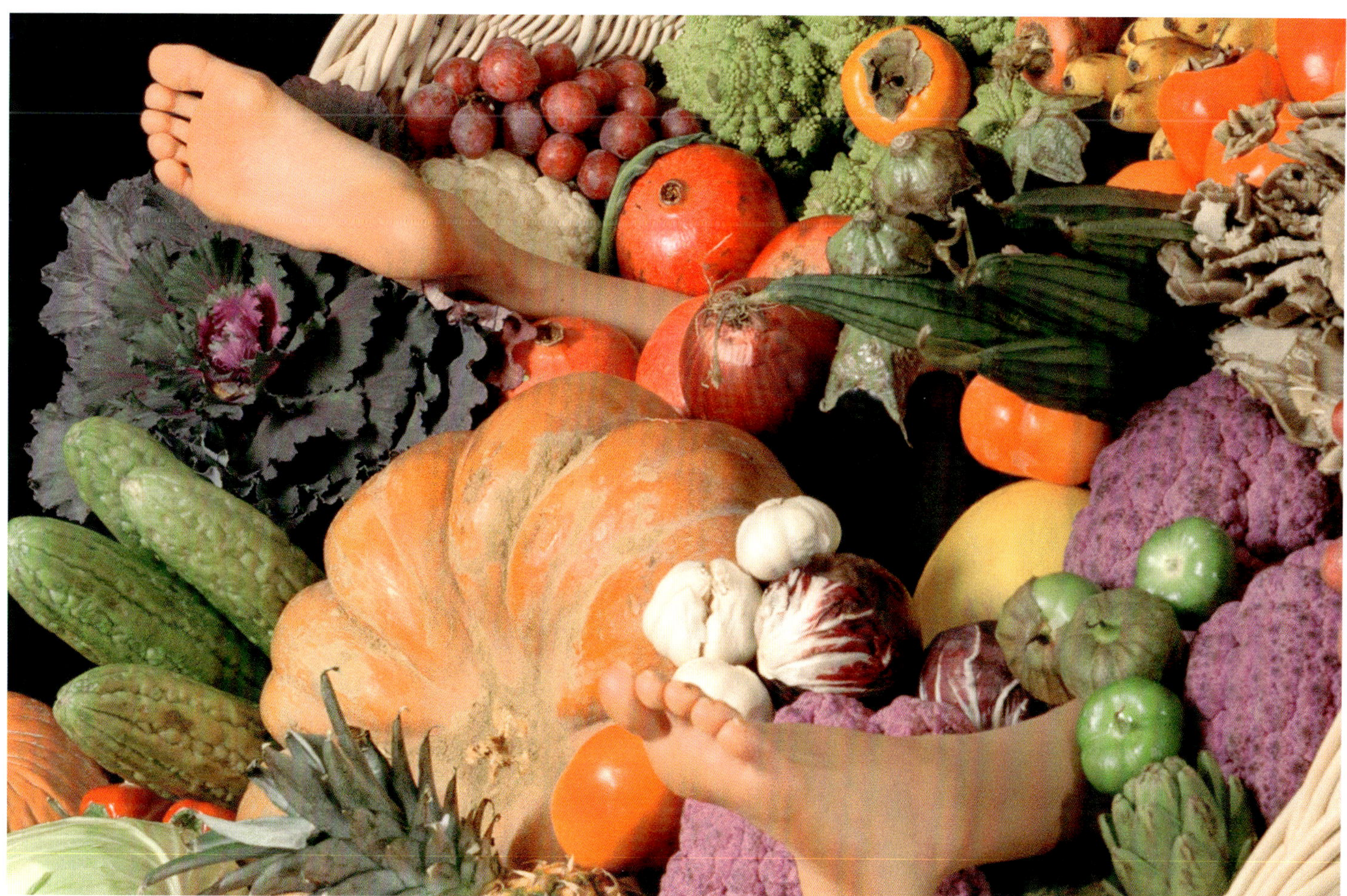

Xavier Cha, *Horn of Plenty* (part 1 of *Holiday Cruise!*) (detail).

days in *The House with the Ocean View* (2002). But never has a performer achieved such virtuosic nullity. "Holiday Cruise!" was like a recital of Morton Feldman's six-hour long crystalline, minimal Second String Quartet performed at a convention of auctioneers: a devastatingly beautiful, crafted individual essence loosed into a loony bin. For Calle and Abramovic, the life and character of the artist stay giddily present as subject. For Cha, the individual artist is subsumed not into the collective, but into the work itself. **TD**

1. P.D. James, *Devices and Desires* (London: Faber and Faber, 1989).

XAVIER CHA

Born in 1980, Los Angeles, California; Lives and works in New York, New York
EDUCATION: 2004, Master of Fine Arts, University of California, Los Angeles; 2002, Bachelor of Fine Arts, Rhode Island School of Design, Providence, Rhode Island; **SOLO EXHIBITIONS:** 2006, "Holiday Cruise 2006!," Taxter & Spengemann, New York, New York; **GROUP EXHIBITIONS AND PERFORMANCES:** 2006, "In Practice: Special Project Series," SculptureCenter, Long Island City, New York; 2005, "Makers," Taxter & Spengemann, New York, New York; 2005, "8:30 AM," New York, New York; 2004, "and if you think you see just with your eyes you are mad," Peres Projects, Los Angeles, California; 2004, "Shadow Cast," Miami, Florida; 2003, "Human Advertisement Series," Los Angeles, California; 2003, "Topiary Tags," Los Angeles, California

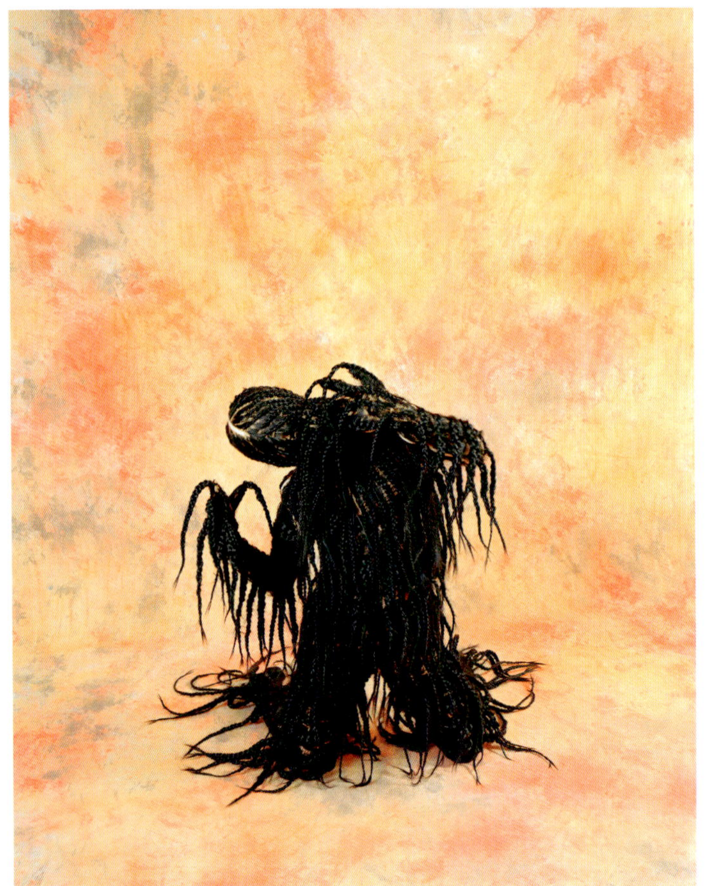

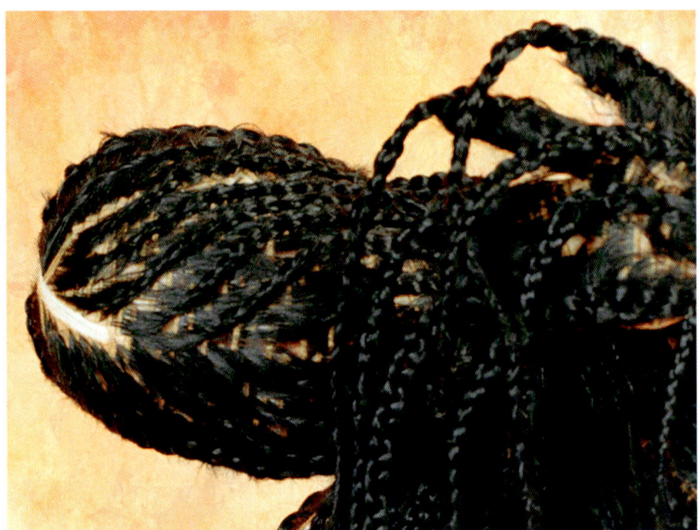

Left: Xavier Cha, *Cornrow Hairbraid* (part 2 of *Holiday Cruise!*), 2006. Spandex, synthetic hair, artist. 62 inches. Collection of John Rubeli. Installation view at Taxter & Spengemann, New York. Above: Xavier Cha, *Cornrow Hairbraid* (part 2 of *Holiday Cruise!*) (detail).

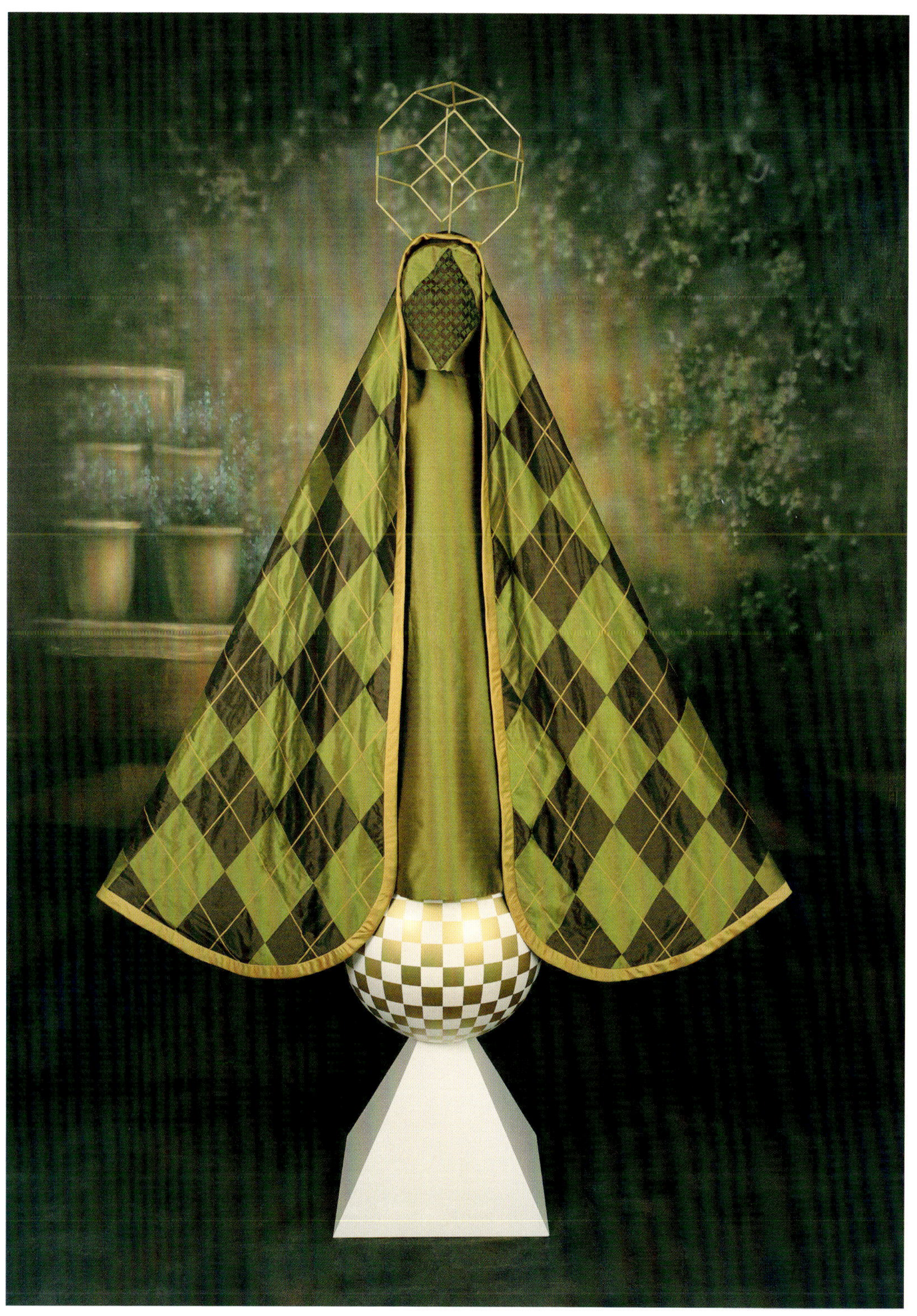

Xavier Cha, *Polyhedra* (part 3 of *Holiday Cruise!*), 2006. Fabric, steel, MDF, paint, artist. 120 x 72 inches. Installation view at Taxter & Spengemann, New York.

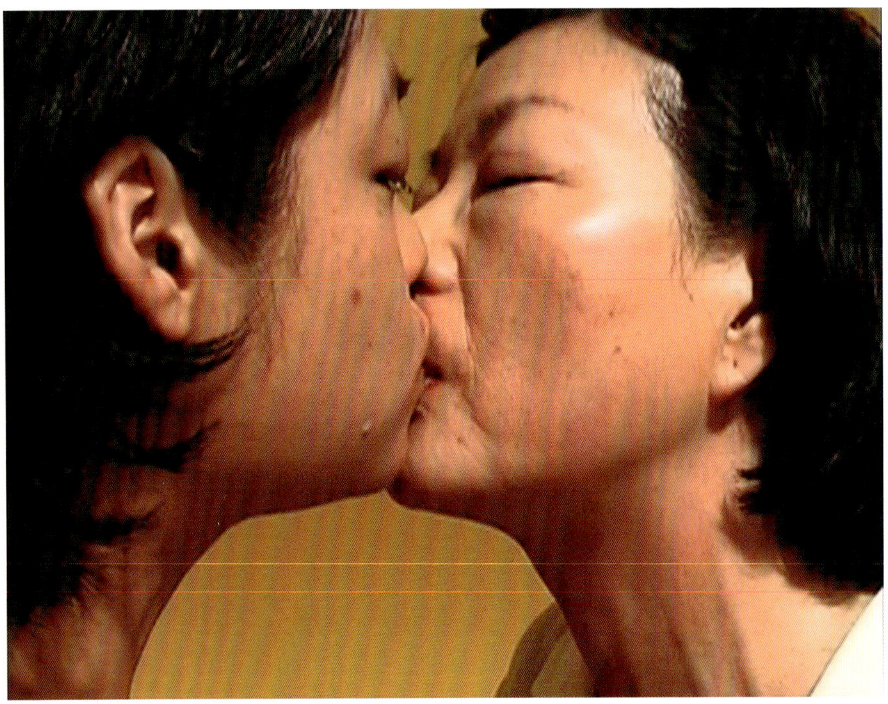

Above and below: Patty Chang, *In Love*, 2001. Two-channel video installation. Dimensions vary on installation; 3 minutes, 28 seconds. Edition of 5.

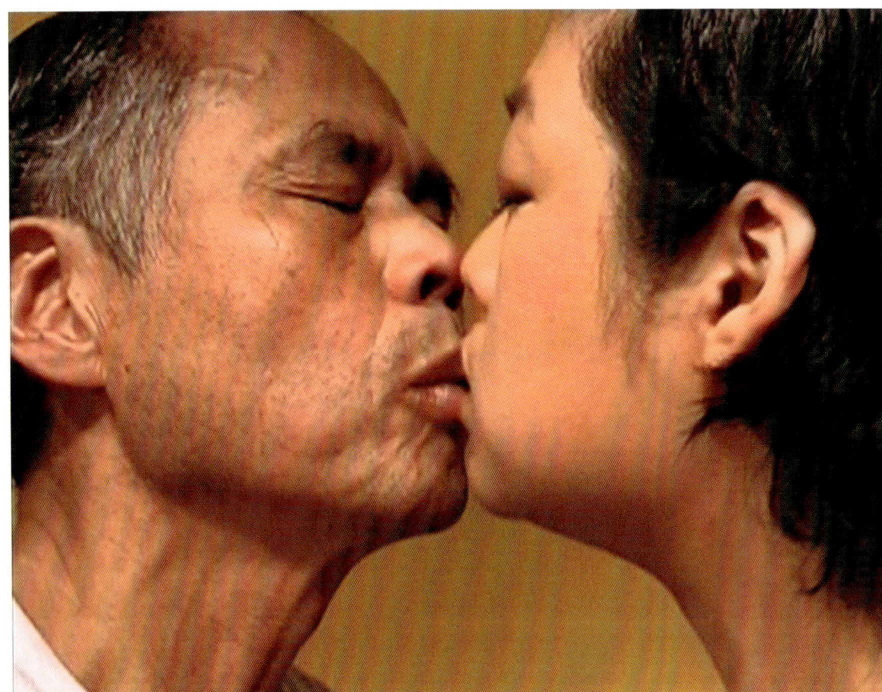

PATTY CHANG

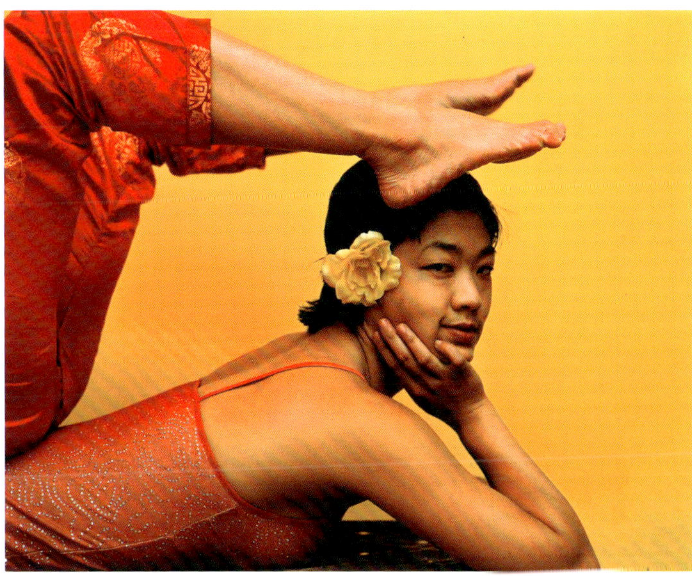

Patty Chang, *Contortion* (video still), 2001. C-print. 40 x 60 inches.

Patty Chang treads along the precarious line between fiction and reality. In her earlier performance-based video works, she combined body-based and experiential art of the 1960s with the technology of fabricating human perception through the use of video. The strategy is paradoxical in that while the tradition of body-based art sought to bridge the conventional divide between art and life, once filtered and framed through the lens of video, any claim to immediacy became suspect to trickery. Chang invests in those illusions the pathos of poetry that engages an empathetic response from the viewer only to expose the deception, leaving the viewer with a feeling being duped.

For instance, *In Love* (2001) shows Chang kissing an older woman and man, who turn out to be her parents. The thought of kissing our aging parents may initially make some of us feel uncomfortable; but then, witnessing them kissing with tears falling down their cheeks brings to mind the idea of enduring familial ties, filled with moments of love as well as pain. Yet, gradually, something emerges out of their mouths and reveals the reality; the video is a rewinding image of the artist and her family consuming a raw onion. As they eat the pungent vegetable they start to cry and their mouths eventually meet in a beguilingly emotional kiss.

In another mesmerizing work entitled *Contortion* (2000), Chang poses as an exotic Chinese contortionist, clad in a silk costume and hair adorned with a blooming peony. She seductively smiles at the viewer while sinuous legs drape over her shoulders in an impossible manner. Her lower body is cropped in the video's frame so that her dexterity appears deceptively truthful. Her coy smile, however, begins to look straight into our hidden desire to objectify her body as a seductive curio. It is, in fact, a curious image of a body since it is performed by two people.

Chang's effective manipulation of vision in the framework of video makes the genre of "documentary" itself the subject of analysis. This becomes most evident in her recent, ambitious video work, *Shangri-La* (2005), produced as part of the Three M Project—a series of works commissioned jointly by the Hammer Museum in Los Angeles, the Museum of Contemporary Art in Chicago, and the New Museum of Contemporary Art in New York. *Shangri-La* documents Chang's trip to Zhongdian County in Diqing Prefecture, located in China's Yunnan Province. This mountainous town near the Tibetan border has such an ethereal atmosphere that in 2002 the Chinese government allowed the town to change its name to

Shangri-La (to attract tourism), the name of a utopia in James Hilton's novel *Lost Horizon* (1933). The artist shows herself interacting with local people in what appears to be an effort to produce some kind of B-movie, starring herself as a heroin who is about to marry a white male character. There is no specific narrative either to her trip or to the imaginary movie. The context of the work becomes more complex when considering the location as the self-declared "real" Shangri-La, whose origin lies within fiction. Chang's video work is about the "truthiness" of Shangri-La and art as a whole; in both, perception matters more than facts. **MT**

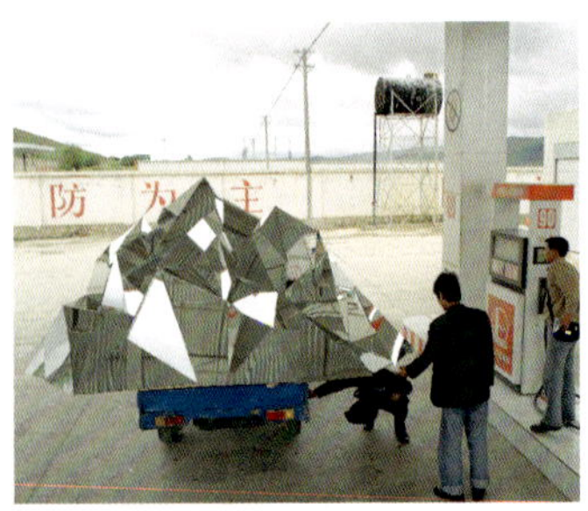

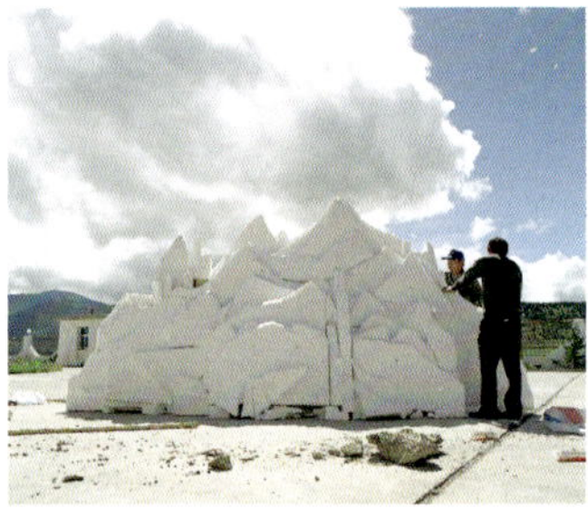

Above left: Patty Chang, *Shangri-La*, 2005. C-print. 20 x 24 inches. Edition of 5. Above right: Patty Chang, *Shangri-La*, 2005. C-print. 20 x 24 inches. Edition of 5.

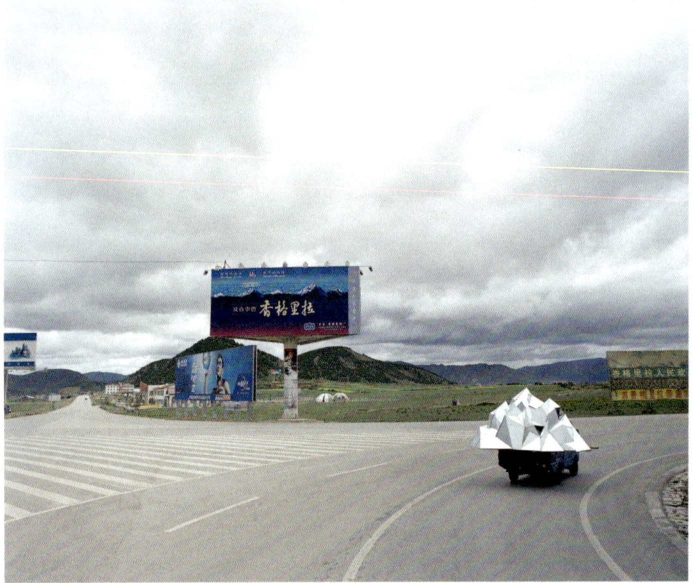

Patty Chang, *Shangri-La* (Mirror Mountain - Billboards), 2005. C-print. 20 x 24 inches. Edition of 5.

PATTY CHANG

Born in 1972, San Francisco, California; Lives and works in New York, New York

EDUCATION: 1994, Bachelor of Arts, University of California, San Diego; **SOLO EXHIBITIONS:** 2005, "Shangri-La," part of the "Three M Project," Armand Hammer Museum of Art and Cultural Center, Los Angeles; New Museum of Contemporary Art, New York; Museum of Contemporary Art, Chicago; 2002, Galerie Gabrielle Maubrie, Paris, France; 2001, Jack Tilton/Anna Kustera Gallery, New York, New York; **GROUP EXHIBITIONS AND PERFORMANCES:** 2003, "Moving Pictures: Contemporary Photography and Video from the Guggenheim Museum Collections," Guggenheim Museum Bilbao, Spain; 2002, "Mirror, Mirror on the Wall," Massachusetts Museum of Contemporary Art (MASS MoCA), North Adams, Massachusetts; 2002, "Moving Pictures," Solomon R. Guggenheim Museum, New York, New York; **GRANTS AND AWARDS:** 2005, Lambert Fellowship in the Arts, Tides Foundation, New York, New York; 2003, The Media Arts Fellowship, The Rockefeller Foundation, New York, New York; 2000, The Louis Comfort Tiffany Foundation, New York, New York

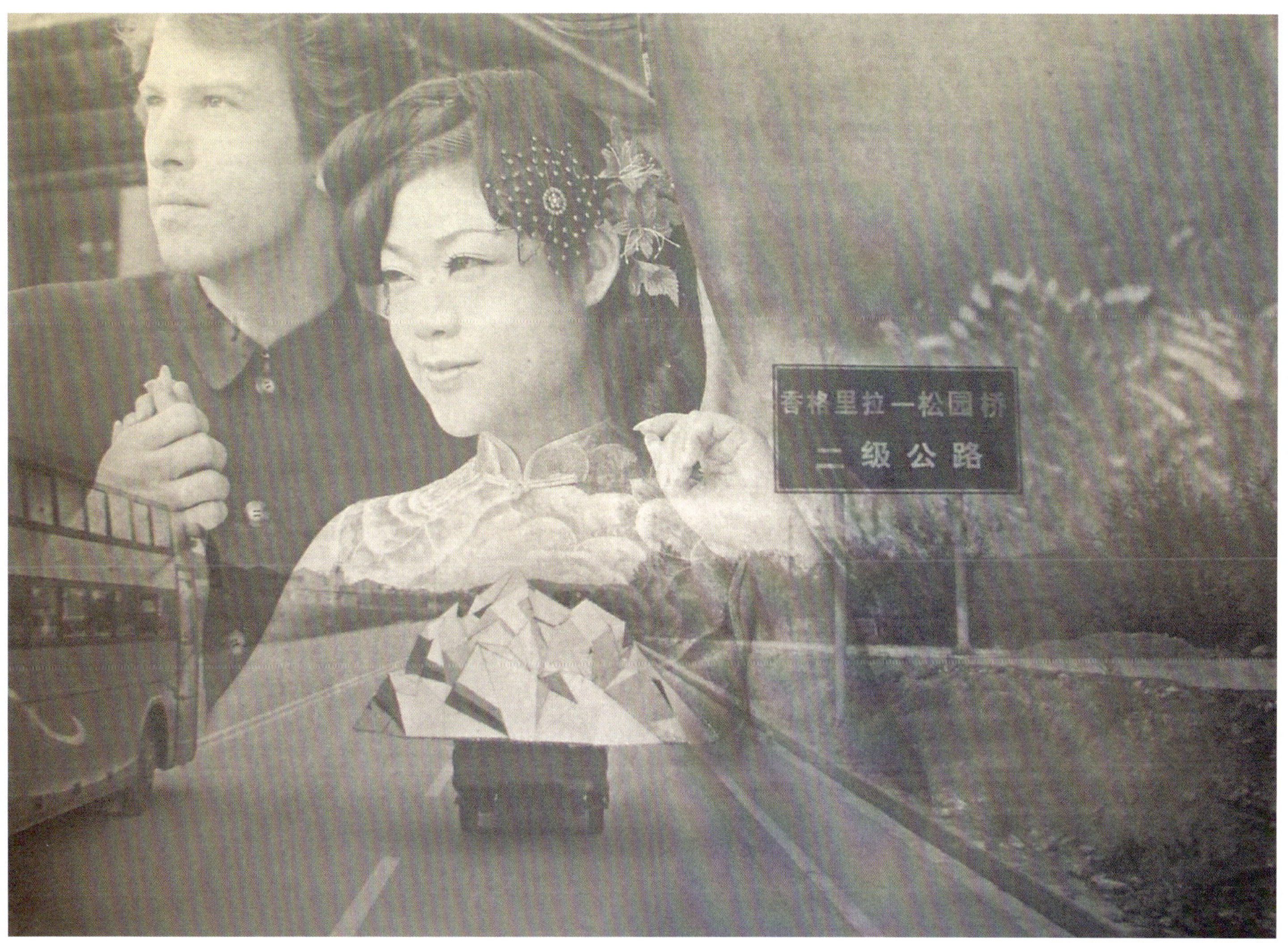

Patty Chang, *Shangri-La Wars no. 1*, 2005. Solar plate etching on paper with chine colle. 22½ x 30¼ inches. Edition of 20. Produced by Art in General.

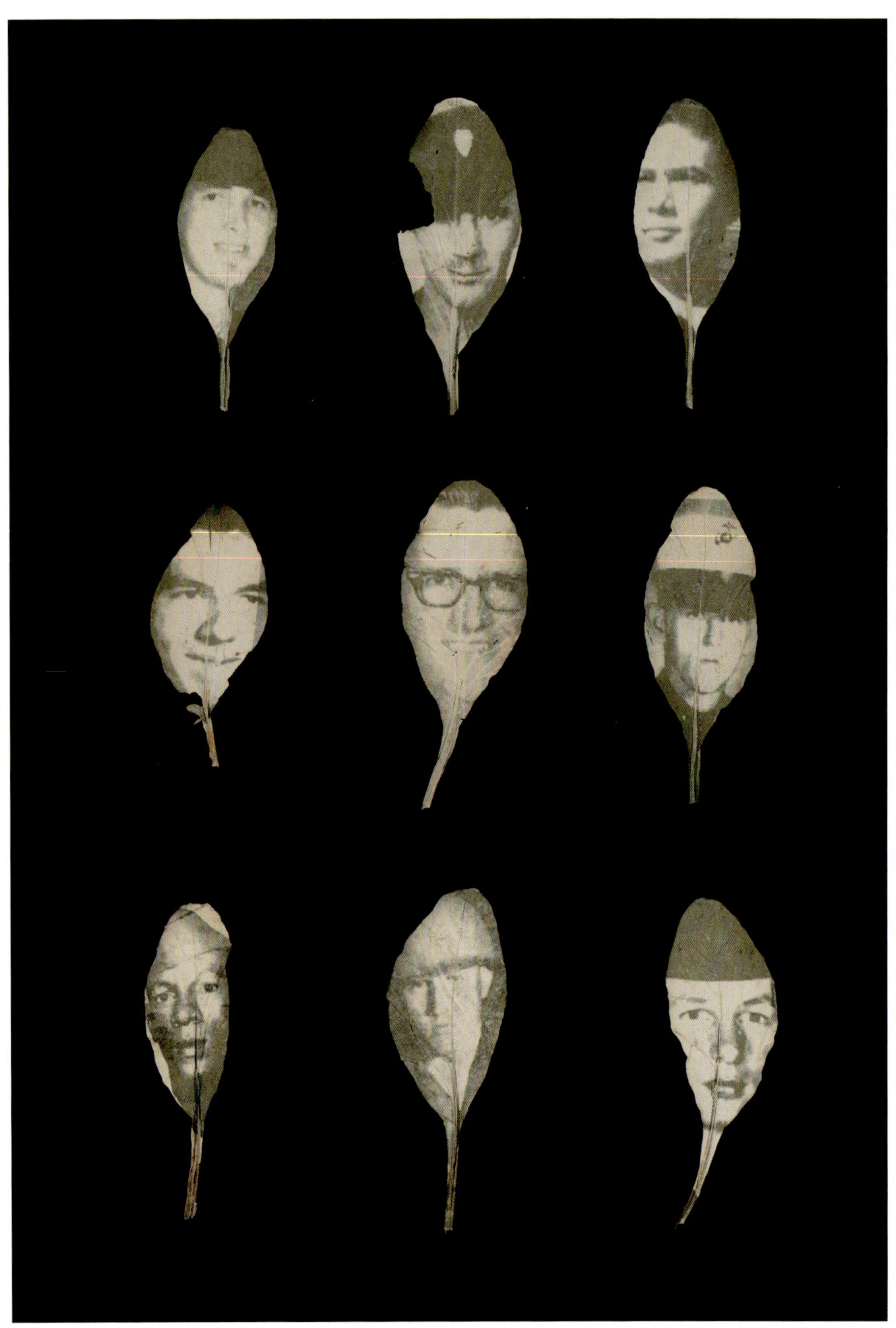

Binh Danh, *Dead*, from the *LIFE: One Week's Dead Series*, 2006. Photo print on leaves arranged in a grid of 9 images. Each image 10 x 8 inches. Collection of the artist.

BINH DANH

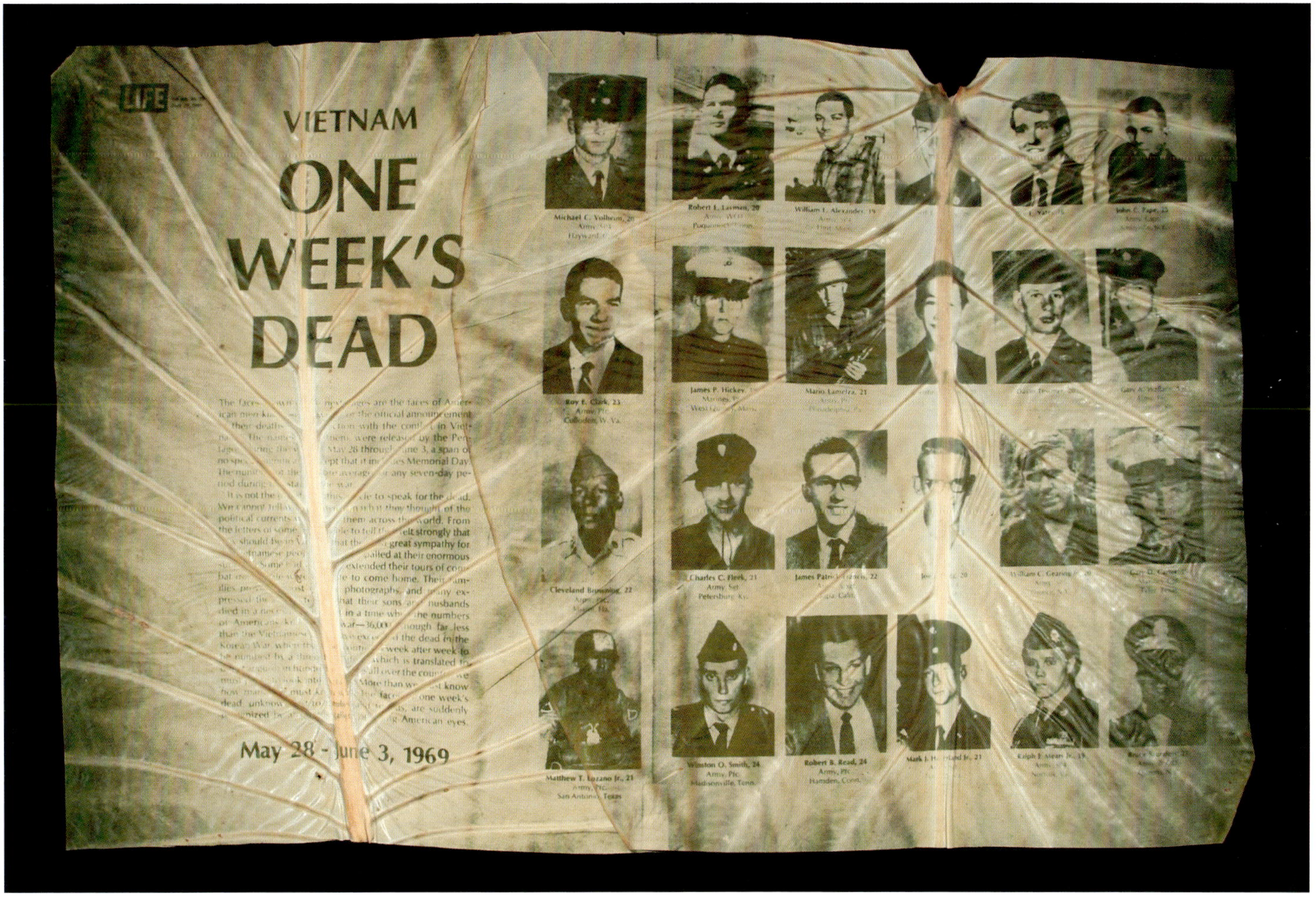

Binh Danh, *One Week's Dead #1*, from the *LIFE: One Week's Dead Series*, 2006. Chlorophyll print and resin. 17½ x 24 inches. Collection of the artist.

Binh Danh is an artist for whom history is of the utmost importance. Key to his work is the idea of an extended teleological thread of time embedded in the earth. For him "history itself is heavy. Through time it sinks, slowly but surely and deeply, into the ground."[1]

His works—historical and personal images photosynthetically imprinted on leaves freshly cut from their source—explore the notion of making evident an invisible but fundamentally extant history. Fragments of written texts as well as images of fallen soldiers, the heavens, or family members are transferred over a period of weeks onto leaves and then preserved, seemingly scientifically, in blocks of resin. His work recalls that of other artists before him, especially Richard Long and Ana Mendieta, who imprint elements of their personal actions and histories onto the landscape. But unlike Long and Mendieta, who documented the marks they left on the earth's surface, Danh's theoretical underpinning is the manifestation of an invisible history embedded in the earth itself.

Binh Danh, *One Week's Dead #2*, from the *LIFE: One Week's Dead Series*, 2006. Chlorophyll print and resin. 27¼ x 21¼ inches. Collection of the artist.

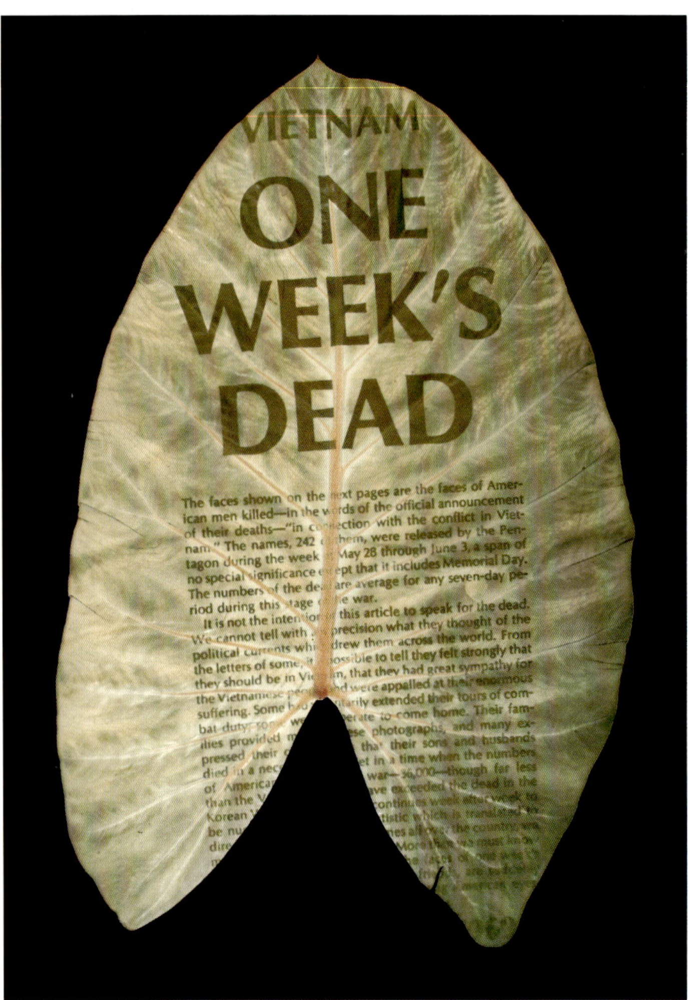

An immigrant to the United States from Vietnam at the age of two, Danh is very much influenced by the history of the Vietnam and American War and often explores his relationship to the United States and to Vietnam in his artworks. He describes a body of work with images of the Vietnam and American War printed on tropical leaves as a "transmigration of matter: the decomposition and composition of matter into other forms. The images of war are part of the leaves and live inside and outside of them. The leaves express the continuum of war. They contain the residue of the Vietnam and American War: bombs, blood, sweat, tears, and metal. The dead have been incorporated into the landscape of Vietnam during the cycles of birth, life, and death. . . . Since matter is neither created nor destroyed, but only transformed, the remnants of the Vietnam and American War live on forever in the Vietnamese landscape."[2]

His most recent body of work includes images from the June 27, 1969 issue of *Life Magazine* entitled "The Faces of the American Dead in Vietnam: One Week's Toll." Printed on leaves and strung with fishnet, the sculptural piece resembles a series of vines, and, more than the bodies of work preceding it, highlights the relationships between the people represented, national histories, and nature. Deeply resonant with current images of the dead from Iraq, the piece also underscores how little we have learned from history. Separated by forty years, the young men in these images could easily be the ones in the newspapers today. Again too, only American faces are represented, indicating the blind spots that facilitate war.

AC

1. Binh Danh, "The Inbetweeners" (MFA thesis, Stanford University, 2004), 11.
2. Ibid., 10.

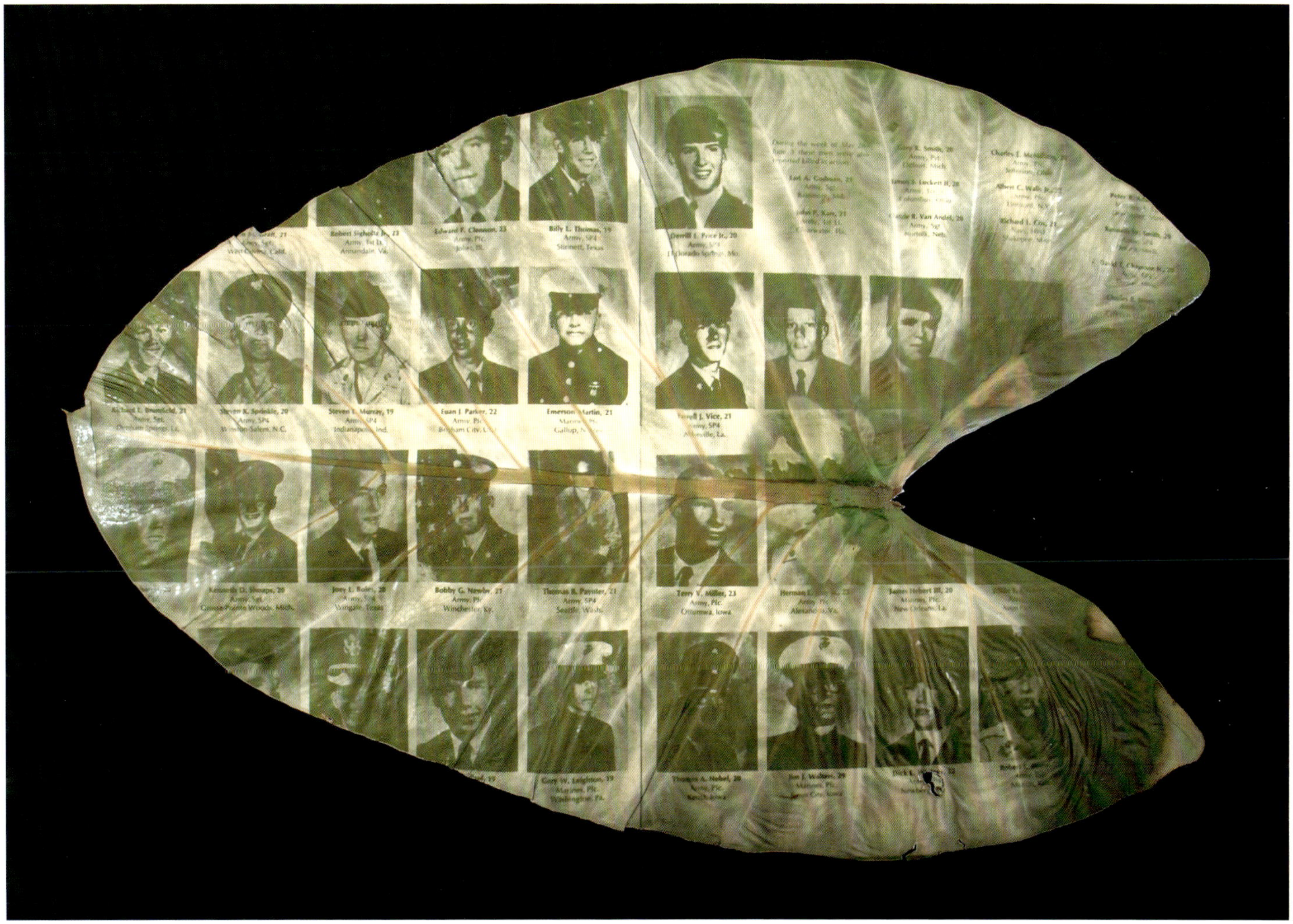

Binh Danh, *Dead #2*, from the *LIFE: One Week's Dead Series*, 2006. Chlorophyll print and resin. 18¾ x 25¾ inches. Collection of the artist.

BINH DANH

Born in 1977, Kien Giang, Vietnam; Lives and works in San Jose, California **EDUCATION:** 2004, Master of Fine Arts, Stanford University, California; 2002, Bachelor of Fine Arts, San Jose State University, California; **SOLO EXHIBITION:** 2004, "human/nature," Haines Gallery, San Francisco, California; **GROUP EXHIBITIONS:** 2005, "Stages of Memory: The Vietnam War," Museum of Contemporary Photography, Chicago, Illinois; 2005, "Persistent Vestiges: Drawing from the American-Vietnam; War," The Drawing Center, New York, New York; 2004, "Collapsing Histories Project," Daigo Fukuryu Maru Exhibition Hall and Gallery ef, Tokyo, Japan; 2003, "Bring Light into the Darkness," SomArts Cultural Center, San Francisco, California

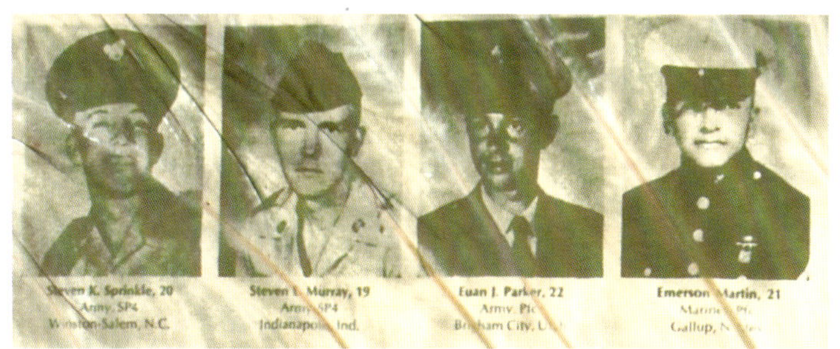

Binh Danh, *Dead #2*, from the *LIFE: One Week's Dead Series* (detail).

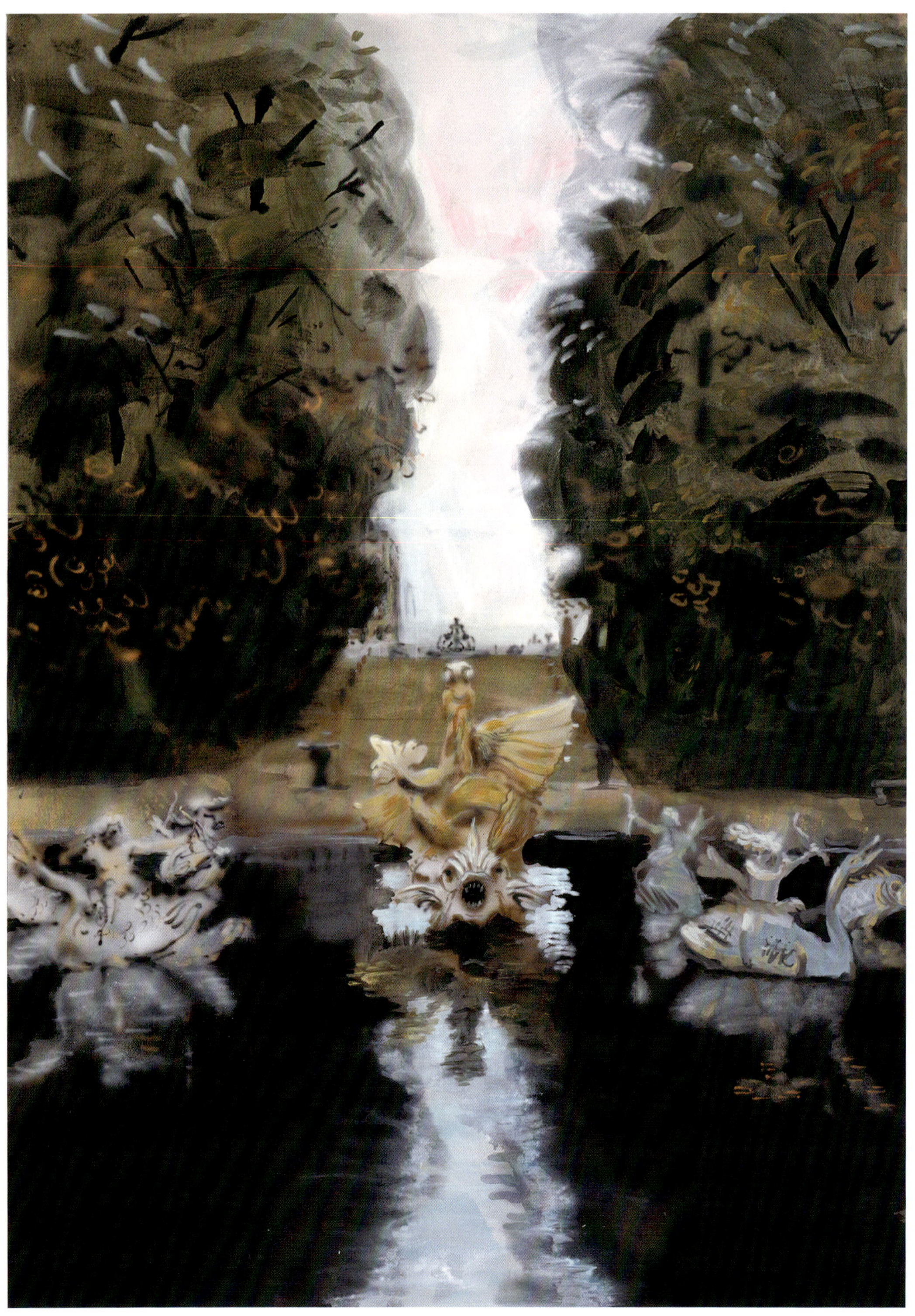

Mari Eastman, *Versailles*, 2004. Acrylic and glitter on canvas. 84 x 60 inches. Collection of Eileen Harris Norton, Santa Monica.

MARI EASTMAN

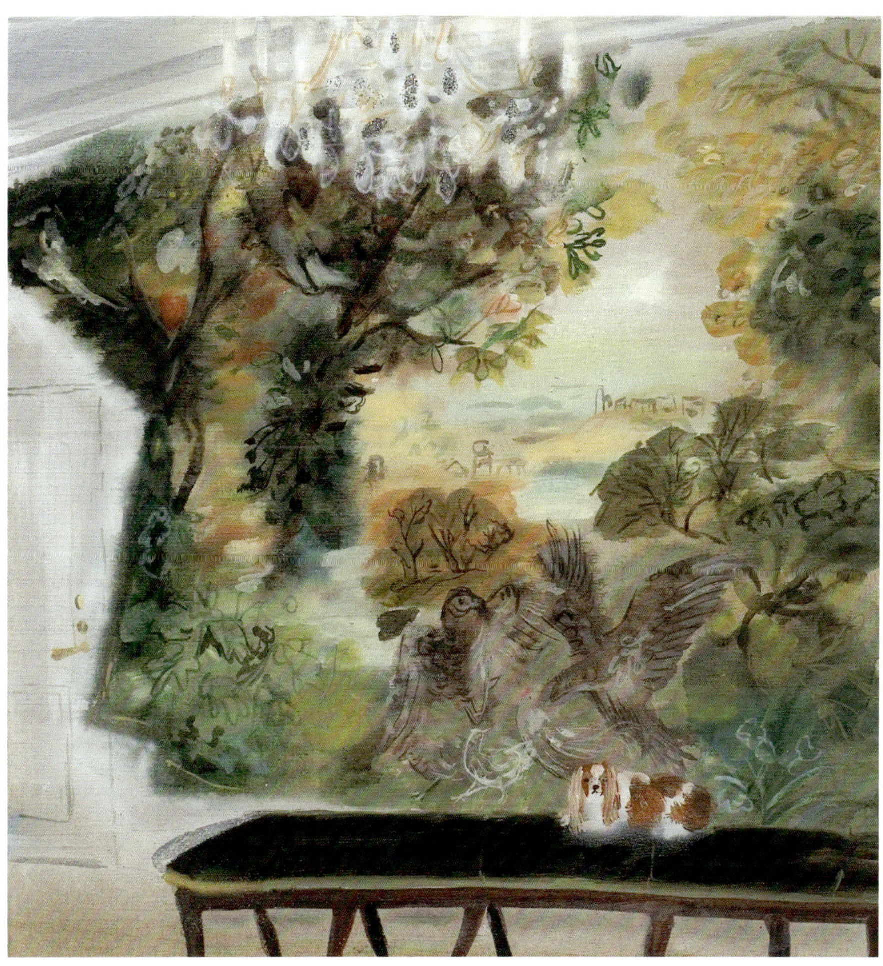

Mari Eastman, *Chelsea on Bench in front of Tapestry*, 2003. Acrylic, oil, glitter on canvas. 32 x 30 inches. Collection of Karyn Lovegrove and Peter Leak.

Mari Eastman's paintings and drawings originate from images, ranging from the unsettling to the banal (or the unsettlingly banal), that we encounter on a daily basis. Working from imagination and from magazines, dollar store calendars, newspapers, and Time-Life books, Eastman uses spray, airbrush, acrylic, oil paints, and other media to render beautifully hazy landscapes, Asian antiquities, war scenes, animals, luxurious interiors, and recently, Native American portraits and early American landscapes.

With their sparkly surfaces and pastel washes Eastman's images can, and have been, read as knowing appropriations of girlishness. While that is undoubtedly an aspect of the work, her use, in the past few years, of source material portraying scenes of war and colonization invite a different read of her oeuvre. She writes of a "desire for equilibrium" but also points out the underlying violence in much of her source material, which includes not only war and hunting scenes, but also, luxury items and splendid interiors (including ones

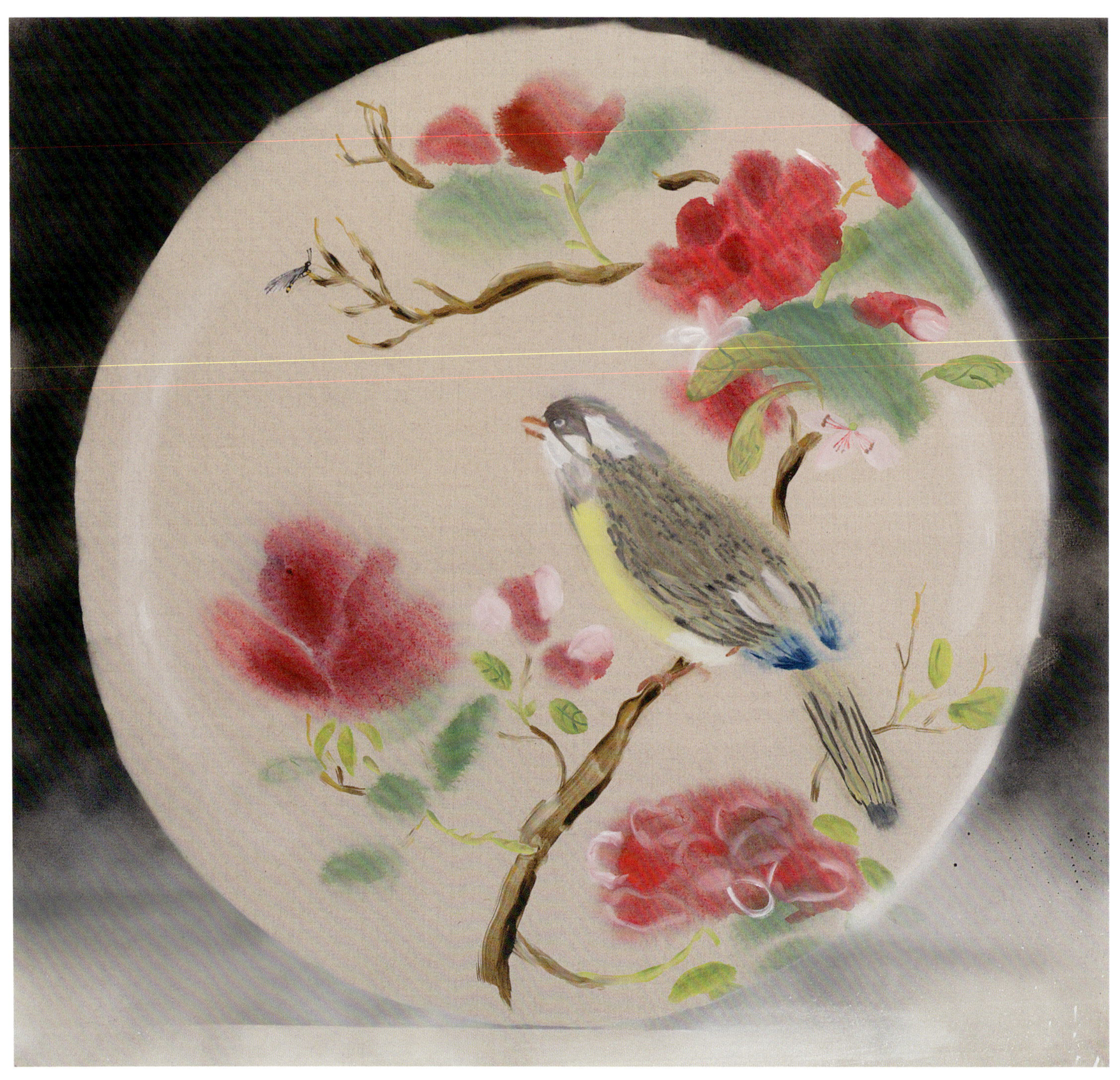

Mari Eastman, *Bird on Flowering Spray: Porcelain Cup, Chieng-lung Period (1736–1750)*, 2004. Acrylic on canvas. 40½ x 43½ inches. Collection of Rosette Delug.

from Versailles). While she indulges in the sheer pleasure of beauty and celebrates the often mundane ways in which we incorporate aesthetic pleasure into our everyday lives she also notes the darker side of much of this pleasure.

In an early piece Eastman stuck a magazine photo to the center of the canvas, thinking that she might paint in the surrounding scene of cameras, lights, and props used to create the image. Ultimately she decided to extend, rather than detract, from the illusion, using her imagination to further the context captured in the photo. Her decision to depict the fantasy constructed in the photograph rather than the reality surrounding it continues to inform her work.

Eastman's signature use of glitter imbues her works with a simultaneous sense of magic—glitter as fairy dust—and kitsch. She refers to glitter as a representation of the gap between an imagined ideal and reality. Laying paint to canvas is an attempt to capture the perfectly envisioned image, which, in spite of any artist's skill, always remains elusive. The lush perfection—verdant forests, gorgeous sunsets, tumbling waterfalls—captured in Eastman's works draws, in part, from traditional Chinese landscape paintings. She describes these as "fantasy lands" in contrast to the punishing, Christian-influenced landscapes of an artist such as Pieter Bruegel. Ironically, many of Eastman's lush paintings now depict war, or in the case of the Native American landscapes, "a lost Eden."

In her exhibitions Eastman treats her paintings as parts of a larger scene, drawing beyond the borders of the canvas with Sharpie markers directly onto the gallery walls. These extensions sometimes include multiple works, incorporating them together as part of a larger holistic landscape. **AC**

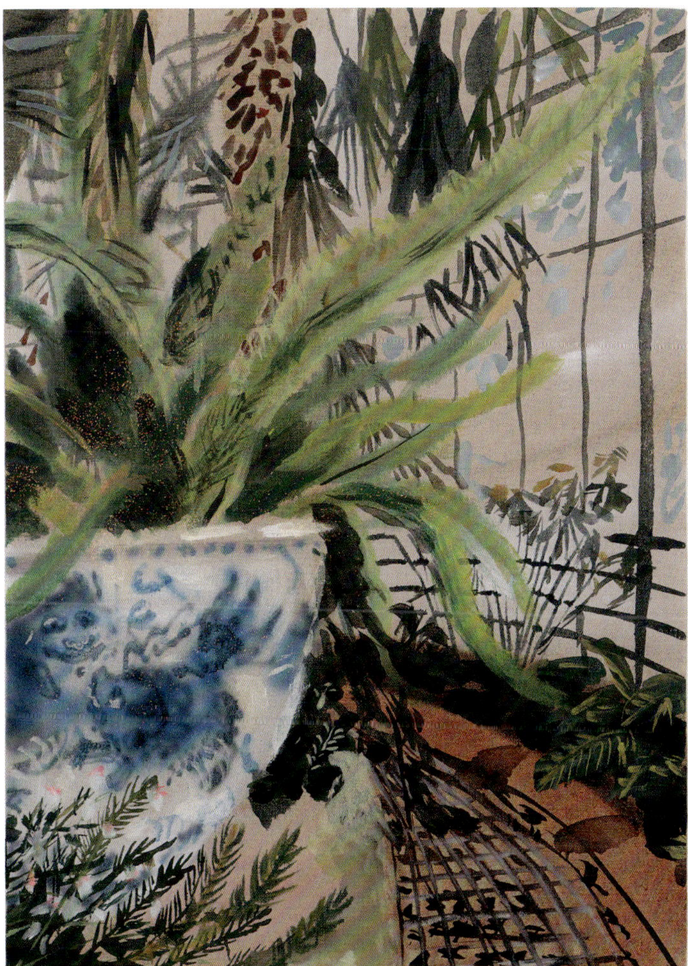

Mari Eastman, *Brussels' Palace*, 2004. Acrylic and glitter on canvas. 22 x 16 inches. Collection of Craig & Lynn Jacobson.

MARI EASTMAN

Born in 1970, Berkeley, California; Lives and works in Los Angeles, California **EDUCATION:** 1996, Master of Fine Arts, School of the Art Institute of Chicago, Illinois, Chicago; 1992, Bachelor of Arts, Smith College, Northampton, Massachusetts; 1991, Chautauqua School of Art, New York; 1990–91, Wesleyan University, Middletown, Connecticut; **SOLO EXHIBITIONS:** 2005, Nicolai Wallner Gallery, Copenhagen, Denmark; 2004, Karyn Lovegrove Gallery, Los Angeles, California; **GROUP EXHIBITIONS:** 2005, "Alex Bircken, Mari Eastman, Maaike Schoorel," Maureen Paley, London, England; 2004, "The Undiscovered Country," Armand Hammer Museum of Art and Cultural Center, Los Angeles, California; 2003, "Girls Gone Wild," Bronwyn Keenan Gallery, New York, New York; **GRANTS AND AWARDS:** 1997, Illinois Arts Council Artists Fellowship Award; 1994, Philip Morris Fellowship for Artists of Color

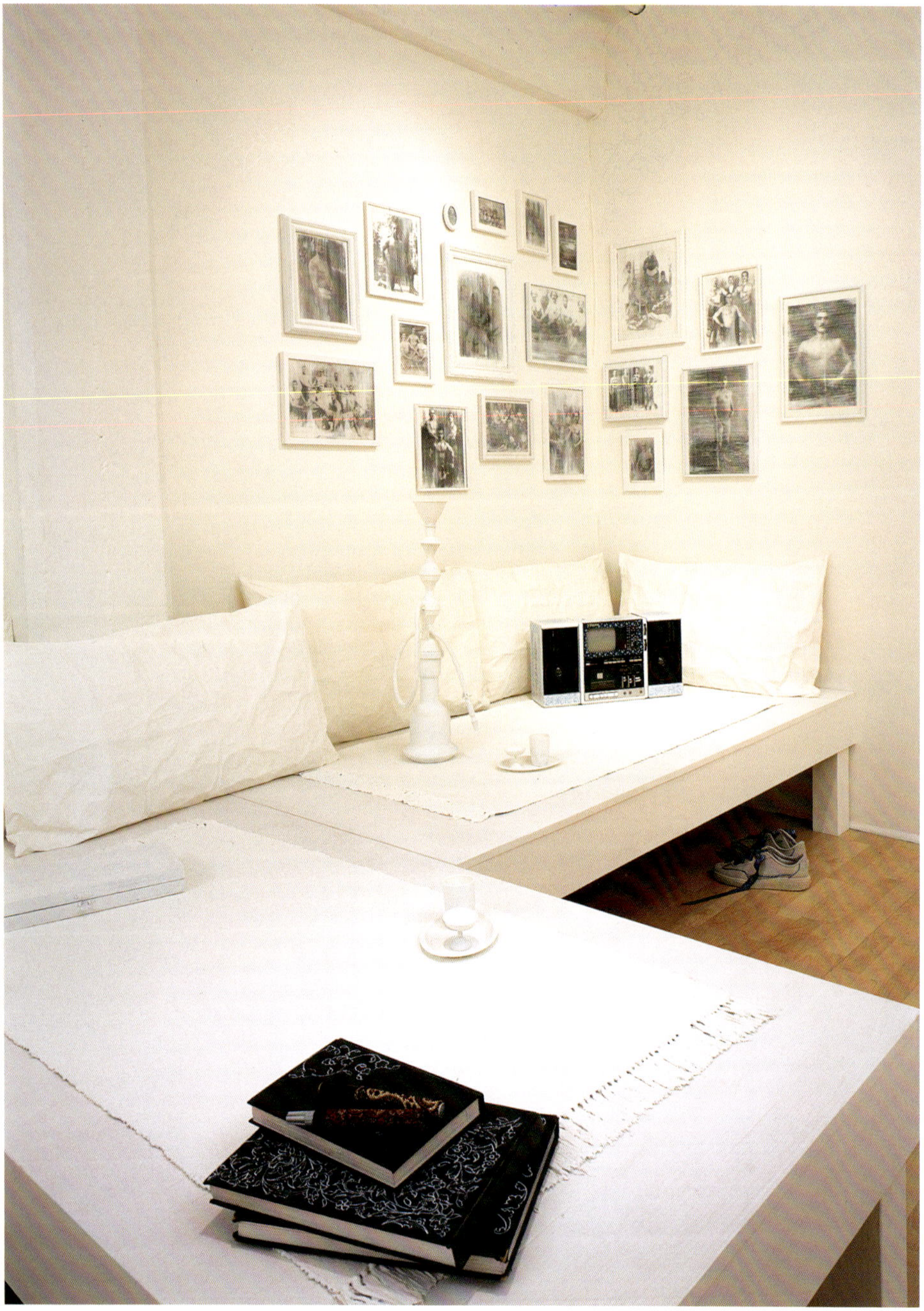

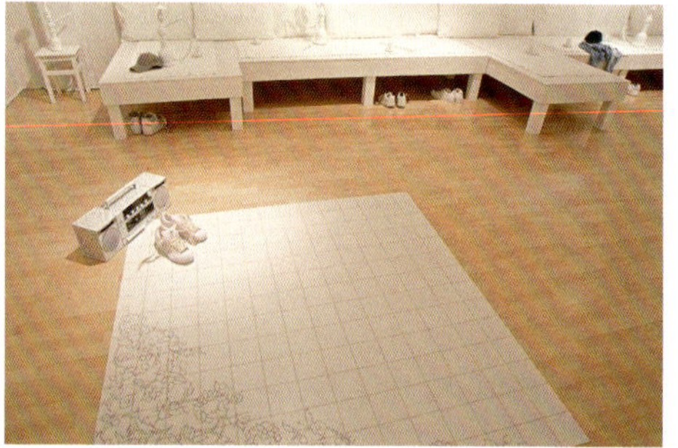

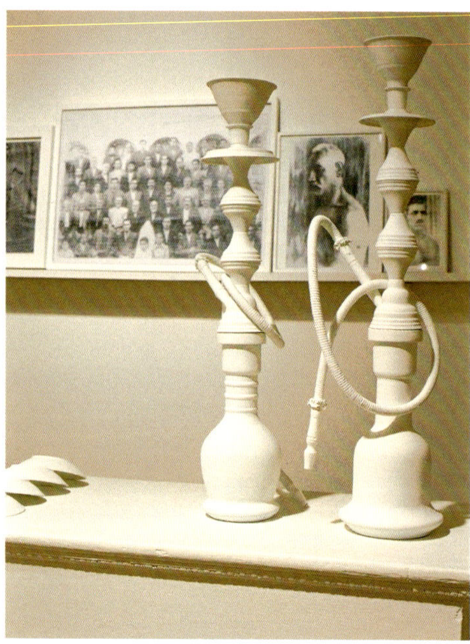

This page and opposite: Ala Ebtekar, *Elemental*, 2004. Mixed media. Dimensions variable (total of 156 x 180 inches footprint area; two benches; 60 x 60 inches linoleum floor; a counter/table with sculptural elements). Collection of the artist.

ALA EBTEKAR

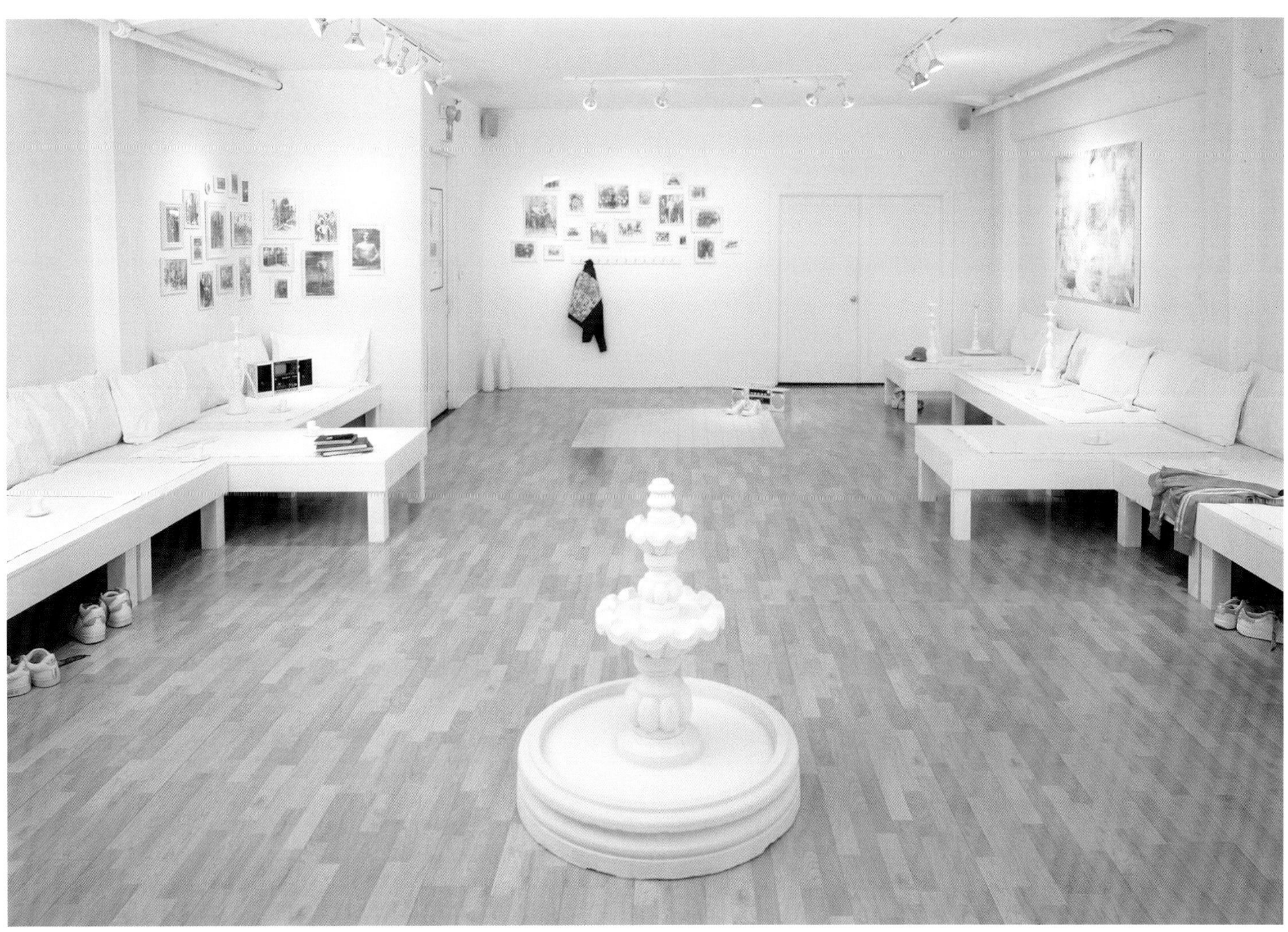

Ala Ebtekar's works over the past four years (during which he received his BFA and began an MFA program) have been profoundly affected by his visits to Iran. At the age of nineteen he returned to his parent's birth land for the first time since the age of one. When a stay of a few weeks was extended to six months, Ebtekar studied at an art school in Tehran. A native of Berkeley, California, Ebtekar was influenced by an exhibition in Tehran of contemporary Iranian Cubist painters and his classmates' interests in Western art. On the contrary, Ebtekar's interest turned to Persian miniature paintings and calligraphy, which he studied with an instructor outside of school, and, later, to Iranian coffeehouse paintings. Two artistic traditions that deal with the same subject matter—heroic epics from *The Book of Kings*—miniature paintings and coffeehouse paintings exist on opposite ends of the class divide. Miniature paintings, often commissioned by the nobility, incorporate written text, while coffeehouse paintings are done on wall hangings or walls in coffeehouses and are narrated for largely illiterate audiences by modern day bards.

Ebtekar was struck by the similarity between the coffeehouse milieu, which has been slowly dying out in Iran, and the hip-hop and graffiti cultures in the United States. Both traditions blend narration and rhythm with visual and physical expression. His first large-scale installation, *Elemental* (2004), appeared as a dream world locale synthesizing these two traditions. Whitewashed coffeehouse paintings and photographs of wrestlers, traditional coffeehouse seating, and hookahs co-existed with boom boxes covered with Persian floral motifs, embroidered track jackets, and beaded Adidas with fat-laces made from Iranian ribbons.

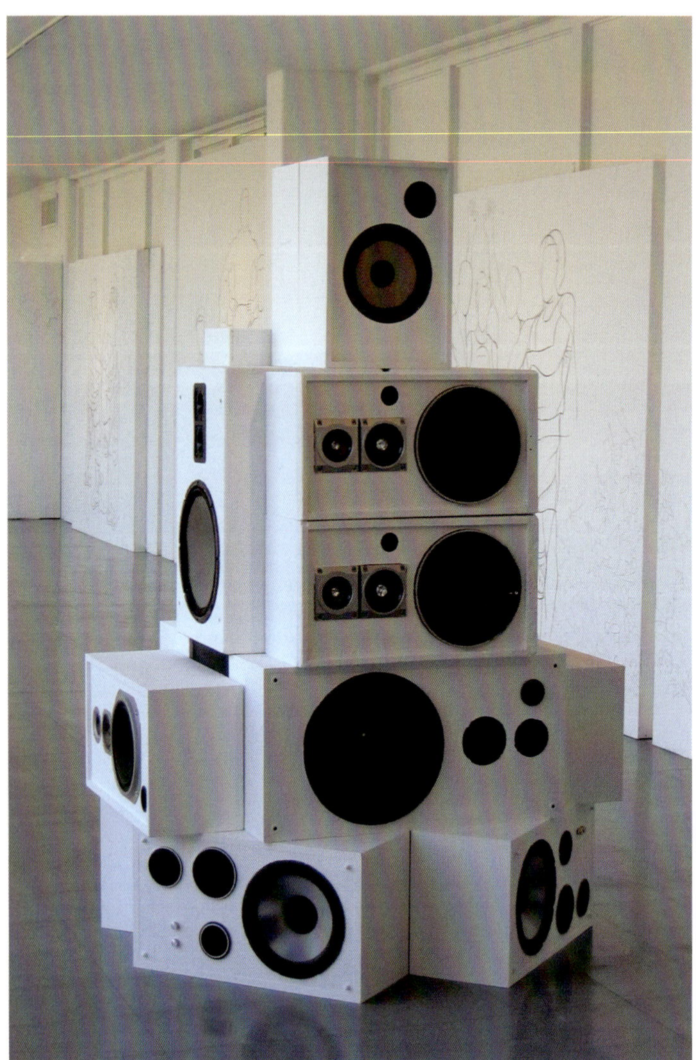

Ala Ebtekar, *Emergence*, 2006. Mixed media. Dimensions variable. Collection of the artist. Installation view at Richmond Art Center, California.

A more recent body of work, *Aahangar Project* (2005), included a falsified ancient text—the first Iranian text on cyborgs—and cartoonish drawings of Transformer-like Iranian heroic figures. Ebtekar plans to issue these drawings, "a re-writing of mythology to create my own mythology," as trading cards in Tehran. For him the re-insertion of these figures into Iranian culture is a "closing of the circle" of his borrowings and re-interpretations.[1]

His most recent works feature sketchy drawings showing faceless figures, layered and seemingly morphing and merging into one another. Their unfinished quality embodies the sense of transience implied in the word "Emergence," a frequent part of the titles of the exhibitions in which that work has appeared. Figures in Iranian wrestler garb pose in B-boy stances: the amalgamation of signifiers indicates a new synthesis. Stacks of painted speakers or boom boxes stand in the center of Ebtekar's 2006 exhibitions at Gallery Paule Anglim in San Francisco and the Richmond Art Center in Richmond, California. Surrounded by the shifting figures populating his drawings, they seem to be beating out a new, but familiar, rhythm.

AC

1. Ala Ebtekar, conversation with the author, February 14, 2006.

ALA EBTEKAR

Born in 1978, Berkeley, California; Lives and works in Berkeley, California **EDUCATION:** 2006, Master of Fine Arts, Stanford University, California; 2002, Bachelor of Fine Arts, San Francisco Art Institute, California; **SOLO EXHIBITIONS:** 2006, "Emergence," Richmond Art Center, California; 2004, "Elemental," Intersection for the Arts, San Francisco, California; **GROUP EXHIBITIONS:** 2005, "Ala Ebtekar & Jeong-Im Yi," Lisa Dent Gallery, San Francisco, California; 2004, "REBUS," Gallery Paule Anglim, San Francisco, California; 2003, "War of the Worlds," in collaboration with Tim Rollins + K.O.S., White Box, New York, New York; 2003, "No War," The Luggage Store Gallery, San Francisco, California; **GRANTS AND AWARDS:** 2005, Jack and Gertrude Murphy Fine Arts Fellowship, The San Francisco Foundation, California

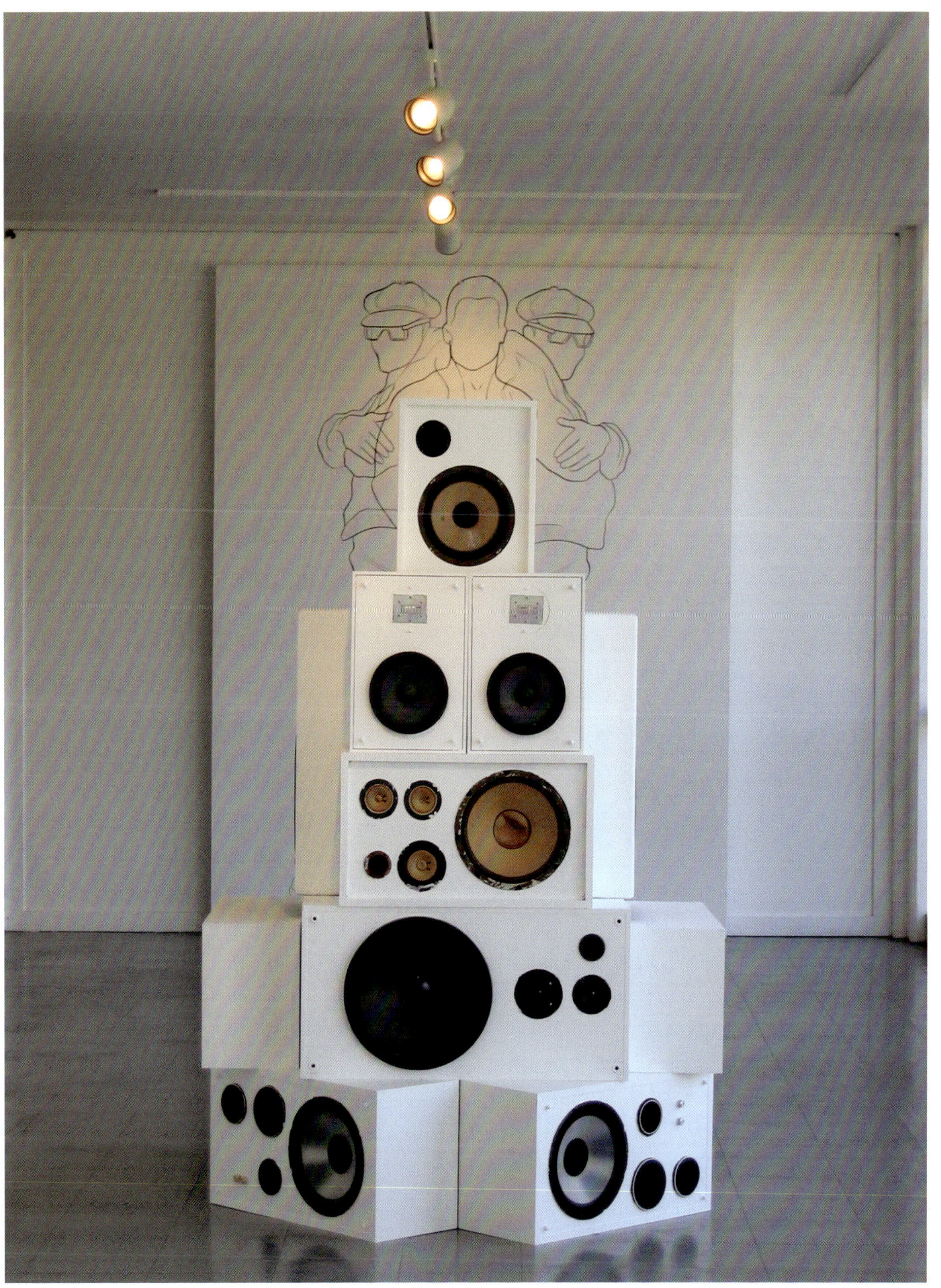

Ala Ebtekar, *Emergence*, 2006. Mixed media. Dimensions variable. Collection of the artist. Installation view at Richmond Art Center, California.

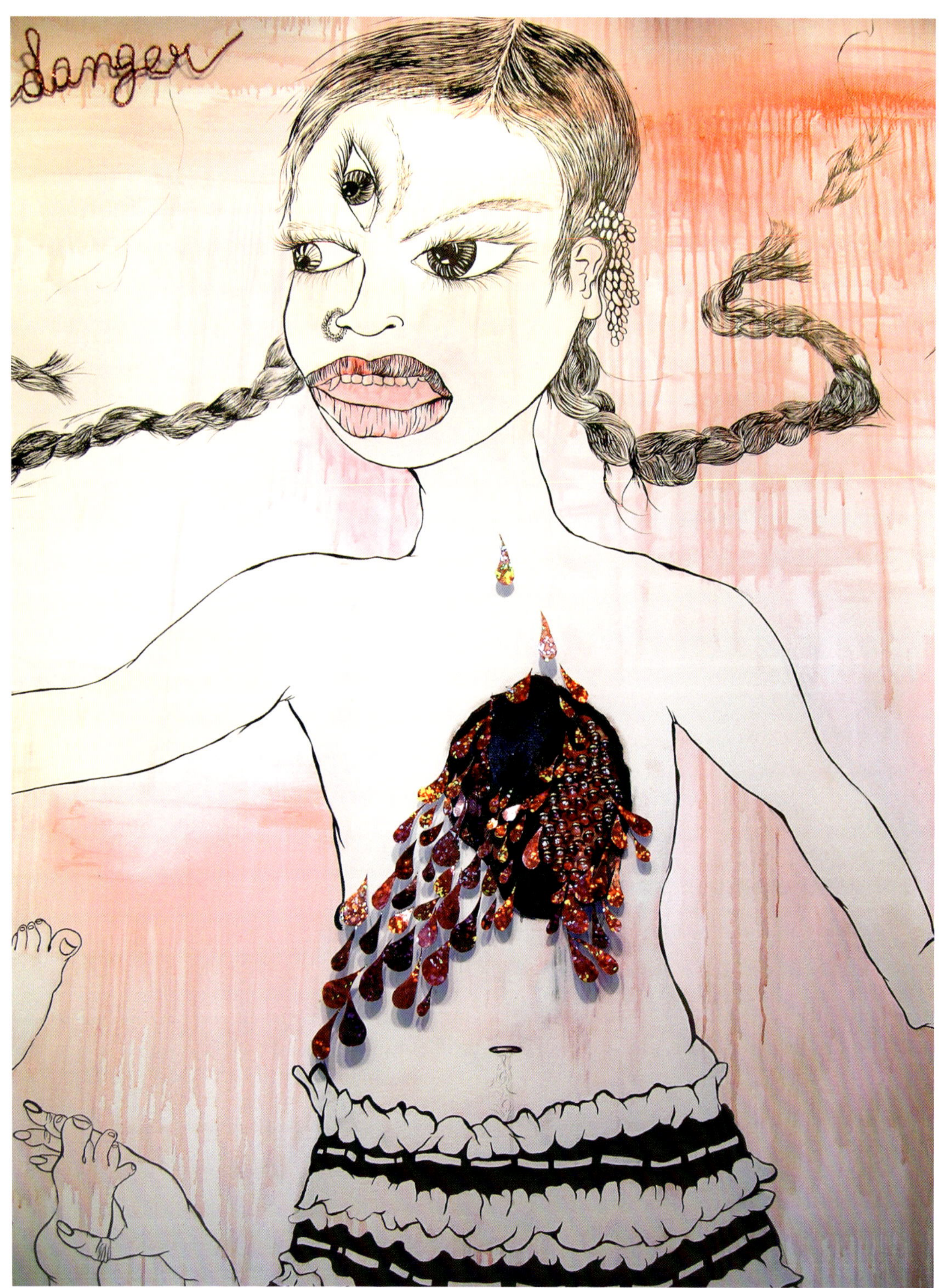

Chitra Ganesh, *Evidence of Past Lives* (detail), 2005. Mixed media. Approx. 120 x 264 inches. Collection of the artist. Installation view at Jersey City Museum, New Jersey.

CHITRA GANESH

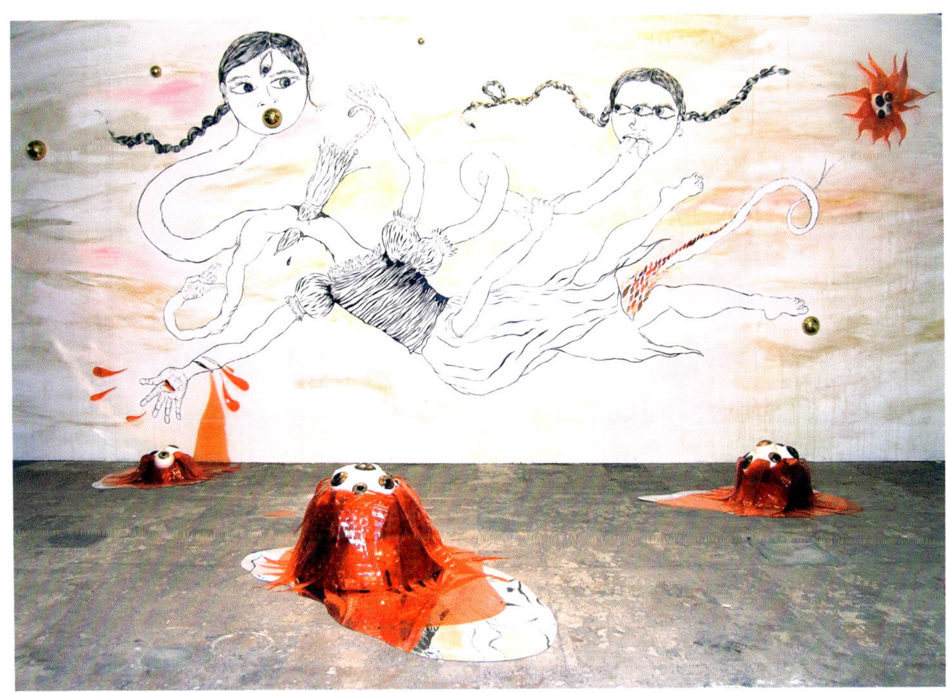

Chitra Ganesh, *Sisters*, 2005. Mixed media. Approx. 120 x 240 x 144 inches. Collection of the artist. Installation view at Lower Manhattan Cultural Council, New York.

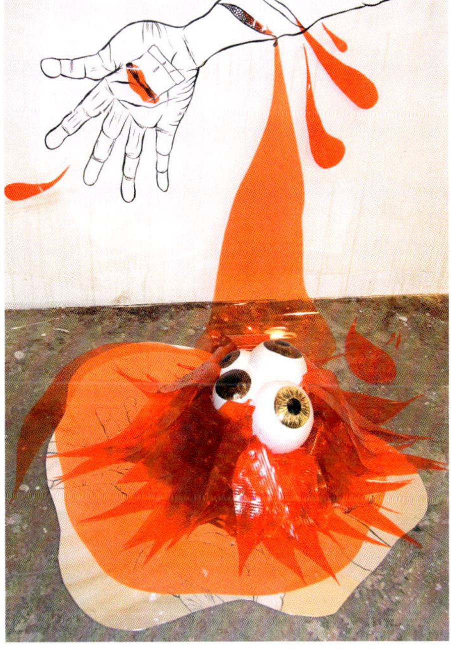

Chitra Ganesh, *Sisters* (detail).

Chitra Ganesh experiments with the multiplicity of meanings in art and language at a time when singular narratives tend to dominate myth, history, religion, and headlines. She reclaims both text and images to offer a retelling of scenes or moments that have often been neglected or forgotten. Ganesh's interest in opening up the making of meaning to diverse groups of viewers mirrors her work as a community activist and educator.

In mural projects such as *Evidence of Past Lives* (Jersey City Museum, 2005), *637 Feet of Running Wall* (Queens Museum of Art, 2002), and *Broken Spell* (Wave Hill, 2005), among numerous others, Ganesh combines drawing, assemblage, and washes of color to create fantastical scenes of re-imagined texts. Drawing upon tales of creation and moral struggle from Hindu, Indian, and Greek mythology, as well as from poetic and current event sources, Ganesh identifies overlooked narratives within the mainstream telling of events. *Broken Spell* identifies the moment in which Surpanakha, a demoness from the Ramayana, is banished to the forest as punishment for expressing amorous desires. Her departure—rather than serving as an appropriate ending—becomes the subject of Ganesh's invigorating image. In a series of other work, Ganesh muses on the notion of "exploration without conquest" by crafting imaginative portraits of Kalpana Chawla, the Indian woman astronaut, who died in the 2003 space shuttle accident.

Sensuous female figures dominate Ganesh's images. Recurring motifs in works such as *Evidence of Past Lives* and *Broken Spells* include a woman's head with black braided hair often detached or tenuously connected to the rest of her body by an elongated neck. Other vital parts, notably her hands, arms, legs, breasts, and eyes

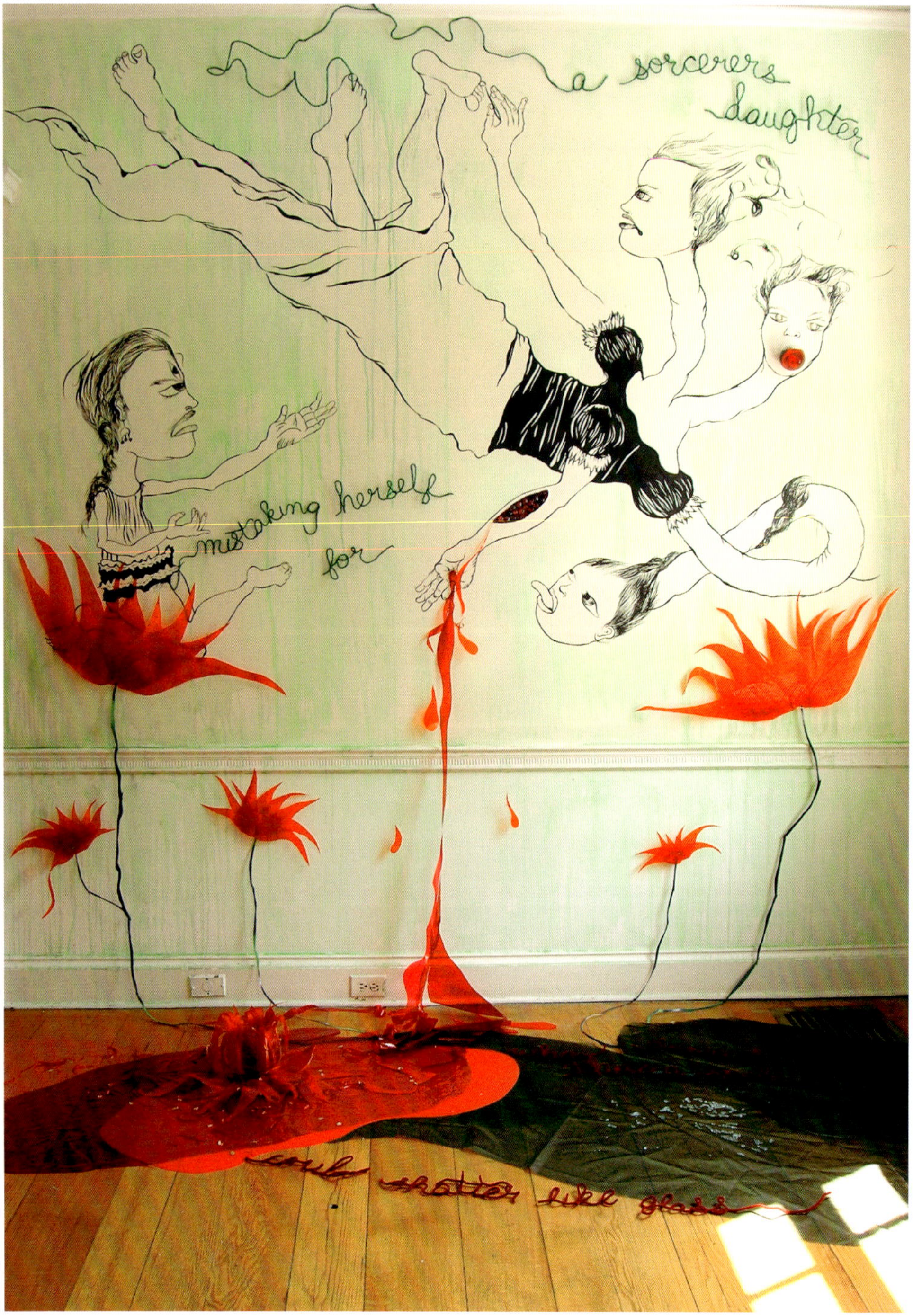

Chitra Ganesh, *Broken Spell*, 2004. Mixed media. Dimensions variable.

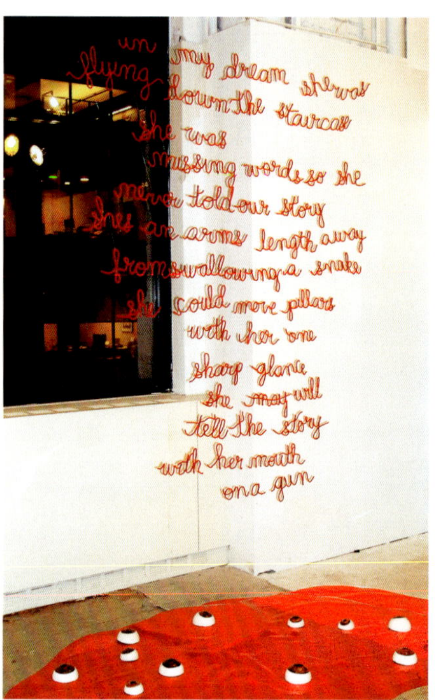

Chitra Ganesh, *In My Dream*, 2005. Mixed media. Dimensions variable. Collection of the artist. Installation view at Lower Manhattan Cultural Council, New York.

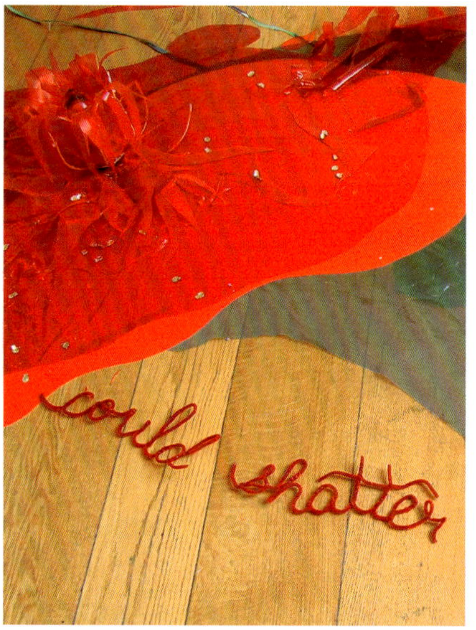

Chitra Ganesh, *Broken Spell* (detail).

multiply in metaphoric numbers. At once seductive, powerful, and dangerous, Ganesh's women are goddess, animal, mother, warrior, and lover. They wield weapons, drip blood from their fangs, offer nourishment, and gaze watchfully all within the same text. Speech also figures into Ganesh's images as phrases float throughout the picture plane in rounded black cursive. The fragmentation of message and disembodiment of her speaker signify space for unspoken stories.

Ganesh embeds casual references to everyday life into her work including brightly colored plastics, textured clothes, and cheap metallic props which rise from the flat surfaces of the wall, sometimes spilling onto the ground. These found, inorganic materials find new purpose as the decaying remains of lush plants and the innards of living creatures. By allowing the mundane and mass-produced to co-exist with icons from myth and history, Ganesh binds the monumentality of text to the everyday existence of her viewers.

Ganesh also uses newspapers, comic-book forms, and other popular graphic imagery sometimes referencing contemporary Bollywood movie posters. Overly dramatized and intensely colored with bands of spoken passages, these tableaux allow her to pose questions between characters and to open additional, alternative views within a prescribed scenic window. *Seeing the Disappeared*, an installation with Mariam Ghani (White Box, Videobox, 2004) utilized missing persons flyers with images of individuals detained and deported as part of post-9/11 homeland security measures to address their lost narrative as well as those missing as a result of 9/11. In her monumental installations, Ganesh continues to examine language as a cultural condition by re-envisioning events and stories of both past and present. **CY**

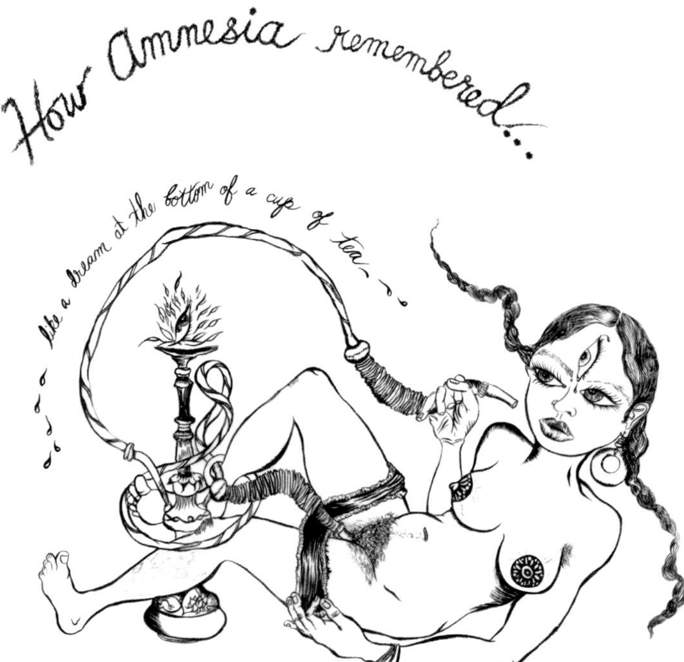

Chitra Ganesh, *Amnesia Remembers*, 2005. Sumi ink on denril paper. 20 x 16 inches. Collection of the artist.

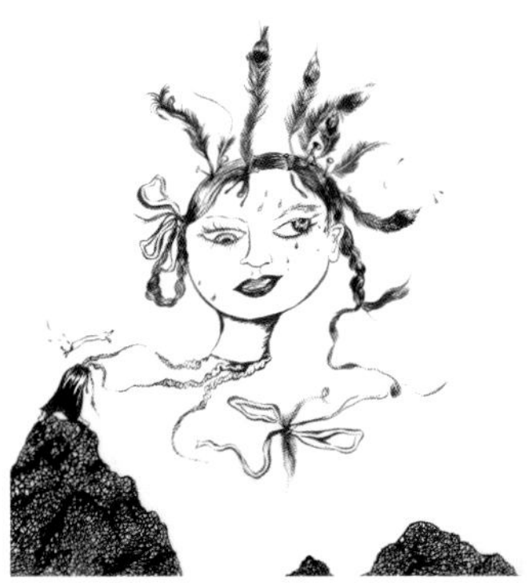

Chitra Ganesh, *Peacocks*, 2005. Sumi ink on denril paper. 16 x 14 inches. Collection of the artist.

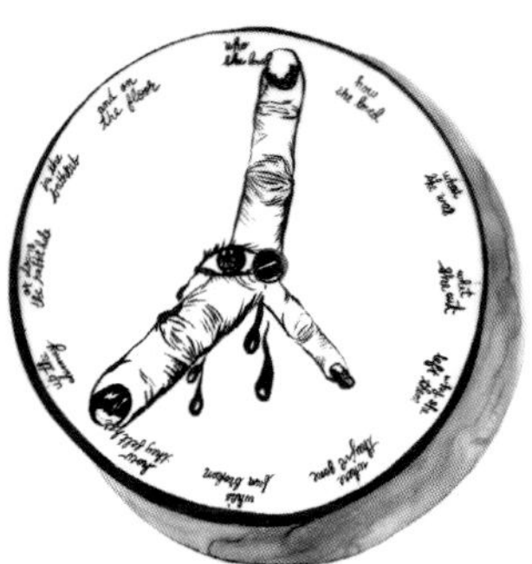

Chitra Ganesh, *Her Body Clock*, 2005. Sumi ink on denril paper. 14 x 11 inches. Collection of the artist.

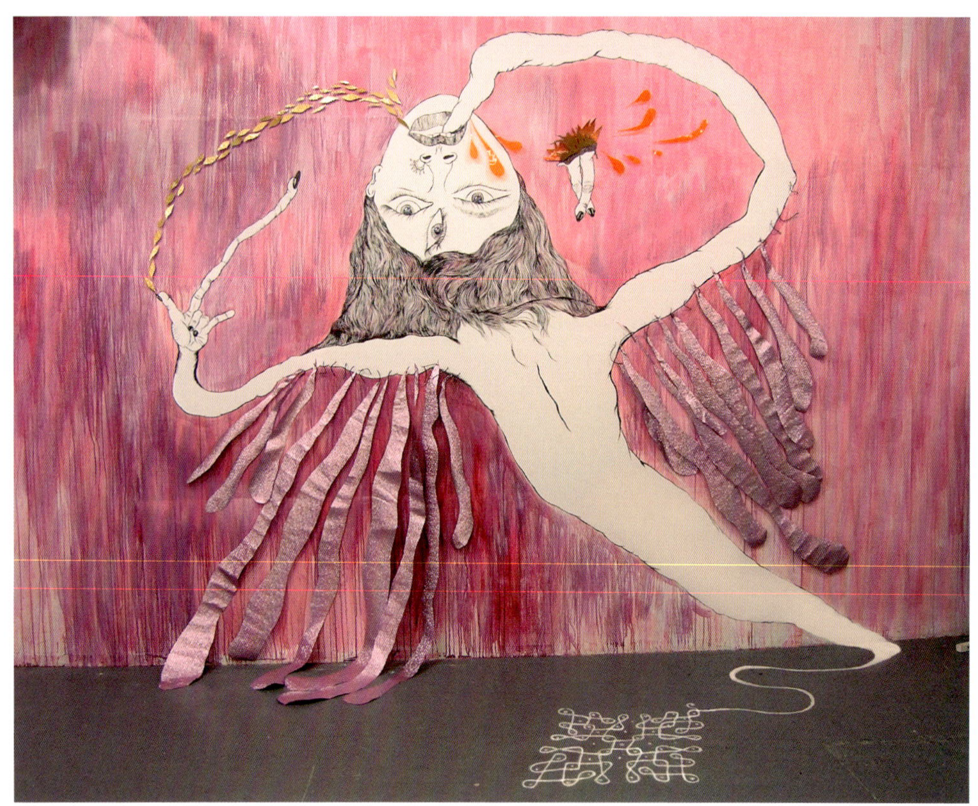

Chitra Ganesh, *Written on Wind and Water* (detail), 2005. Mixed media. Approx. 144 x 216 x 96 inches. Collection of the artist. Installation view at Goliath Visual Space, New York.

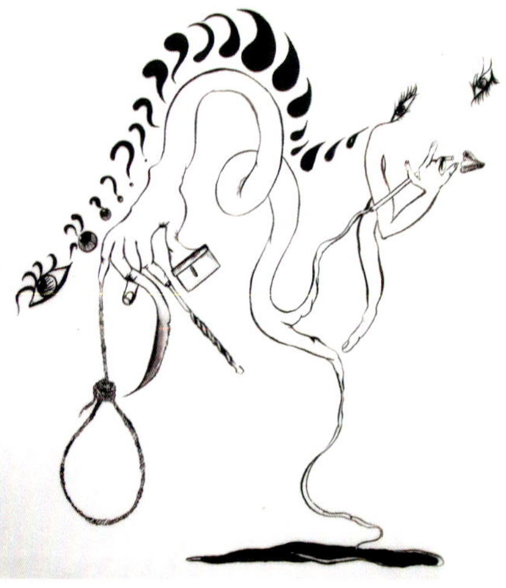

Chitra Ganesh, *Weapons in Hand*, 2005. Sumi ink on denril paper. 14 x 11 inches. Collection of the artist.

CHITRA GANESH

Born in 1975, Brooklyn, New York; Lives and works in Brooklyn, New York **EDUCATION:** 2002, Master of Fine Arts, Columbia University, New York, New York; 1996, Bachelor of Arts, Brown University, Providence, Rhode Island; **SOLO AND TWO PERSONS EXHIBITIONS:** 2005, "Evidence of Past Lives," 1 x 1 Artist Commission, Jersey City Museum, New Jersey; 2003, "Her Secret Missions," Momenta Art, Brooklyn, New York; **GROUP EXHIBITIONS:** 2006, "Nicola Durvasula, Chitra Ganesh, Tejal Shah," Thomas Erben Gallery, New York; 2005, "Fatal Love," Queens Museum of Art, New York; 2004, "Treasure Maps," Apex Art, New York; **AWARDS AND RESIDENCIES:** 2005, Artist's Fellowship, New York Foundation for the Arts; 2005, Gregory Millard Fellow; 2005, Project Space Residency, Headlands Center for the Arts, Sausalito, California; 2004, Astraea Visual Arts Award; 2002, Artist in the Marketplace Program, Bronx Museum of the Arts, New York, New York; 2002, Artist-in-Residence, Abrons Arts Center, Henry Street Settlement, New York, New York

Right: Chitra Ganesh, *Jungle Beneath*, 2004. Mixed media. Approx. 210 x 180 x 96 inches. Collection of the artist. Installation view at White Columns, New York. Below: Chitra Ganesh, *Jungle Beneath* (details).

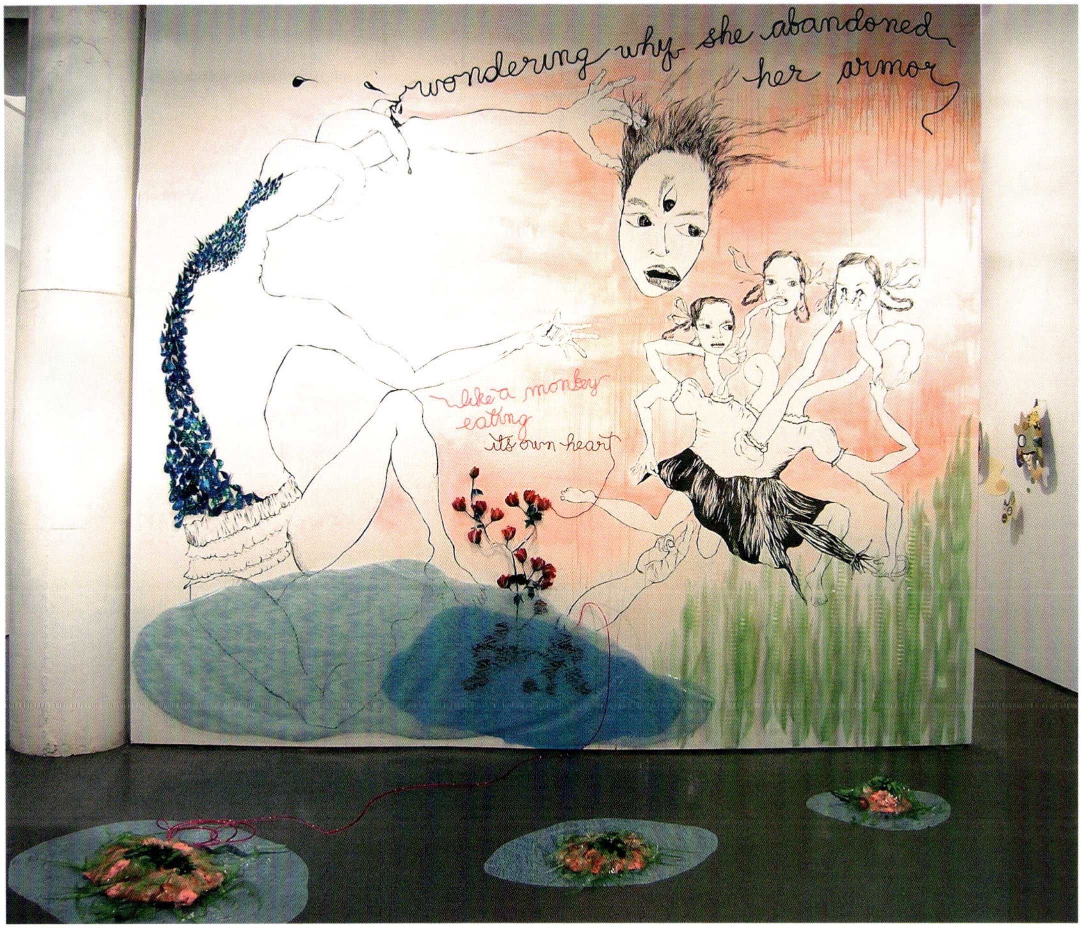

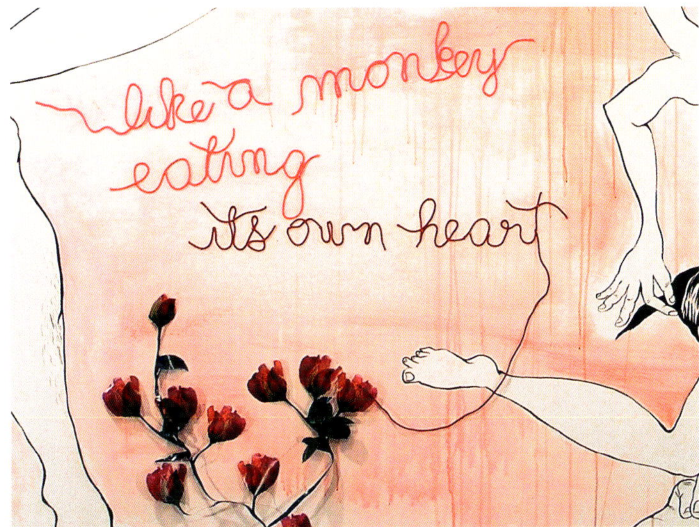

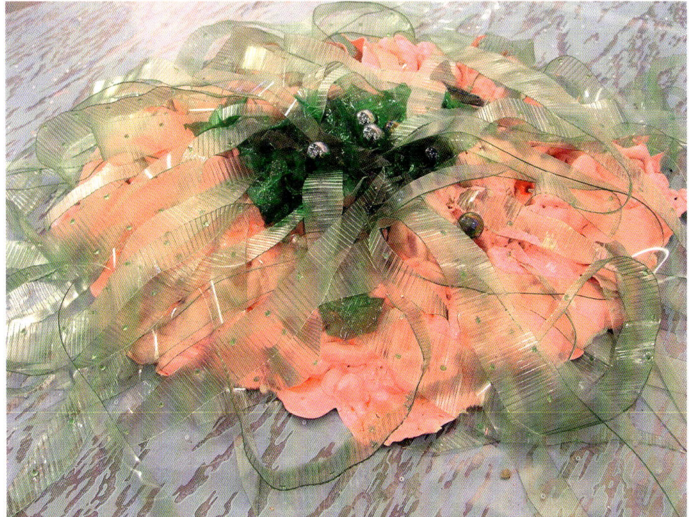

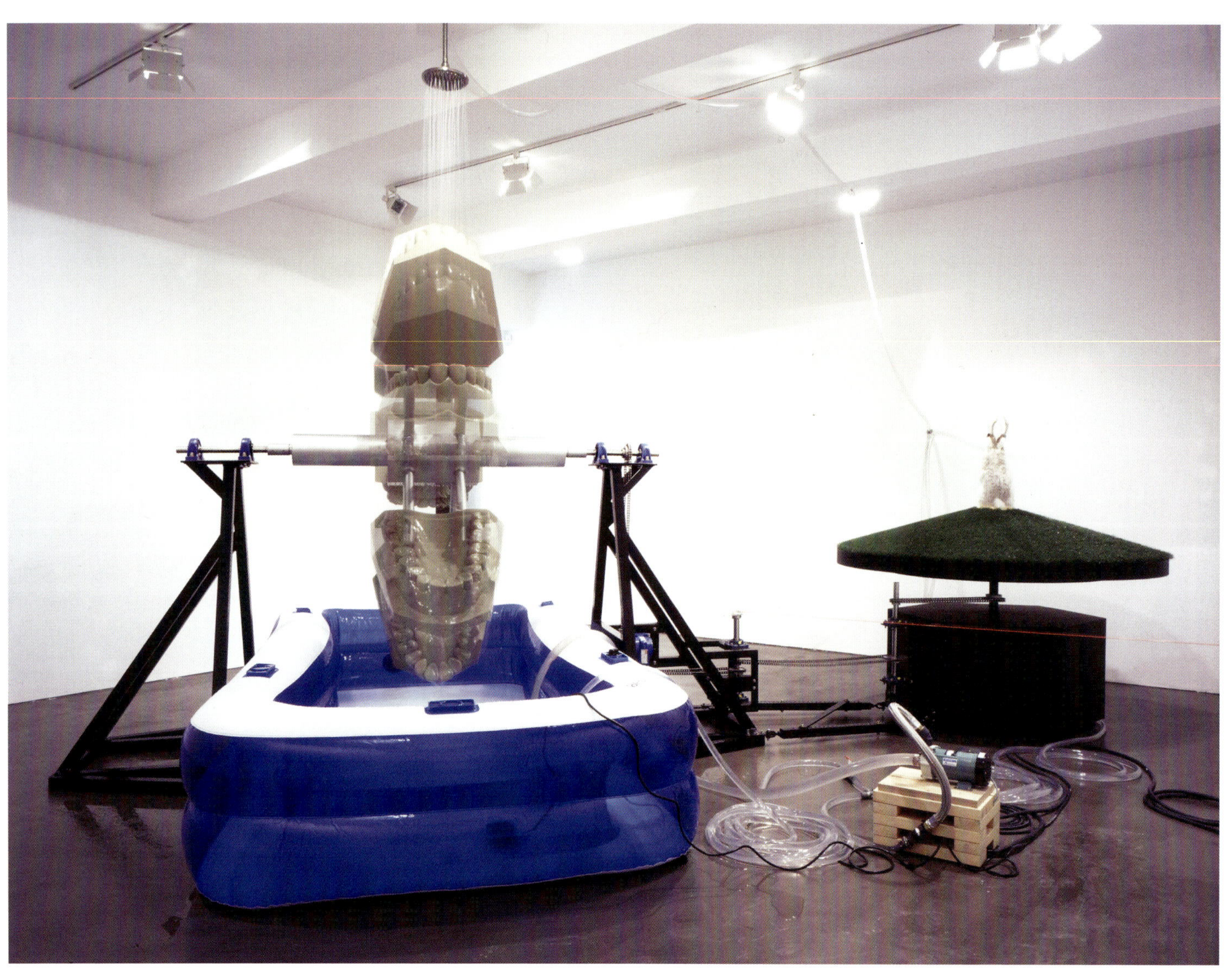

Glenn Kaino, *Simple System for Dimensional Transformation*, 2003. Mixed media. Dimensions variable. Installation view at the Bronx Museum of the Arts, New York.

GLENN KAINO

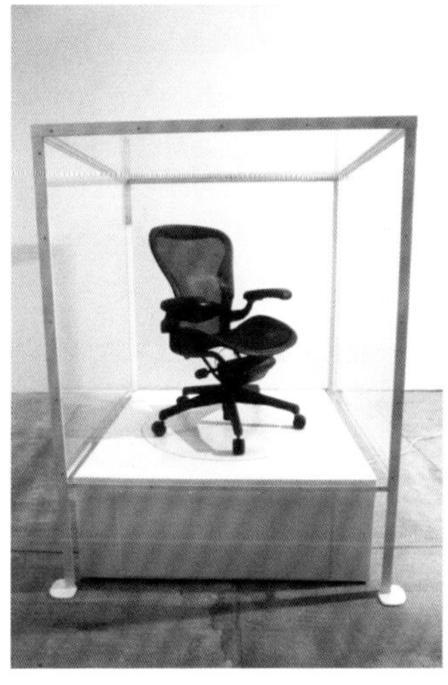
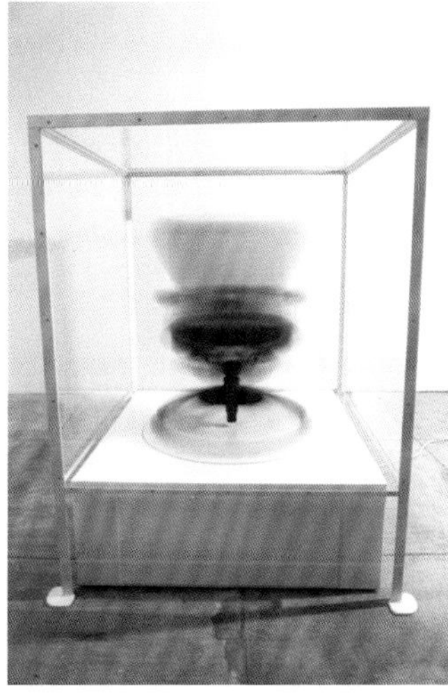

Glenn Kaino, *The Siege Perilous*, 2003. Aeron chair, electric motor, vitrine. 65 x 49 x 49 inches. Collection of Bill Cisneros. Installation view at The Project, New York.

Glenn Kaino is a conjurer. In a sense, all artists are conjurers—they are makers of images, shapes, and forms. But Kaino's sculpture specifically presents possibilities of unexpected formal changes and disguised conceptual detours in objects whose references and functions may appear familiar at first glance. Take for instance works such as *Desktop Operation: There's No Place Like Home (10th example of Rapid Dominance: Em City)* (2003), which effects transformation on what is itself a symbol of disguise and transformation—the Emerald City from *The Wizard of Oz* (1939). Collapsing the familiar cultural reference with the borrowed format of a miniature Zen garden, a banal commodity that promises spiritual calm, Kaino remakes the soaring fantasy castle that is all surface glitters and filled with empty hopes into a turgid, impersonal monument, while supplanting the promised peace of mind with an imposing sense of doom and obduracy. *The Siege Perilous* (2003) consists of an Aeron chair, supposedly the most ergonomically sound chair available in the market, simply framed in a vitrine. As the chair revolves at breakneck velocity, it turns into, or spectrally conjures up the shape of a chalice, perhaps the Holy Grail. In its transformative movement, the supreme cipher of Christian religiosity is replaced by the most dignified holder of the postmillennial, late-capitalist human body entrapped in the electronic workstation—or the two representations become inseparably one.

Kaino also creates mechanisms for the transubstantiation of energy into form and vice versa. *Simple System for Dimensional Transformation* (2003), a Rube Goldberg machine-like contraption, is an elaborate sculptural flowchart whose monumental constituents are fitted with incredible complexity to generate just enough energy to flap the wings of a tiny origami crane. As can be seen in the last two examples, Kaino's work also offers a vision for kinetic sculpture at the turn of the century. He updates on important art historical precedents, such as Marcel Duchamp's Rotoreliefs and Jean Tinguely's metamechanics, by proffering, in lieu of the modernist privileging of optical experience and the mid-century existentialist response to industrialism, works that give form to more fluid concepts drawn from quantum physics. In his work, artistic content and political consciousness, and visual form and viewership find more mutually implicated relationships.

Graft (2006), conceived and produced for the present exhibition, consists of a pair of taxidermic animals—a pig and a salmon

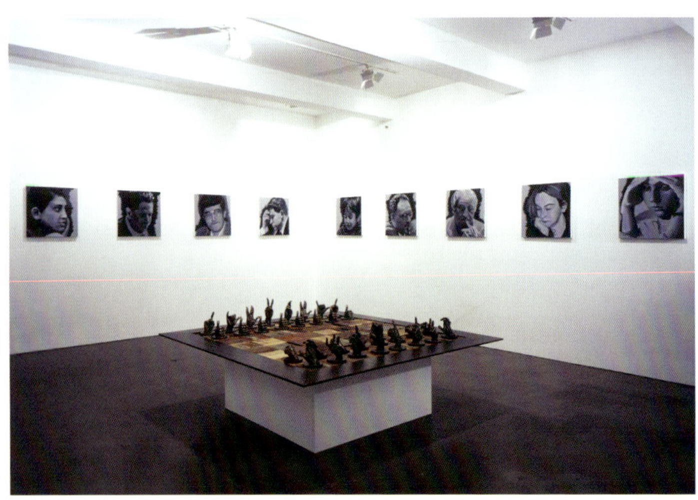

Above and below: Glenn Kaino, *Learn to Win, or You'll Take Losing for Granted*, 2005. Wood and bronze. Chess board: 84 x 84 x 20 inches; Chess pieces: 10 inches high. Installation view at The Project, New York.

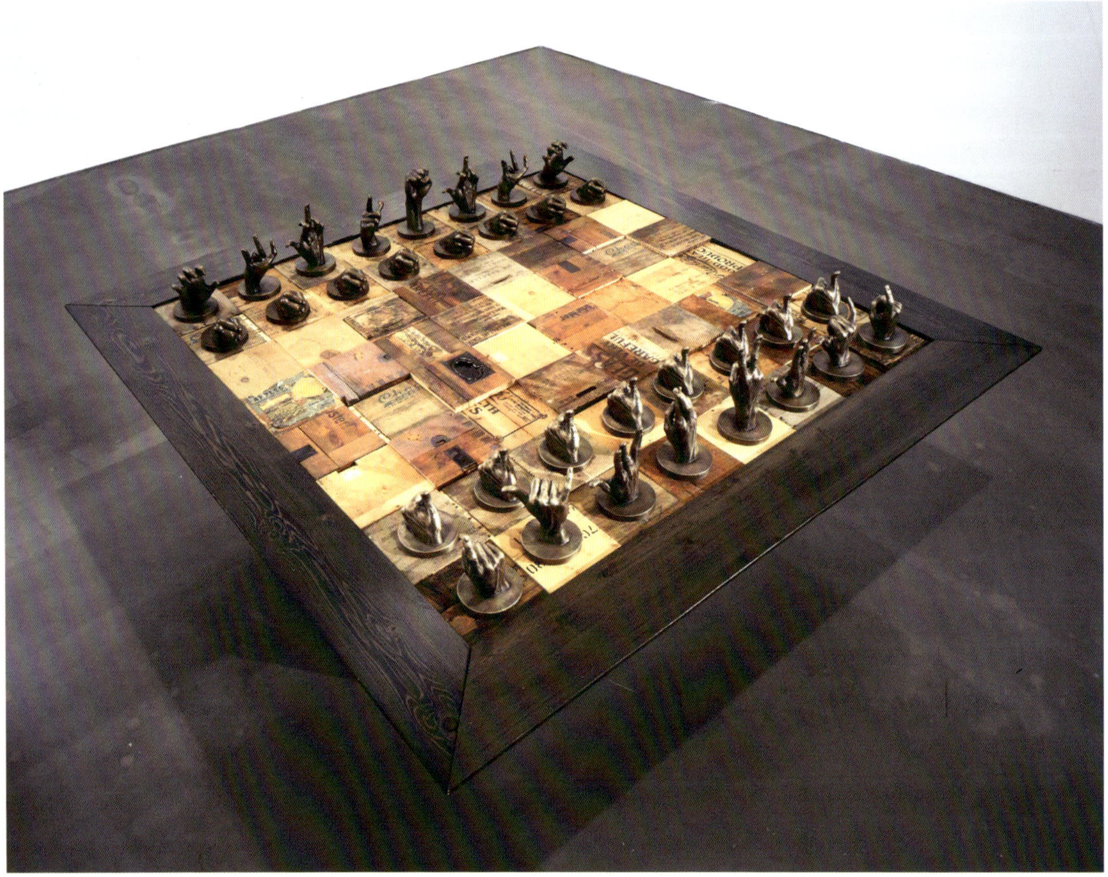

whose respective epidermis have been swapped with those of a cow and a shark. The work was inspired by the news of the partial face transplant recently performed on a French woman who had been mauled by her dog. It also references the spate of TV programs hawking "make-overs"—personal transformations by means of plastic surgery, diet, and "personality coaching"—presented to the public with the "reality" effect produced by highly manipulative editing and presentational tactics. While the work touches upon the problematic notion of race in its formal concern with species and skin, it also serves more broadly as a metaphor for the very impossibility of locating any form of social identity as well as the increasingly troubled place of the science of evolution in the landscape of social ideologies. *Graft* reinforces formal stability and conceptual destabilization, or vice versa, a strategy that has always been and continues to be evident in Kaino's work. **DC**

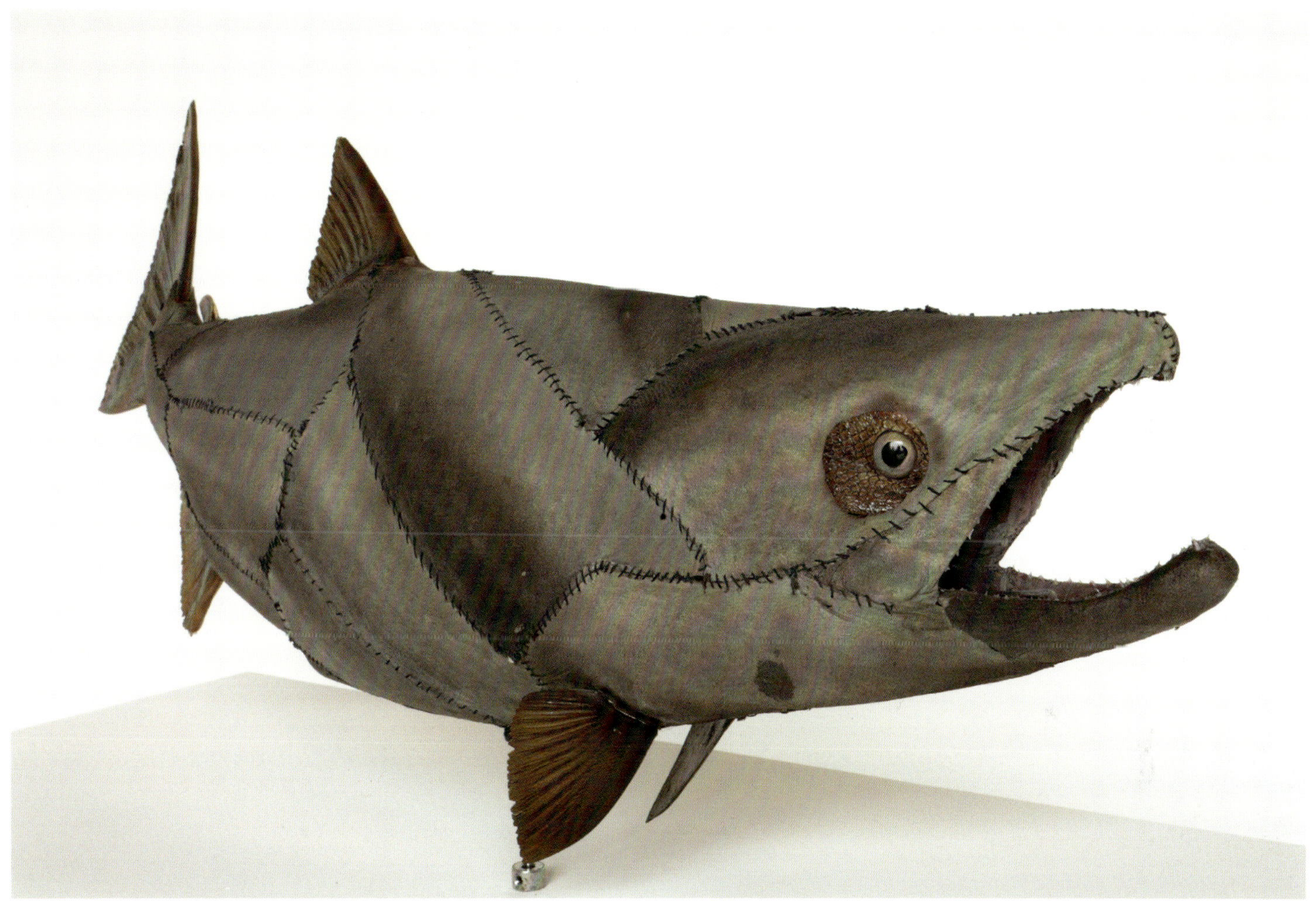

Glenn Kaino, *Graft* (salmon), 2006. Shark skin, thread, salmon skin, plastic. 36 x 12 x 4 inches. Collection of the artist.

GLENN KAINO

Born in 1972, Los Angeles, California; Lives and works in Los Angeles, California **EDUCATION:** 1996, Master of Fine Arts program, University of California, San Diego; 1993, Bachelor of Arts, University of California, Irvine; **SOLO AND TWO PERSONS EXHIBITIONS:** 2004, "Bounce: Glenn Kaino and Mark Bradford," Roy and Edna Disney/CalArts Theater (REDCAT) Gallery, Los Angeles, California; 2004, "Simple System for Dimensional Transformation," The Project, New York, New York; 2001, "Style Telegraphique," Rosamund Felsen Gallery, Santa Monica, California; **GROUP EXHIBITIONS:** 2004, "2004 Whitney Biennial," Whitney Museum of American Art, New York, New York; 2003, "Black Belt," Studio Museum in Harlem, New York, New York; 2001, "One Planet under a Groove," Bronx Museum of the Arts, New York

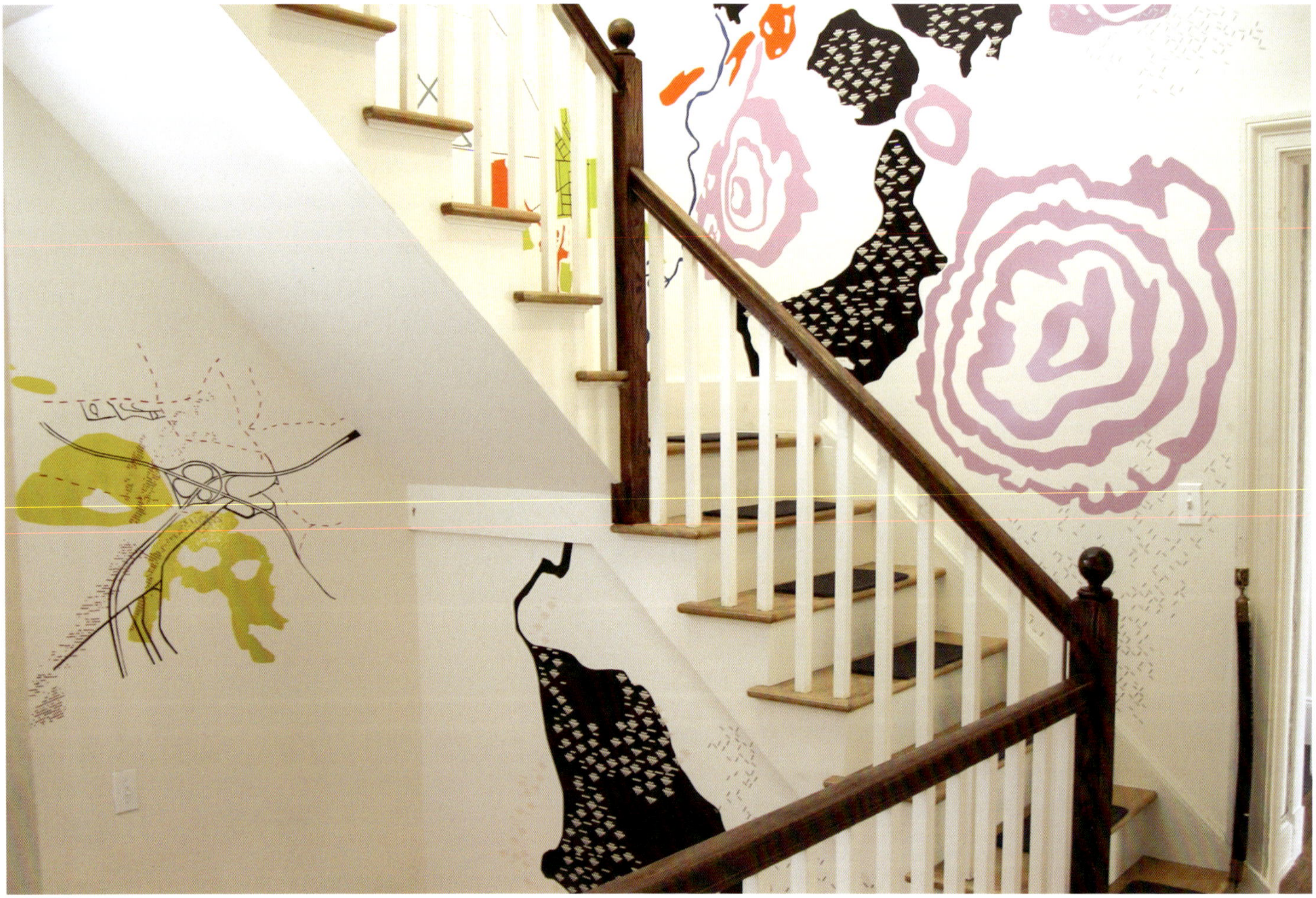

Geraldine Lau, *Information Retrieval, #118*, 2005. Vinyl on wall. Dimensions variable. Collection of the artist. Installation view at Wave Hill Gallery, New York.

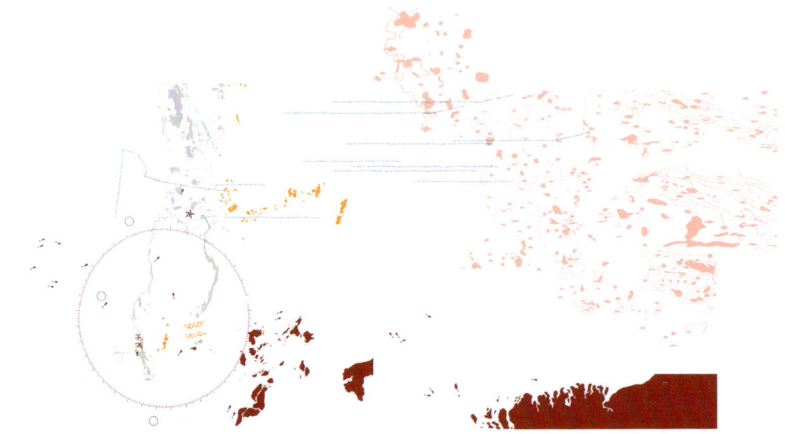

Geraldine Lau, *Information Retrieval, #125*, 2006. Digital drawing. Dimensions variable. Collection of the artist.

GERALDINE LAU

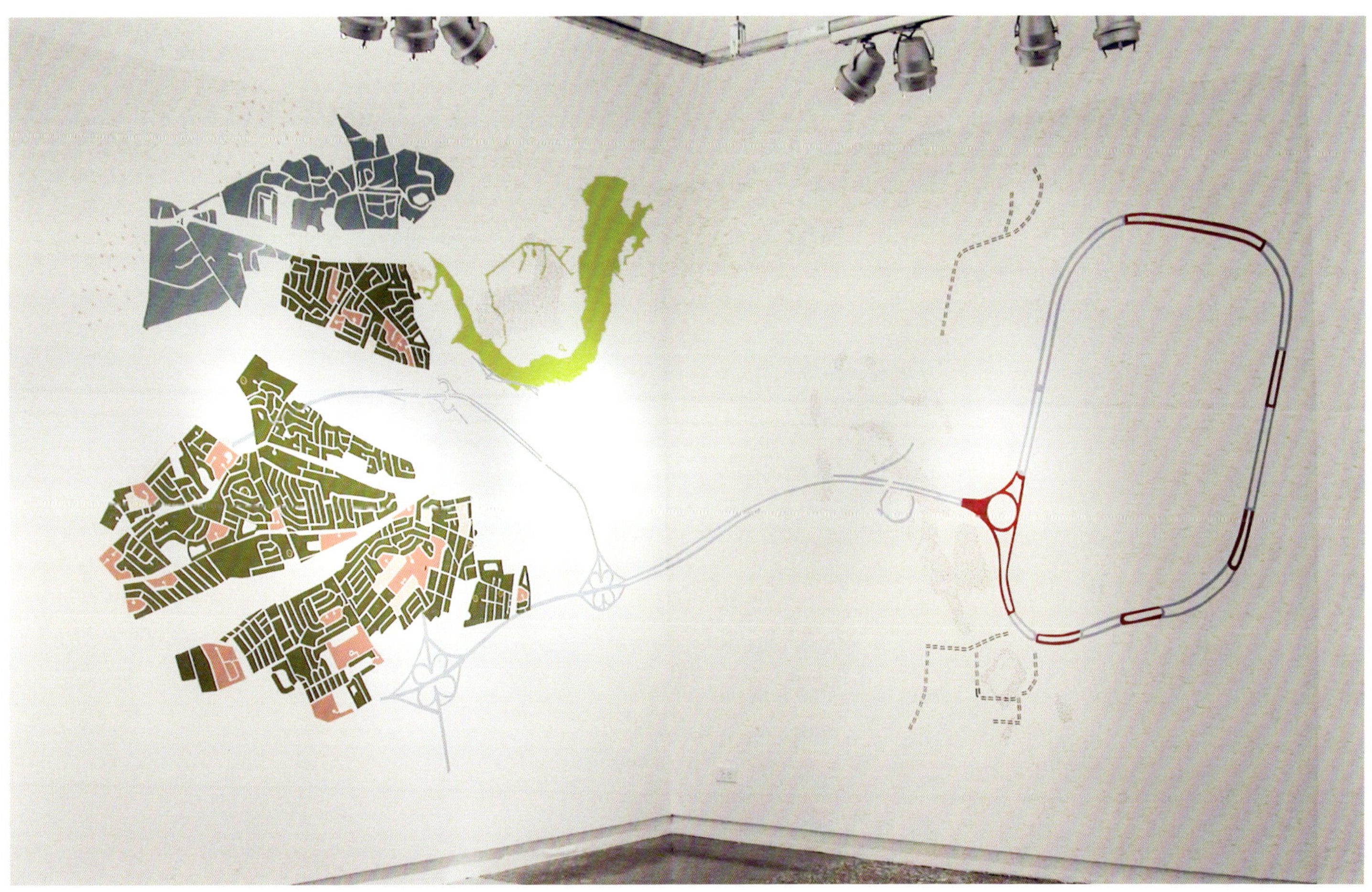

Geraldine Lau, *Information Retrieval, #111 (Distribution Through Five Points)*, 2004. Vinyl on wall. Dimensions variable. Collection of the artist. Installation view at Visual Arts Gallery, New York.

Maps—evidence of vital sites—are encoded abstractions, systems of representation, and a form of governorship over geography. Ancient mapmaking was based on conjecture, extrapolation, and manipulation—an art that became a science. Professor of geography J. B. Harley explains, "By substituting an analogical space for a real space in the process of mapping, human beings acquired intellectual mastery over their world. In many societies maps preceded both writing and mathematical notation."[1]

For this exhibition at Asia Society, Lau installed the site-specific vinyl piece *Information Retrieval # 125* (2006), which extends from the third floor wall onto the second floor landing, and partly reflects onto the ceiling. Generally, she begins a project by selecting elements from several topographical maps of a selected subject. She then reconfigures landmarks and elevations in temporary site-specific, large-scale, process-oriented drawings fashioned from vinyl, tape, and glue—supplies that are commonly used in signage and design industries. Previously cutting the patterns by hand, she now uses a computerized vinyl cutter, which removes her hand from the production process. Her work invokes a mixture of Guillermo Kuitca, Lordy Rodriguez, and Nic Hess—other artists working with cartography and similar materials.

Derived from pictographs and satellite imaging, maps are spatial representations of the real world; Lau takes it a step further by plotting evolution and fiction. Reflecting the spatial growth and development of cities around transportation and distribution nodes, she intends that her maps be read as narrative rather than didactic. These representations embrace contradictions of reality and fiction, past and present, absence and presence, the subjective and the objective, some existing as sites of collective memory. By basing these configurations on existing maps, she partially retrieves what was lost in the purportedly factual and scientific process of cartography. Lau reveals the inaccuracies of mapmaking that are often accepted as truth and deployed as instruments of political power. Conversely, J. B. Harley states, "maps were a means of resistance by which colonized peoples sought to oppose the appropriation of their culture and territory."[2] Despite the sophistication of global positioning technology, cartography is not unaffected by social biases for maps are "created and defined by human agents, exploited by elites, to materialize a world seen through a veil of ideology."[3]

Born in Singapore in 1970, Geraldine Lau received her MFA in painting at the School of Visual Arts in New York, her current city of residence. In 2001, she received a Pollock-Krasner Foundation

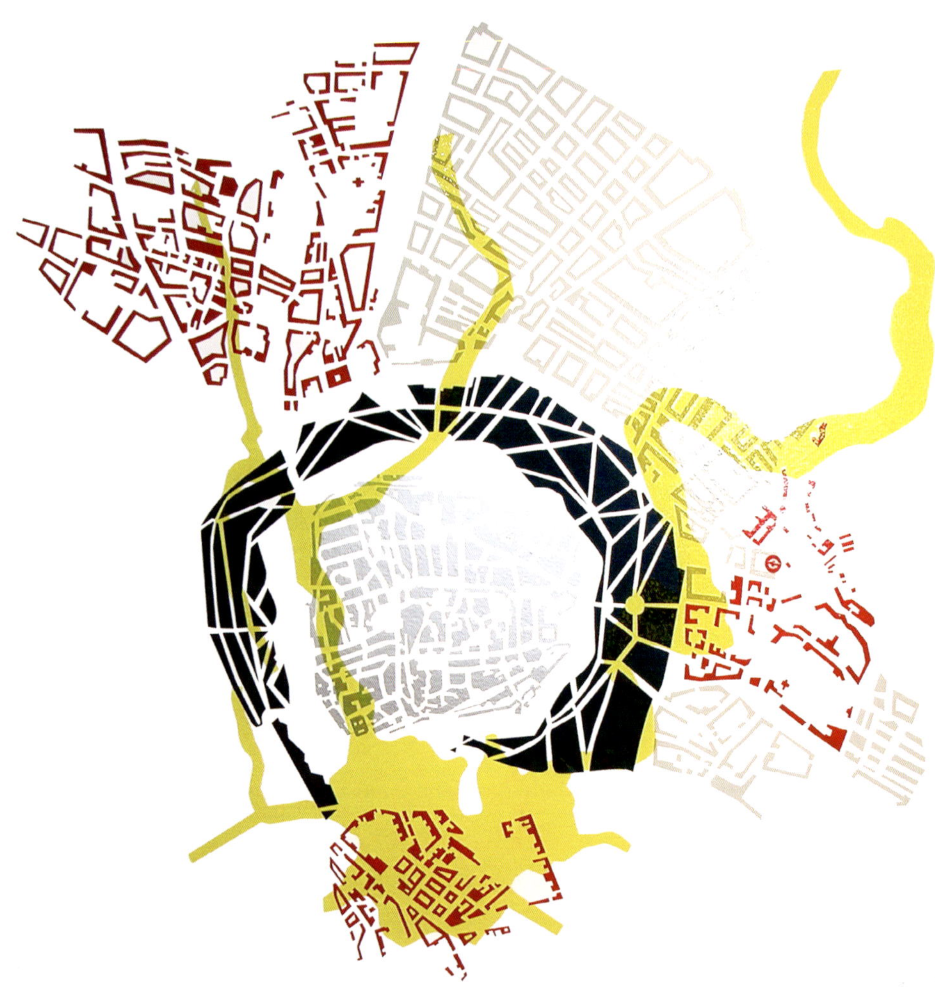

Geraldine Lau, *Information Retrieval, #117 (Ironbound)*, 2004. Vinyl on wall. Dimensions variable. Collection of the artist. Installation view at Visual Arts Gallery, New York.

9/11 Emergency Grant, an award given to artists directly impacted by the events of September 11th; Lau saw parallels between the calamity of 9/11 and the traumatic razing of her ancestral home and neighborhood in Singapore. **KJB**

1. J. Brian Harley, "The new history of cartography," *UNESCO Courier*, June 1991, http://www.findarticles.com/p/articles/mi_m1310/is_1991_June/ai_10940835.
2. Ibid.
3. Ibid.

GERALDINE LAU

Born in 1970, Singapore; Lives and works in New York, New York
EDUCATION: 1997, Master of Fine Arts, School of Visual Arts, New York, New York; 1994, Bachelor of Arts, Royal Melbourne Institute of Technology University, Australia/Singapore; **GROUP EXHIBITIONS:** 2006, "Speed," Staubkohler Gallery, Zurich, Switzerland; 2005, "Organized Spaces," Asian American Arts Centre, New York, New York; 2004, "Subway Series: The New York Yankees and the American Dream," Bronx Museum of the Arts, New York, New York; 2004, "Subway Series: The New York Mets and Our National Pastime," Queens Museum of Art, New York, New York; 2002, "Painting Lately," Abrons Art Center, Henry Street Settlement, New York, New York; 2001, "World Views," New Museum of Contemporary Art, New York, New York

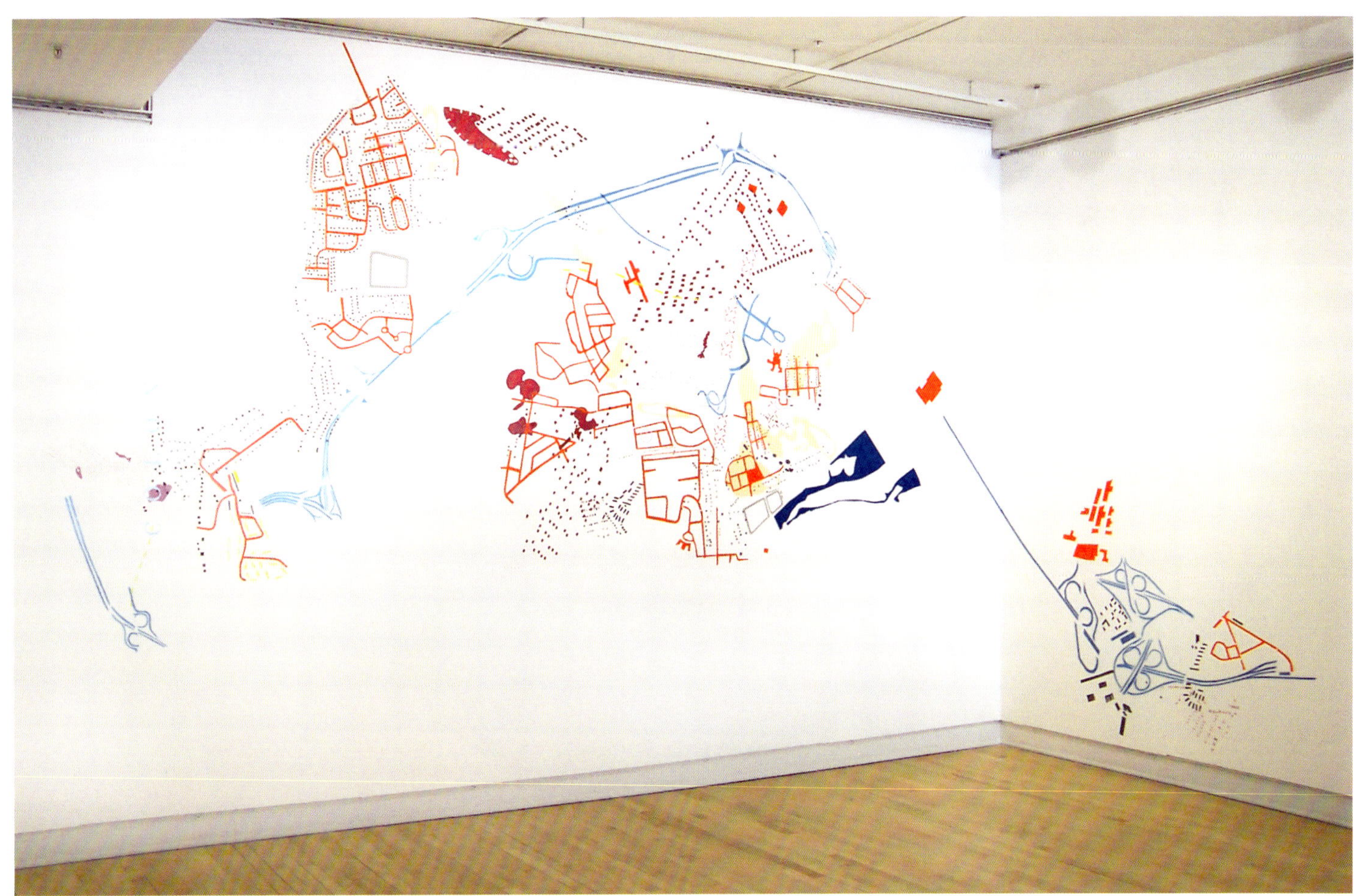

Geraldine Lau, *Information Retrieval, #104 (Troy, North and South in a Day)*, 2004. Vinyl on wall. Dimensions variable. Collection of the artist. Installation view at The Arts Center of the Capital Region, Troy, New York.

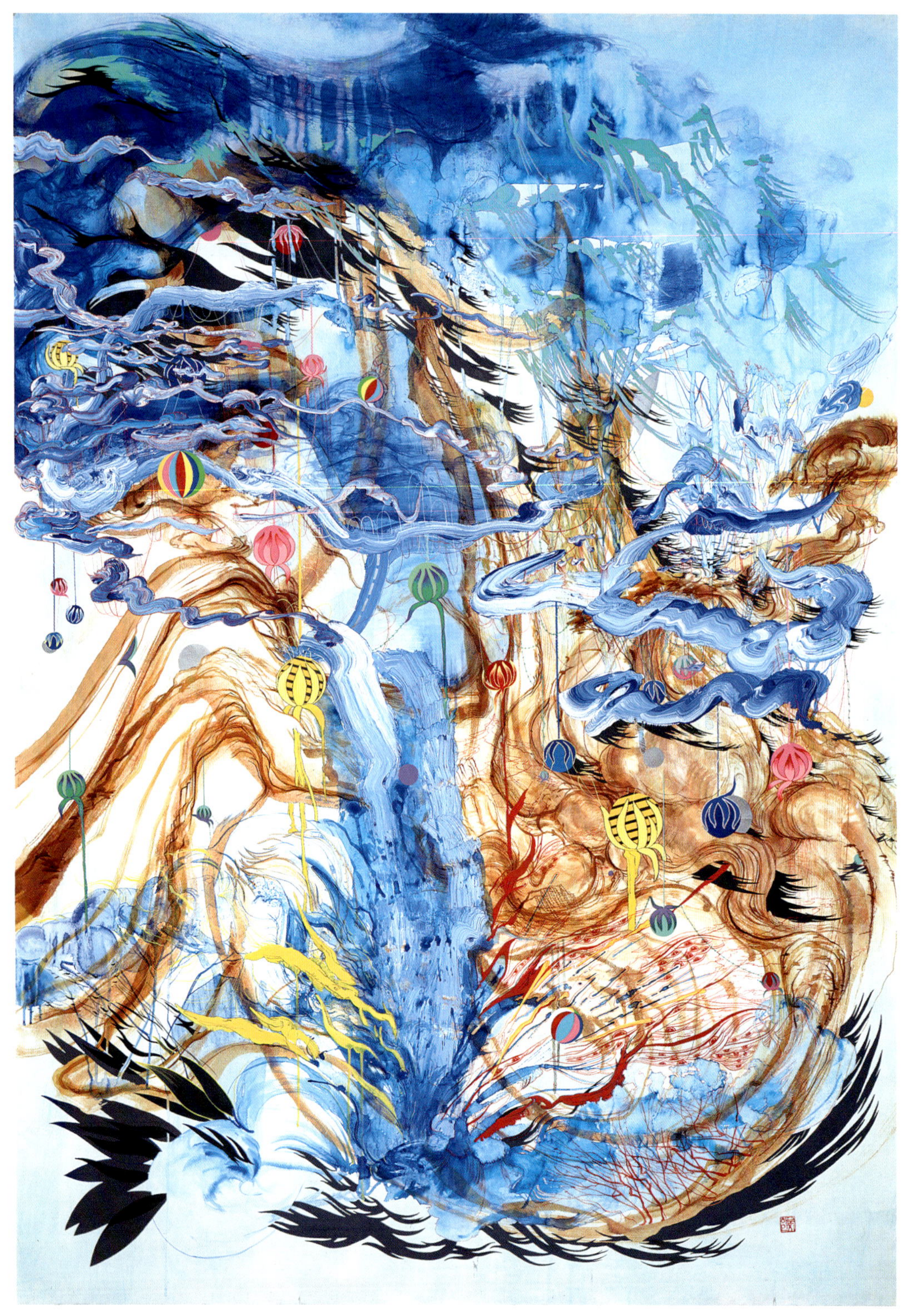

Jiha Moon, *Haven*, 2006. Ink and acrylic on hanji. 80 x 60 inches. Collection of the artist.

JIHA MOON

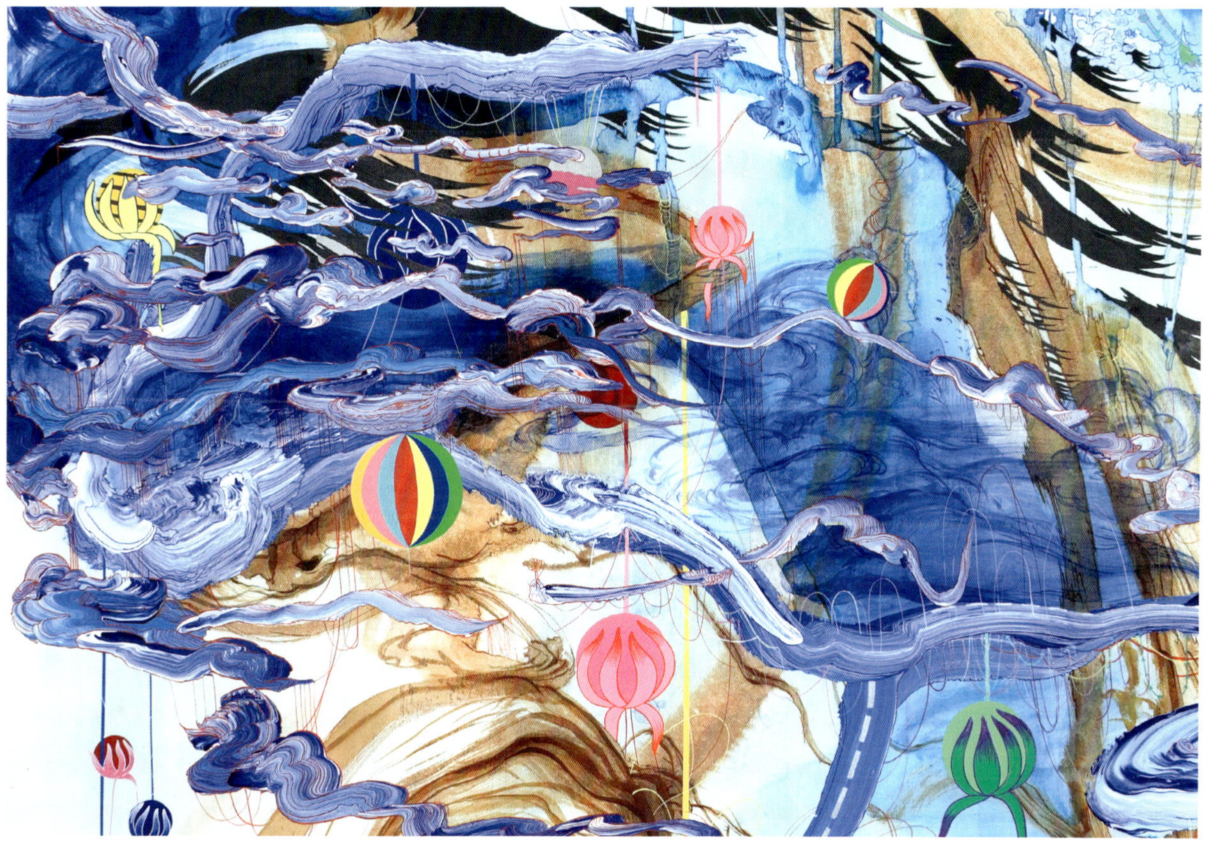

Jiha Moon, *Haven* (detail).

Painter Jiha Moon confronts the ongoing confluence and clashes between Asia and America, past and present, nature and culture. "Symbioland," the title of a 2005 exhibition at the Curator's Office, a gallery in Washington, DC, hints at the concept of symbiosis, a term borrowed from the realm of biology that refers to a deeply intertwined, prolonged dependency between organisms of varied species that may or may not be mutually advantageous for all involved. By masterfully balancing a mélange of styles and art-historical references, Moon's paintings are an interesting—and contradictory—mix of both conflicting cultures and cultural hybridity.

The slim, drawn lines in her work suggest the outlines of draped fabric or natural topographical forms such as those found in Chinese brush paintings. Moon's layers of iconography are not always quite what they seem. She might include, for example, forms that could be interpreted as dangerous puffs of smog or serene, natural clouds. Either way, Moon's mix of intriguingly ambiguous elements

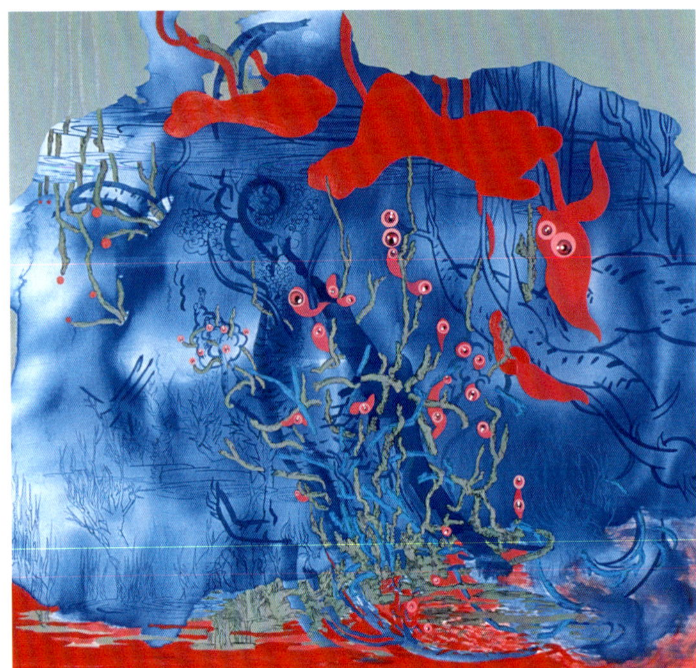

Jiha Moon, *Secret of Swamp*, 2004. Ink and acrylic on silk. 24 x 26 inches. Private collection.

suggests a simultaneous sense of harmony and cacophony. In fact, she calls her images visions of "paradoxical Utopia." She states, "I always try to visualize combinations of opposing themes in art and life. In my painting, I explore complex relationships."[1]

Fittingly, Moon cites a wide range of influences. While her complex paintings might bring to mind those of contemporary artists Arturo Herrera and Julie Mehretu, Moon states that her references range instead from such highly abstract works like *10,000 Ugly Ink Dots*, by Ming dynasty (1368–1644) artist Shitao—whose playful marks Moon finds particularly inspirational—to the dramatic canvases of fifteenth-century Northern Renaissance painter Hieronymous Bosch with their multiple narratives.

Another influence is the little known Chosŏn dynasty (1392–1910), sixteenth-century female artist Sin Sa-im-dang, who created abstract paintings that were often inspired by everyday images such as a stain on a dress. A more contemporary influence is the twentieth-century American Outsider artist Henry Darger, whose fantasy-driven watercolors Moon sees as a model for conveying bizarre, dream-like settings with a delicate palette.

Moon chooses her own palette carefully. She is hyper-aware of how colors carry deep associations, ranging from pop culture references to national symbols. She explains, "The blue in the Korean flag always reminded me of Superman's uniform, and the red always reminded me of Wonder Woman's."[2] Moon is fascinated by the quality of line and the fluidity of classical East Asian ink paintings. For the Asia Society exhibition, she worked on her first monumental, 80-by-60 foot work. She has consciously chosen to work in acrylic, a medium that is typically considered "Western," and ink on Korean handmade hanji paper, to suggest a blend—or dichotomy—of American and Asian elements.

At the same time, Moon relies upon a spontaneous painting process. Experimentation and chance allow for the artist to devise surprising combinations of forms and colors. By balancing artistic control and abandonment, she pushes the boundaries between abstract and representational imagery, forging brave new worlds with each complex composition.

RJ

1. Jiha Moon, conversation with the author, February 19, 2006.
2. Ibid.

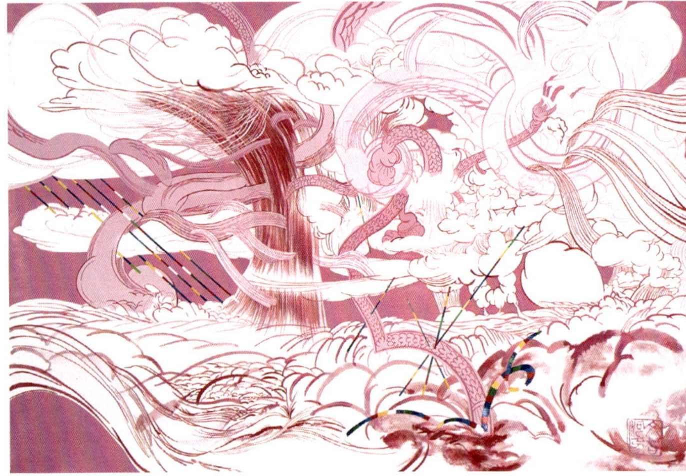

Jiha Moon, *Windfield Circle*, 2004. Ink and acrylic on paper. 20 x 26 inches. Collection of the artist.

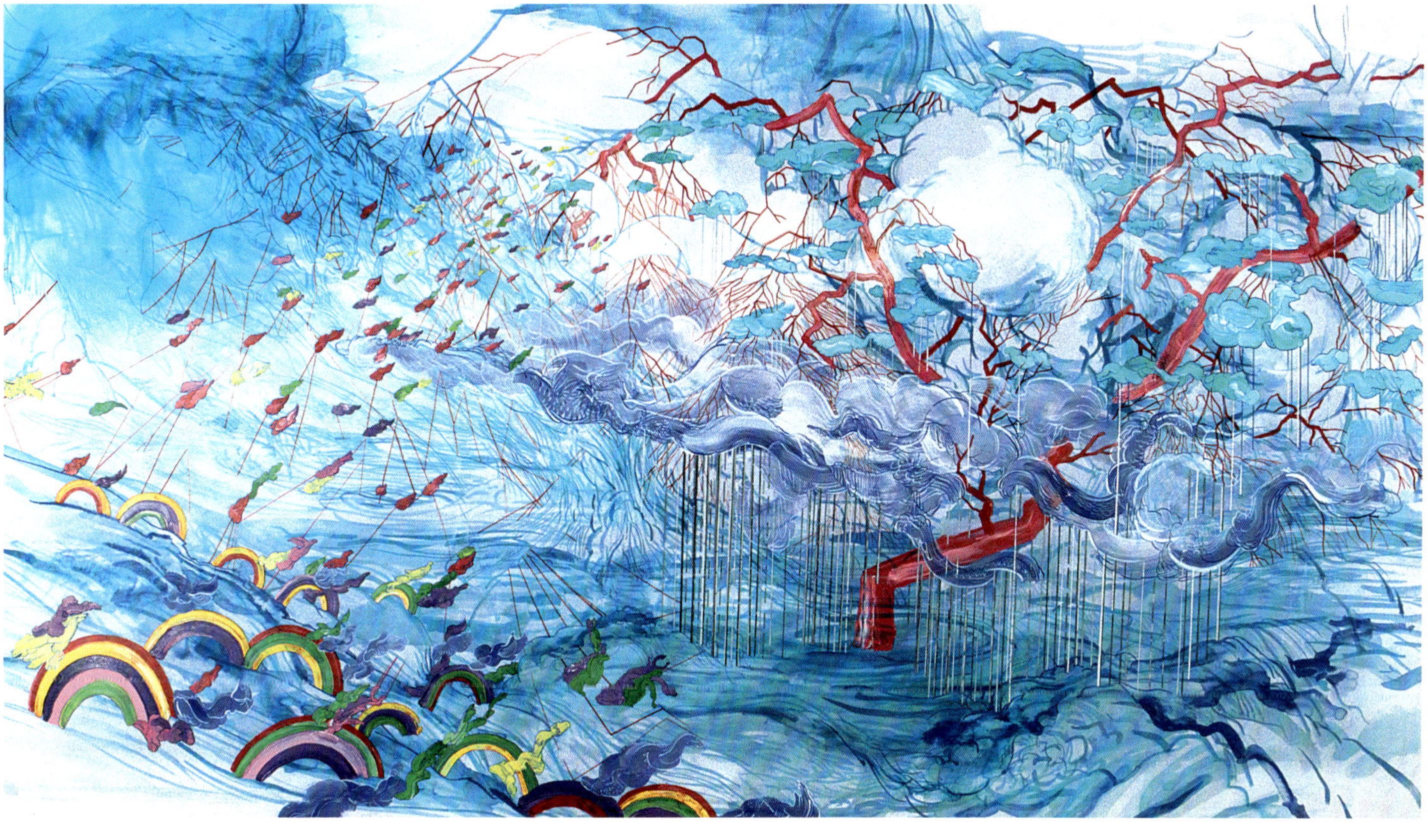

Jiha Moon, *Lucky Red Cedar*, 2005. Ink and acrylic on silk. 26 x 46 inches. Collection of Carol Hawick.

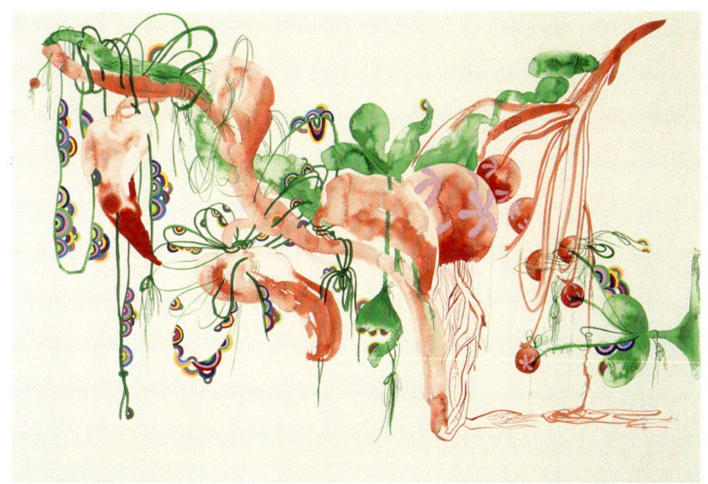

Jiha Moon, *Tie the Knot*, 2005. Ink and acrylic on paper. 20 x 26 inches. Private collection.

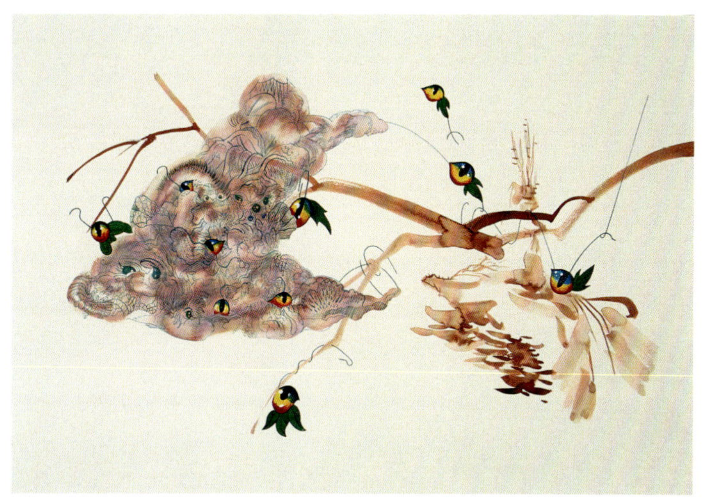

Jiha Moon, *Hooks*, 2005. Ink and acrylic on paper. 20 x 26 inches. Collection of the artist.

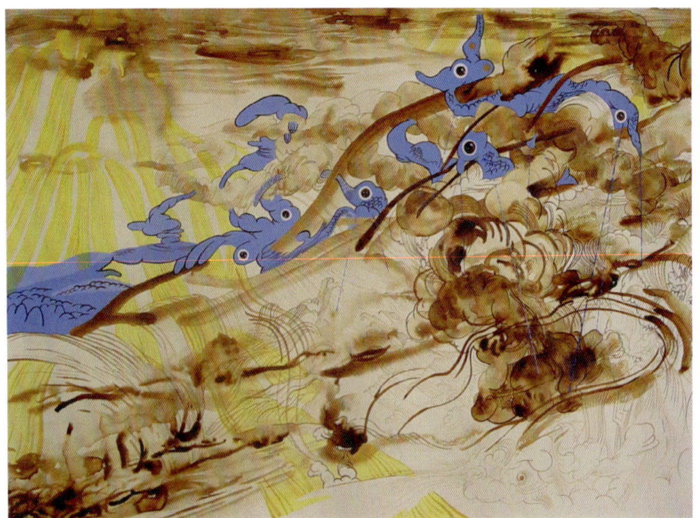

Jiha Moon, *Watcherhill*, 2004. Ink and acrylic on paper. 20 x 26 inches. Private collection.

JIHA MOON

Born in 1973, Taegu, Korea; Lives and works in Atlanta, Georgia **EDUCATION:** 2002, Master of Fine Arts, University of Iowa, Iowa City, Iowa; 1999, Master of Fine Arts, Ewha Womans University, Seoul, Korea; 1996, Bachelor of Fine Arts, Korea University, Seoul, Korea; **SOLO EXHIBITION:** 2005, "Scope Miami," Miami Beach, Florida; 2005, "Symbioland," Curator's Office, Washington, D.C.; 2004, Elizabeth Roberts Gallery, Washington, D.C.; 2003, "I'll Meet You There," Korean Cultural Service, Washington, D.C.; **GROUP EXHIBITIONS:** 2006, "ANIMALIA," Irvine Contemporary, Washington, D.C.; 2006, "Red Beans and Rice," Atlanta Contemporary Art Center, Georgia; 2004, "Semi-Lucid," White Columns, New York, New York; 2004, "Technature," Kunstoffice, Berlin, Germany; **GRANTS, AWARDS, AND RESIDENCY:** 2005, Best in Show, Trawick Prize, Bethesda Arts & Entertainment District, Maryland; 2004, Artist-in-Residence, The Henry Luce III Center for the Arts and Religion, Wesley Theological Seminary, Washington, D.C.; 2002, Fellowship, Virginia Center for the Creative Arts, Sweet Briar, Virginia

Jiha Moon, *White Dog*, 2005. Ink and acrylic on paper. 10 x 10 inches. Private collection.

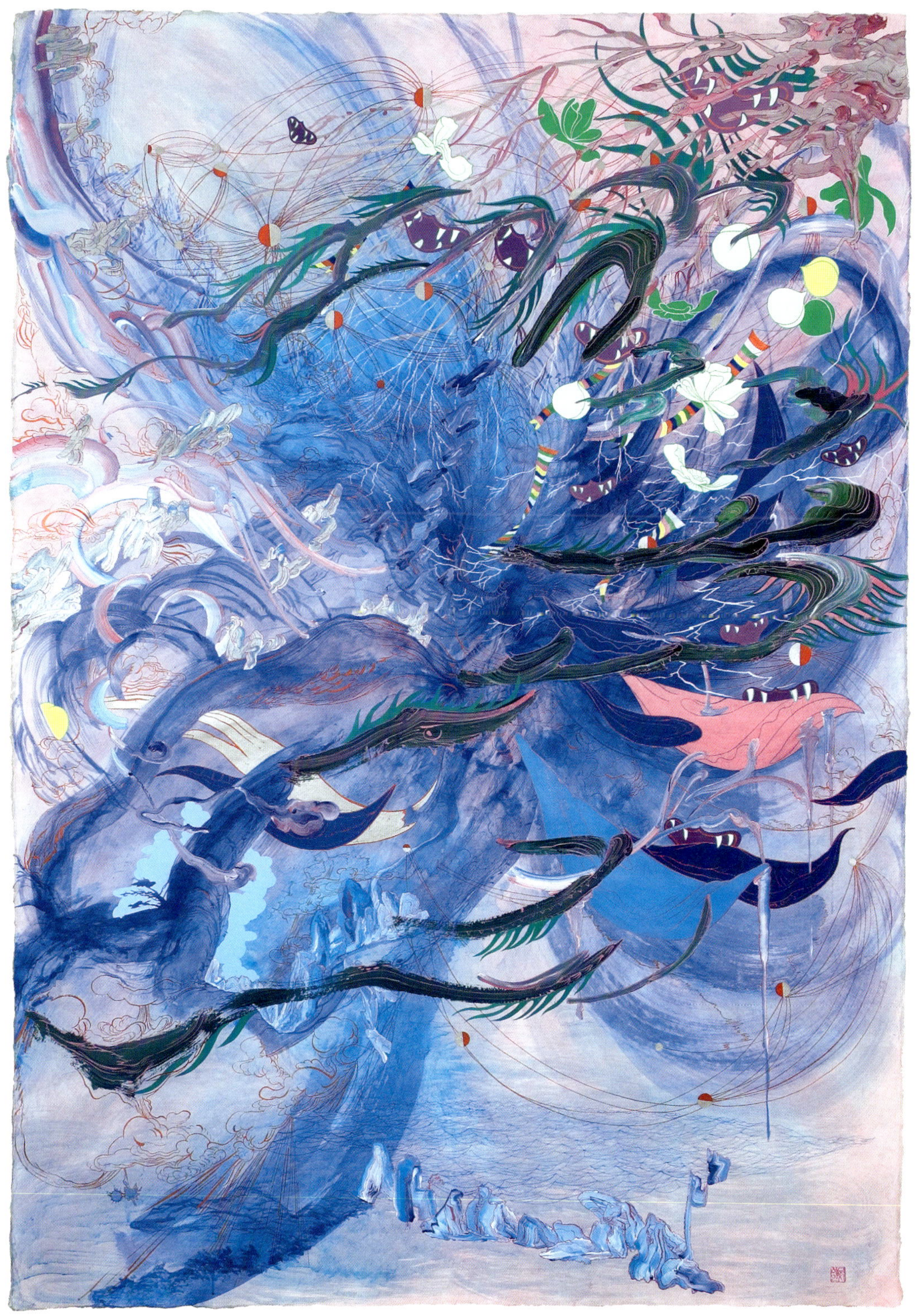

Jiha Moon, *Whirlwind Wheel*, 2006. Ink and acrylic on hanji. 79 x 59 inches. Collection of the artist.

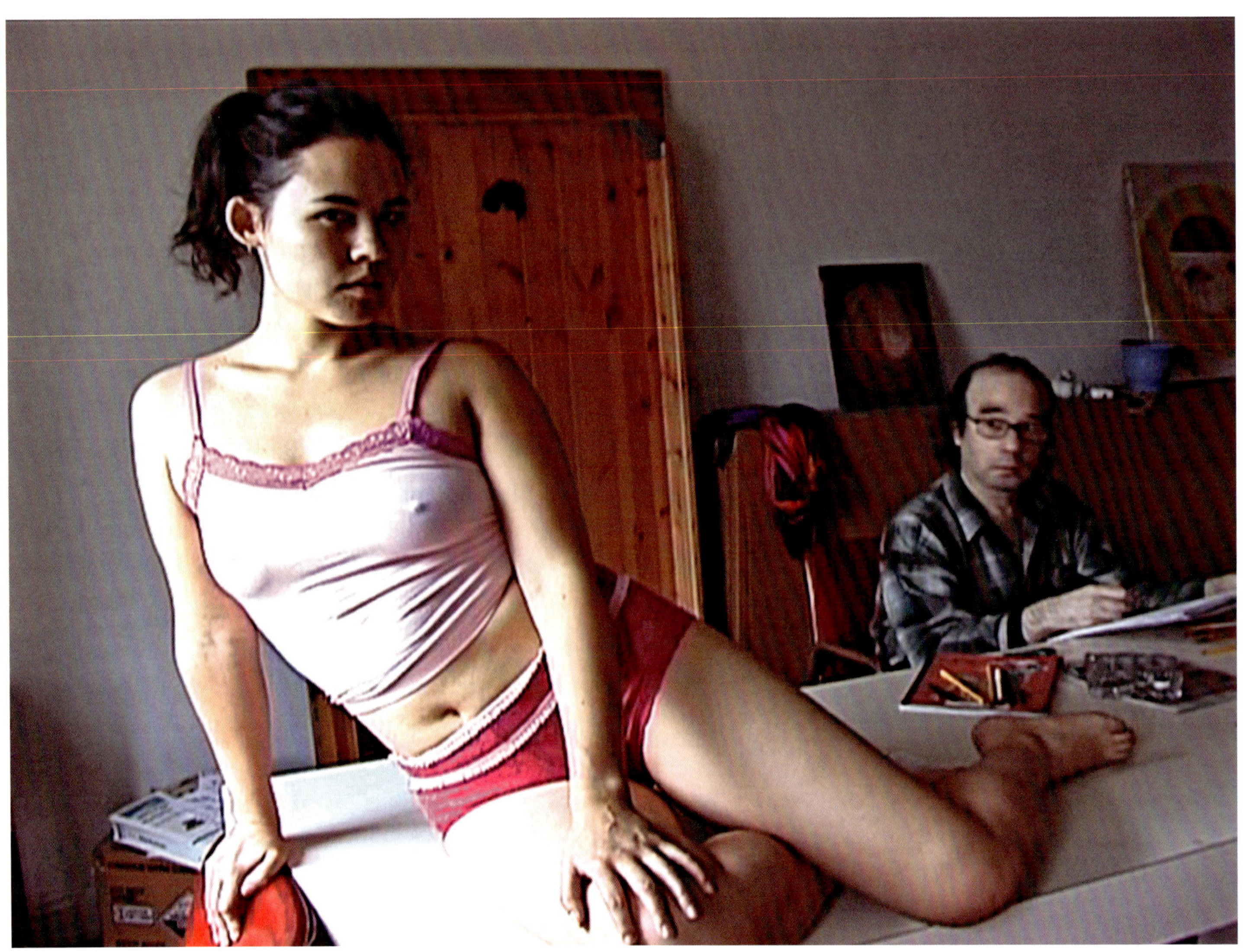

Laurel Nakadate, *Untitled* (video still from *Lessons 1–10*), 2002. Video. 11 minutes, 20 seconds. Collection of the artist.

LAUREL NAKADATE

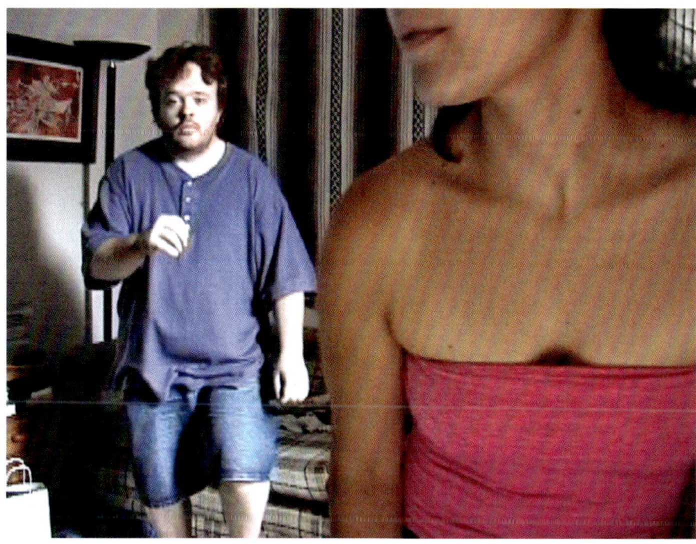

Laurel Nakadate, *Untitled* (video still from *I Wanna Be Your Mid-life Crisis*), 2002. Video. 14 minutes, 33 seconds. Collection of the artist.

How does a girl negotiate solitude? If she picks up a camera, how might she direct its gaze? When race enters the picture, will difference impact its reading? Through photographic stills and short video-journals, Laurel Nakadate's complication of woman, self, and other strikes to the heart and expands consciousness.

Nakadate was born in Austin, Texas in 1975 and raised in Iowa. She was selected for the 2001 publication *25 Under 25: Up-and-coming American Photographers* and received her first New York solo show in 2002 at the Daniel Silverstein Gallery in New York. While preparing her first video works, *I Wanna Be Your Mid-Life Crisis* (2002–2005) and *We Are All Made of Stars* (2002–2005), Nakadate reflected:

> I make little videos. . . . I drive around the Midwest and east coast looking for men to star in my videos. The men have to be single and childless. It's important to me that the men have no one to care for, nor anyone that cares for them. I ask these men to care for me for just a little bit . . . For the time it takes to make a video. . . .
>
> I make videos about men I don't know and by performing girlish activities with these men. I hope to create a virtual, video relationship . . . The men in my videos don't know about . . . Britney Spears and the bedroom . . . dances that fill the afternoons of pre-teen adolescence . . . playing dead and emergencies and make pretend games of fantasy where one person dies and the other happily weeps and screams for help. But there is something about playing pretend that is secret and sexy and lonely, and at times, a little dangerous.[1]

As her subject "I" moves fluidly between "making videos" and "performing girlish activities"—between directing a scene to acting in it—our complicity as outside viewers is easily drawn into her world of uneasy fantasy. The pathos of her characters and the quirky premise that brings them together exposes a classic scenario where the desiring (male) gaze of the director/auteur establishes power over the (female) subject. Nakadate's reversal of that equation leaves us to wonder whether control can be fixed or if more complex relationships are possible.

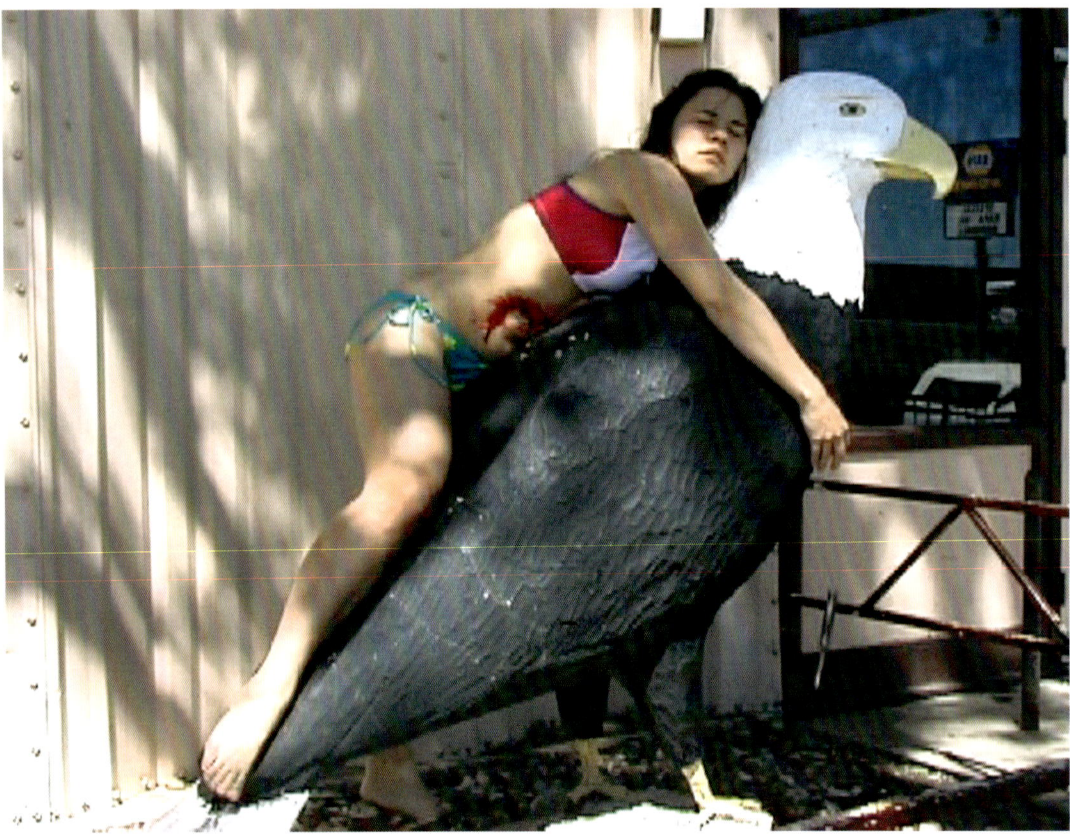

Laurel Nakadate, *Untitled* (video still from *Where You'll Find Me*), 2005. Video. 11 minutes, 53 seconds. Collection of the artist.

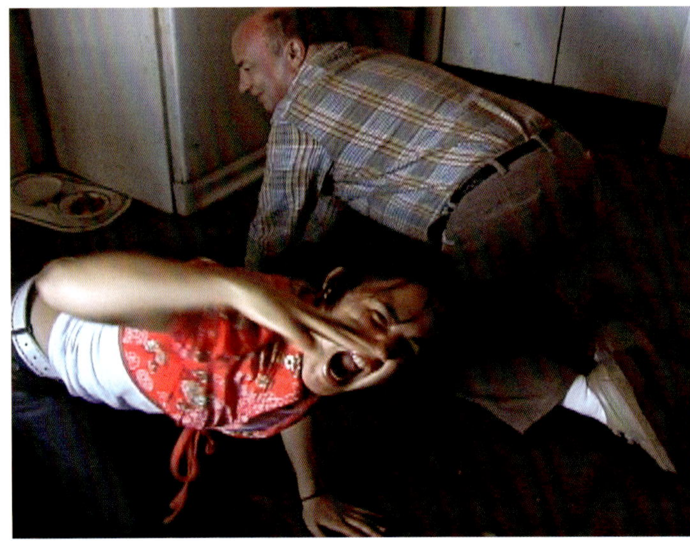

Laurel Nakadate, *Untitled* (video still from *Love Hotel and Other Stories*), 2005. Video. 13 minutes, 50 seconds. Collection of the artist.

Nakadate's activities culminated in 2005 with her second solo show at Danziger Projects, New York and the acclaimed emerging artist exhibition "Greater New York" at PS1 Contemporary Art Center where four new series of works were on view. *Lessons 1–10* (2002), wherein the artist becomes a model for a middle-aged artist of uncertain talent, eviscerates the artistic project begun by Edouard Manet's *Olympia* (1863) whose infamous gaze marked a modernist beginning. Presented as a three-channel installation, *Stories* (2005) enacts various scenarios where the artist and her newly found male friends crouch in cages, crawl around like dogs while she imitates cats, and engage in other acts of role-play. Like odd therapy sessions, these skits re-enact childhood games with adults laying bare the codes of social behavior.

Nakadate's latest bodies of work, *Love Hotel and Other Stories* (2005) and *Where You'll Find Me* (2005) re-envision the spectator by eliminating the male character from the screen. Staged in Japanese

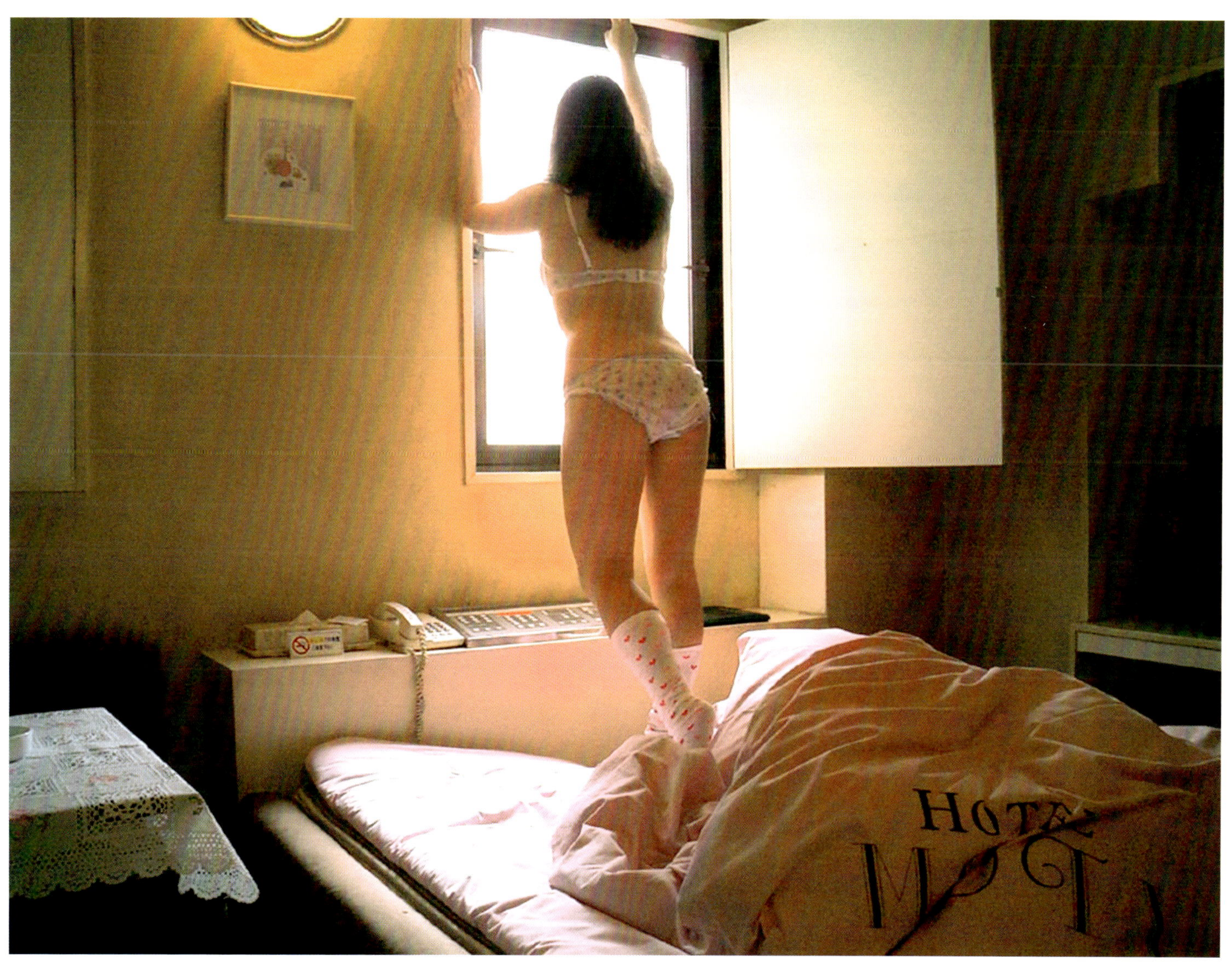

Laurel Nakadate, *Untitled* (video still from *Love Hotel and Other Stories*), 2005. Video. 13 minutes, 50 seconds. Collection of the artist.

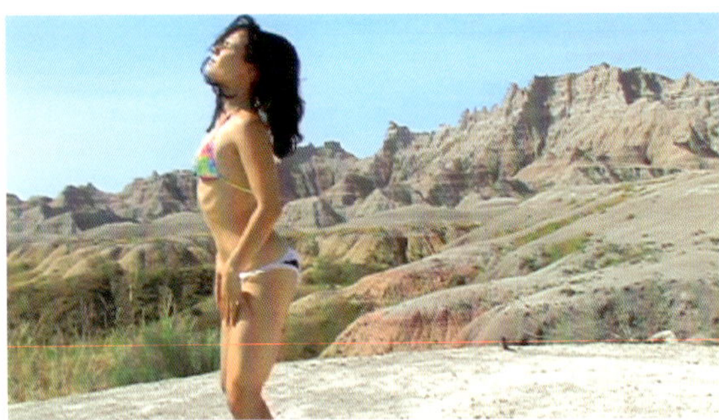

Laurel Nakadate, *Untitled* (video still from *Untitled 2005*), 2005. Video. 5 minutes, 12 seconds. Collection of the artist.

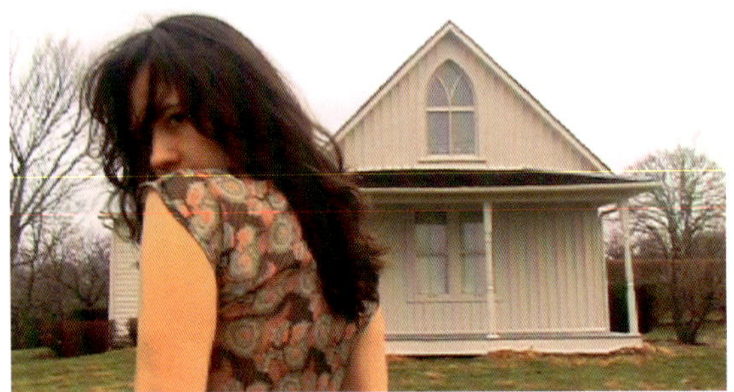

Laurel Nakadate, *Untitled* (video still from *American Gothic*), 2006. Video. 9 minutes, 36 seconds. Collection of the artist.

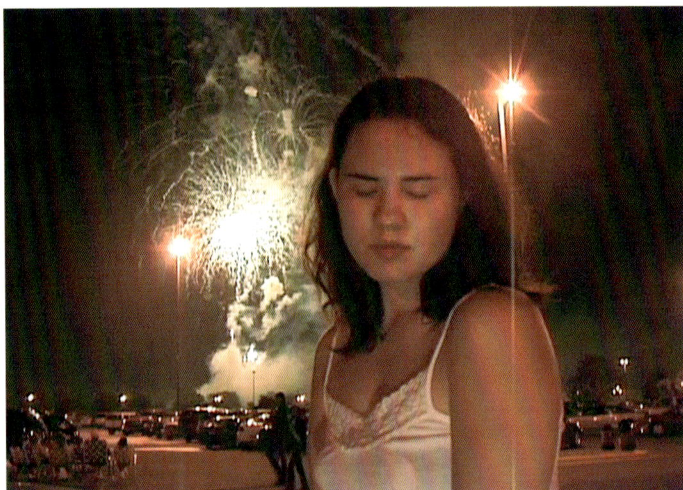

Laurel Nakadate, *Untitled* (video still from *We Are All Made of Stars*), 2003. Video. 17 minutes, 20 seconds. Collection of the artist.

hotel rooms, which are at times rented to call girls, *Love Hotel and Other Stories* makes the artist explicitly available to the viewer. Nonetheless, her women are always alone, waiting, or left behind, counting time and money until their job is done. *Where You'll Find Me* grounds itself on a similar seam between transaction and transformation. In her staging of suicides in suburban and rural America, Nakadate builds on an unspoken relationship with an enraptured audience. As an homage to 1970s performance art as well as a contemporary interpretation of Edward Hopper's anonymous working heroes, these images are both a poignant search for and a proclamation about identity. With her previous work rife with nostalgic popular music of the 1950s and 1960s—Connie Francis, The Everly Brothers, The Doors—Nakadate evokes a vision of America where difference and masquerade endlessly gain momentum. **CY**

1. "AK Diary: Laurel Nakadate," *Artkrush*, 2002, http://beta.artkrush.com.

LAUREL NAKADATE

Born in 1975, Austin, Texas; Lives and works in New York, New York **EDUCATION:** 2001, Master of Fine Arts, Yale University, New Haven, Connecticut; **SOLO EXHIBITIONS:** 2005, "Love Hotel and Other Stories," Danziger Projects, New York, New York; 2004, Central Atlantic Modern Museum, Canary Islands; 2003, "We Are All Made of Stars," Daniel Silverstein Gallery, New York, New York; **GROUP EXHIBITIONS:** 2005, "Oh Boy," New Center for Contemporary Art, Louisville, Kentucky; 2005, "I Was Only Acting," Museo Nacional Centro de Arte Reina Sofía, Madrid, Spain; 2005, "Greater New York 2005," PS1 Contemporary Art Center, New York, New York; 2005, "KunstFilmBiennale 2005," Cologne, Germany; 2003, "Towards a Low-End Theory," Minnesota Center for Photography, Minneapolis, Minnesota; 2002, "Enough About Me," Momenta Art, Brooklyn, New York

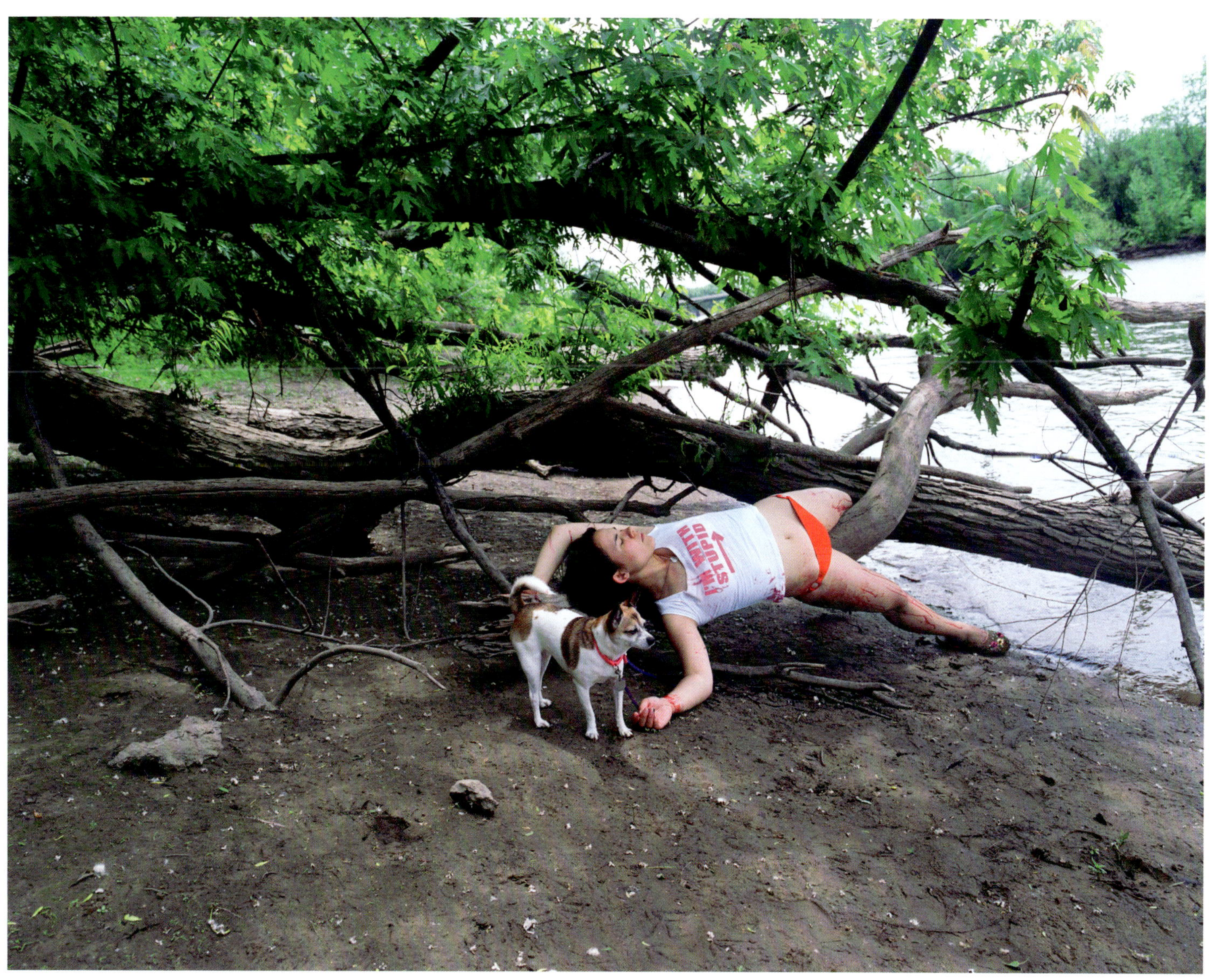

Laurel Nakadate, *Untitled* (video still from *Where You'll Find Me*), 2005. Video. 11 minutes, 53 seconds. Collection of the artist.

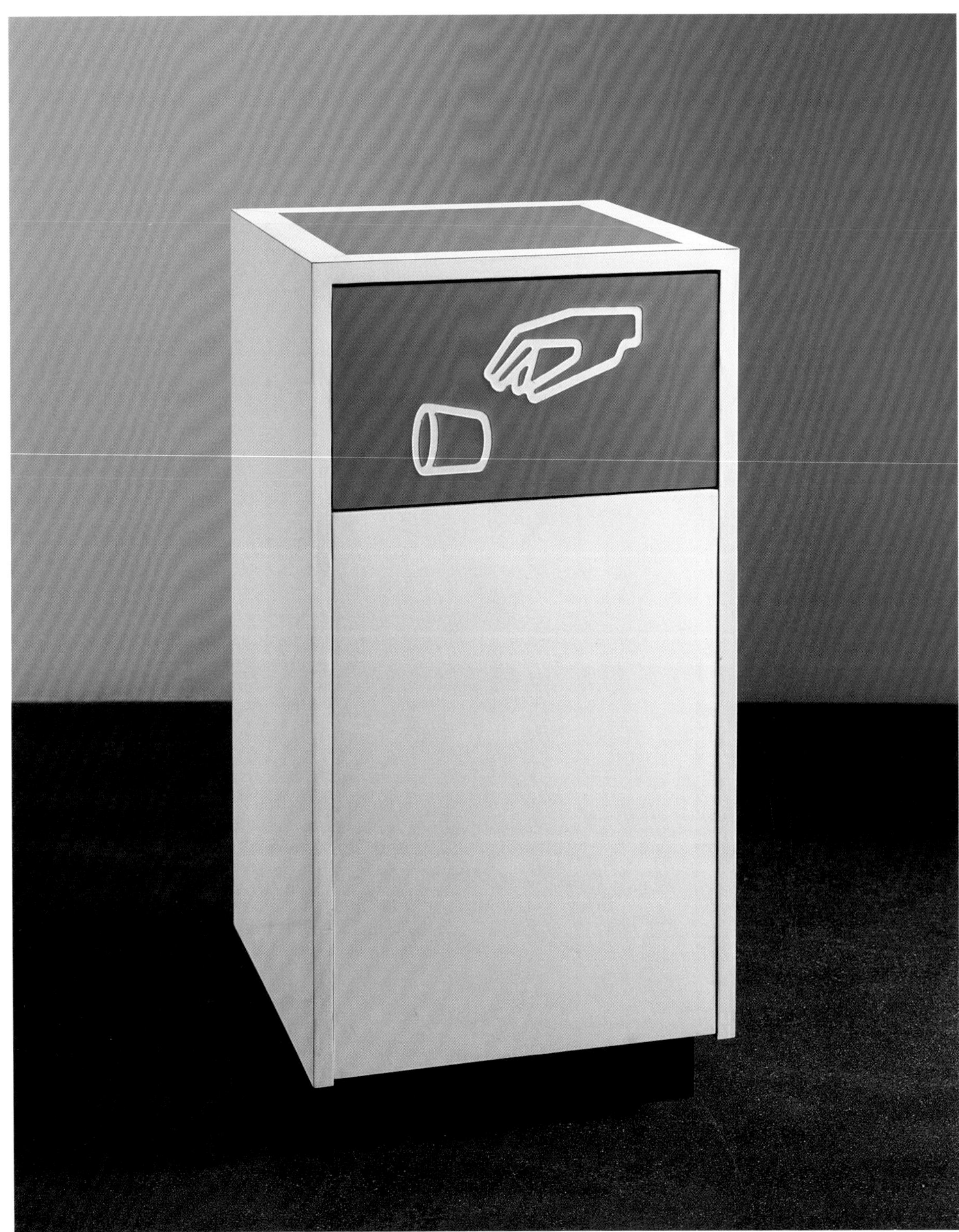

Kaz Oshiro, *Trash Bin #10*, 2006. Acrylic on stretched canvas. 39¾ x 20 x 20 inches. The Paul Rusconi Collection, Los Angeles.

KAZ OSHIRO

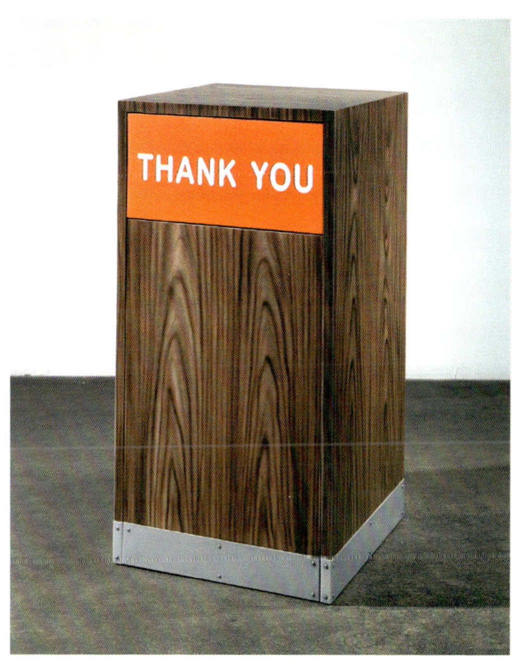

Kaz Oshiro, *Trash Bin #3*, 2003–04. Acrylic and bondo on stretched canvas. 39⅛ x 20⅛ x 20⅛ inches. The Paul Rusconi Collection, Los Angeles.

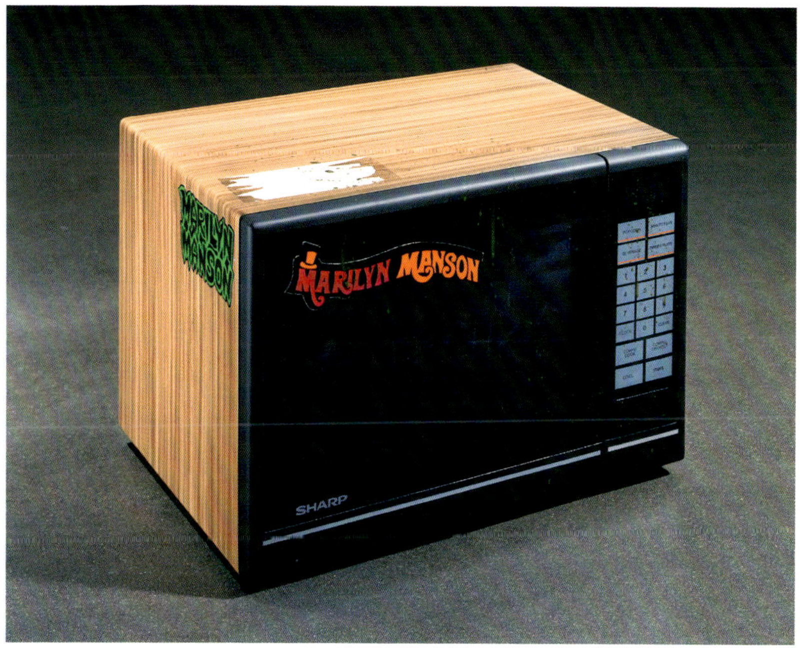

Kaz Oshiro, *Microwave Oven # 1 (Marilyn Manson)*, 2003–04. Acrylic and bondo on stretched canvas. 15¾ x 23⅛ x 16 inches. The Paul Rusconi Collection, Los Angeles.

With meticulous craftsmanship Kaz Oshiro stretches the conventional medium of painting—acrylic on canvas—on both a literal and conceptual level. The result is a three-dimensional trompe-l'oeil of prosaic items such as refrigerators, washing machines, and microwave ovens. These works realistically represent mass-produced commodities, and through their modular forms, simulate Minimalist art. However, the deadpan geometry in the vein of Donald Judd is unsettled by fabricated traces of stickers of post-punk avant-garde bands such as Sonic Youth, or of spilled detergent by way of Jackson Pollock. These marks appear incidental, yet they immediately turn run-of-the-mill objects into indexes of their imagined owners or users. In this manner, Oshiro invites us into the private sphere of the everyday environment.

For instance, one of his series of objects in mock wood grain, *Microwave Oven #1 (Marilyn Manson)* (2003–2004), appears like a relic from a college dormitory. The sense of nostalgia is intensified

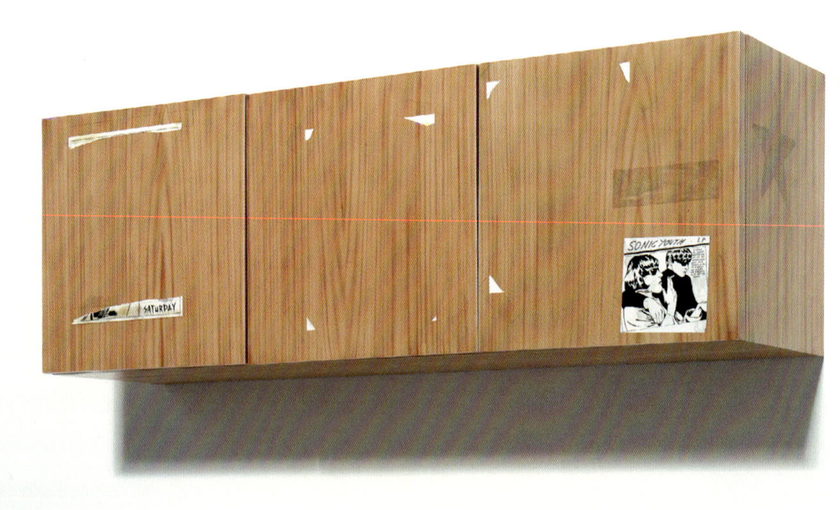

Kaz Oshiro, *Wall Cabinet #2 (Sonic Youth)*, 2003–04. Acrylic on stretched canvas. 15⅛ x 45½ x 12 inches. Private collection of Niels Kantor, Los Angeles.

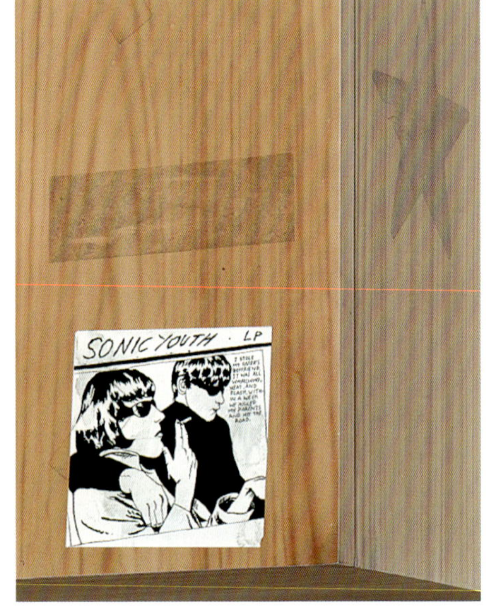

Kaz Oshiro, *Wall Cabinet #2 (Sonic Youth)* (detail).

by the outdated design of this benign home appliance. Close inspection reveals Oshiro's artistry of meticulous painting and molding of details with bondo, a putty used for auto repair. This object then reverts back into the realm of art. The artist's early interest in punk music crawls in, however, with Manson's stickers and scratched letters on the front side reading "ANTI-CHRIST." This microwave is as much an intensely laborious artwork as a sly slap in the face—reproaching the life of convenience and consumerism, which can domesticate an anti-mainstream icon as controversial as Marilyn Manson into superficial decoration.

Recently, Oshiro's interest has shifted toward what he describes as an "incidental aspect between space and object." Particularly, his works disguised as trash bins of the sort commonly found in fast food restaurants take on their own life cycle by chance, making their subject matter "the life of objects." For instance, in the present exhibition, Oshiro's trash bin-shaped painting allures visitors to mistakenly deposit litter into the work with its universal symbol of a hand that visually instructs them to: "Trash it here." The focus is placed upon questions of how misunderstanding a certain entity—in this case, mistaking the artwork for a receptacle of garbage—can actually enliven the object, however discreetly. The transformative characteristic of his oeuvre remains active, and the visitors' real life gestures (whether successfully completing the mission or not) become a component of Oshiro's illusionist art. Revelation of the hollowness of formal art is replicated in the generic form of an empty garbage can, which might be refilled by daily acts of consumption and resulting productions of waste. The work is cynical, humorous, and also somehow hopeful.

Born in U.S. occupied Okinawa in 1967, Kaz Oshiro received his formal art education in the United States. While keeping a close tie with his hometown, today he considers himself simply as an artist based in Los Angeles. **MT**

KAZ OSHIRO

Born in 1967, Okinawa, Japan; Lives and works in Los Angeles, California
EDUCATION: 2002, Master of Fine Arts, California State University, Los Angeles; 1998, Bachelor of Arts, California State University, Los Angeles; **SOLO EXHIBITIONS:** 2006, Steven Wolf Fine Arts, San Francisco, California; 2005, "Drone," Rosamund Felsen Gallery, Santa Monica, California; 2005, "Room Acoustics," Tokyo Hipsters Club, Inart Gallery, Tokyo, Japan; 2002, "Pop Tatari (Curse of Pop Music)," Rosamund Felsen Gallery, Santa Monica, California; **GROUP EXHIBITIONS:** 2005, "Thing: New Sculpture from Los Angeles," Armand Hammer Museum of Art and Cultural Center, Los Angeles, California; 2004, "Rock," Mark Moore Gallery, Los Angeles, California; 2004, "Nothing Compared to This," Contemporary Art Center, Cincinnati, Ohio; 2004, "2004 California Biennial," Orange County Museum of Art, Newport Beach, California

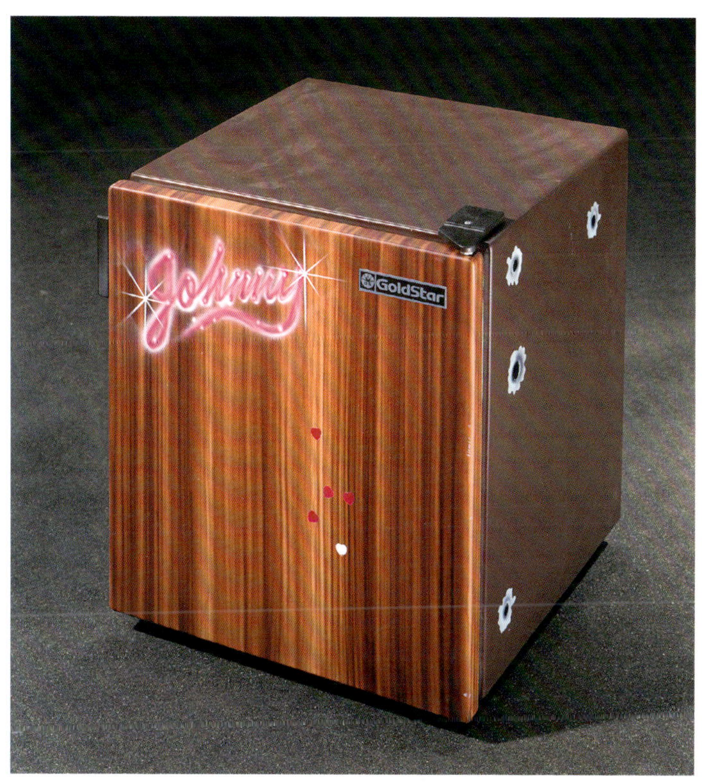

Kaz Oshiro, *Small Fridge # 4 (Johnny)*, 2003–04. Acrylic and bondo on stretched canvas. 19⅛ x 17¾ x 17⅛ inches. Private collection of James and Susan Phillips.

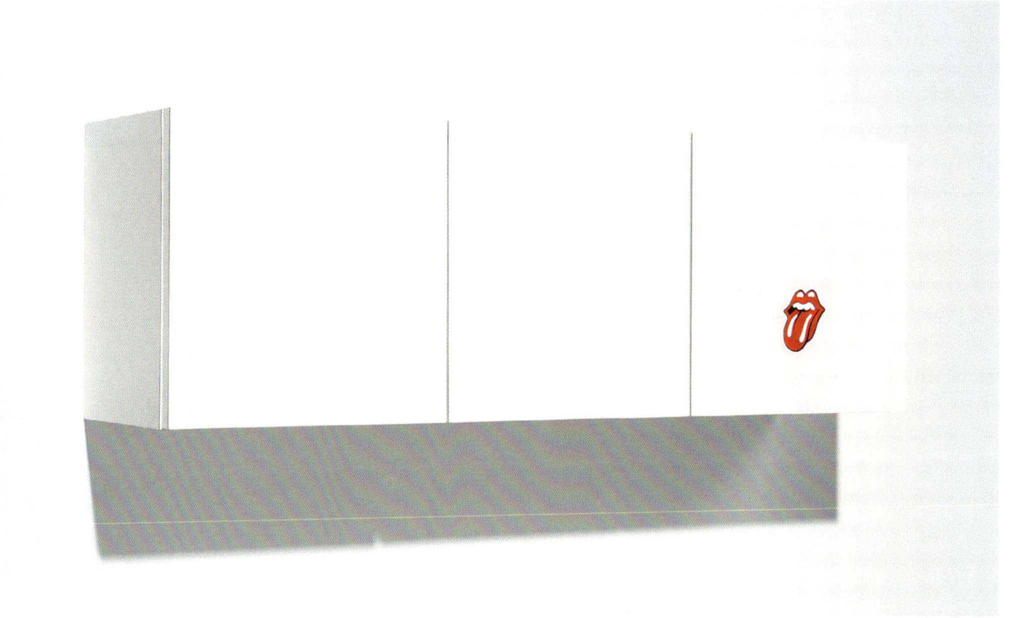

Kaz Oshiro, *Cabinet #5*, 2005. Acrylic on stretched canvas. 15 x 45⅜ x 12 inches. Private collection of Steven Molasky, Las Vegas.

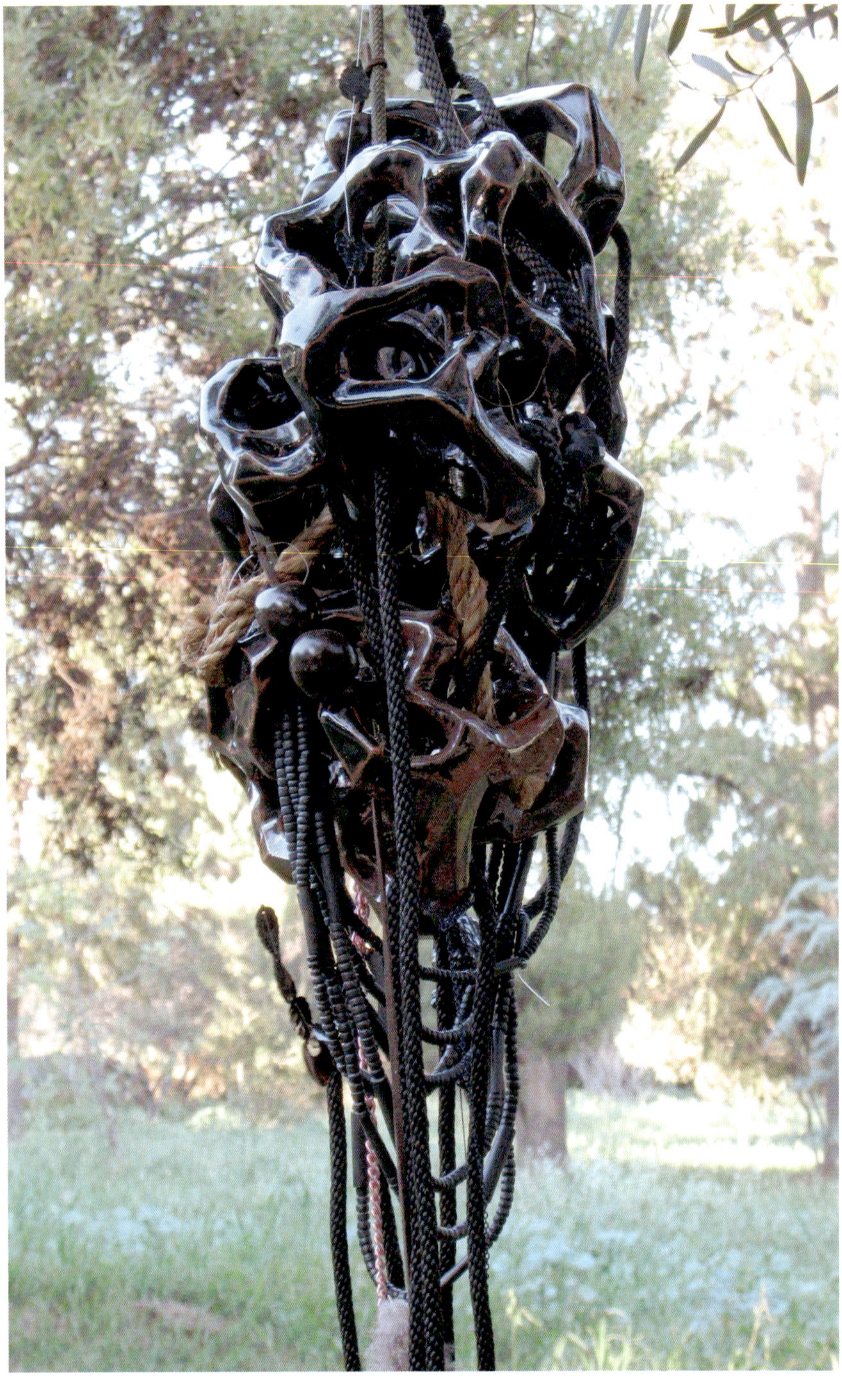

Anna Sew Hoy, *Black Noir*, 2004. Fired ceramic, rope, beads, charms, chain, charms. Dimensions variable, approx. 14 x 20 x 13 inches (ceramic piece). Collection of the artist.

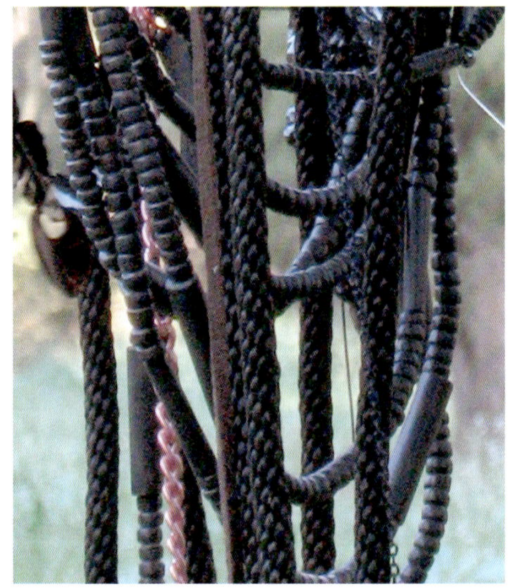

Anna Sew Hoy, *Black Noir* (detail).

ANNA SEW HOY

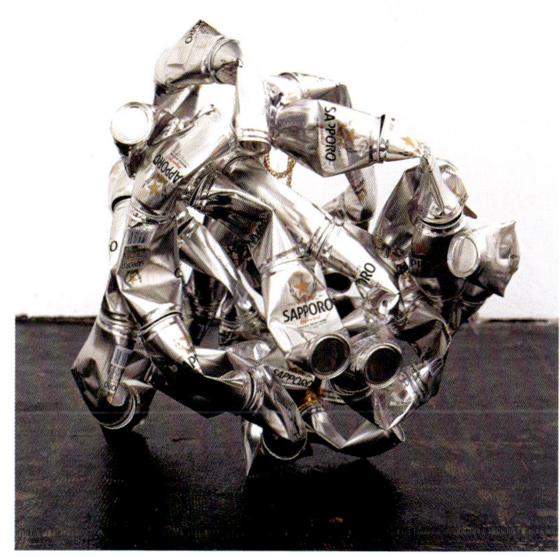

Anna Sew Hoy, *Calm Day*, 2003. Sapporo Beer cans, PC-7. 25 x 28 x 26 inches. Private collection.

Two consistent themes emerge in Anna Sew Hoy's growing body of work. One is a sense of a holistic relationship between the natural and the artificial. Another is the deployment of traditional Japanese and Chinese traditions in tandem with strategies common in modern and contemporary Western art.

Sew Hoy turns to the Japanese tradition of ikebana, the practice of harmonious flower arrangement, when composing some of her playful sculptures. She incorporates artful juxtapositions of disparate, found elements, such as used perfume bottles, logs, and store-bought knives. Another East Asian reference that Sew Hoy has appropriated is the concept of the Chinese scholar's rock, an idea dating back to the Tang dynasty (618–907). Traditionally, Chinese scholar's rocks are untouched stones found in natural settings that display unusual, seemingly sculpted shapes—and are deemed beautiful for display as an art object.

She applies the traditions of ikebana and the Chinese scholar's rock when assembling the detritus of everyday American life. By working with found, commercial elements, Sew Hoy's work not only nods to the Duchampian readymade, but also recalls that of other installation artists of roughly the same generation who share a hip, flea-market sensibility—Cady Noland and Rachel Harrison come to mind. Yet Sew Hoy arrives at an original variation on a popular thread in contemporary art. She offers a clever sampling and remix of practices, stretching across national boundaries and art-historical and cultural references.

Sew Hoy transforms her installations in relation to the spaces where they are shown. One series, *Dreamcatcher* (2006)—the title refers to a Native American craftwork intended to provide owners with pleasant dreams—can either hang from the ceiling or from a sculptural stand. Another work, *Haiku* (2006)—named, obviously, after a style of minimalist Japanese poetry—is a stripped-down piece featuring an amorphous foam shape that leans into a mirror placed on the ground (see fig. 21, page 40). The configuration recalls Narcissus looking vainly at his reflection. Inserted into the backside of the foam blob are a group of knives. By calling the piece *Haiku*, Sew Hoy suggests a simple narrative although it is clearly up to the viewer to interpret the story.

Beyond her installations featuring found objects, she has also made a line of T-shirts. In keeping with her focus on giving new life to found objects, she silkscreened some of her drawings onto used

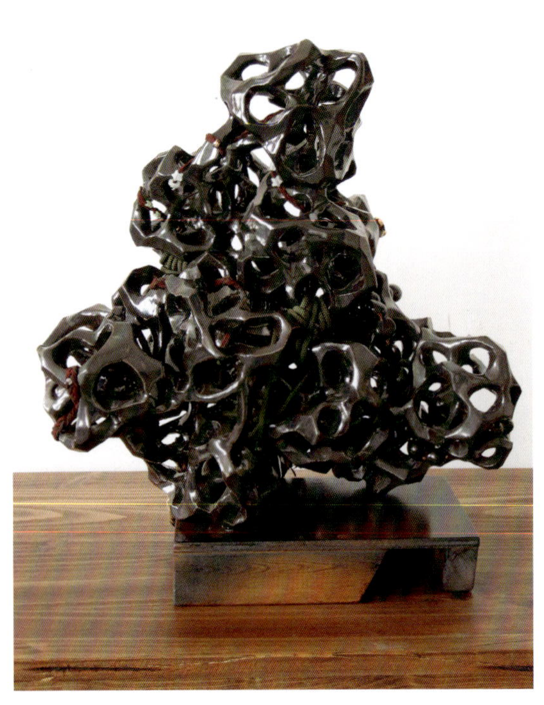

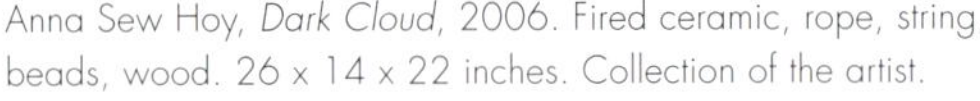

Anna Sew Hoy, *Dark Cloud*, 2006. Fired ceramic, rope, string, beads, wood. 26 x 14 x 22 inches. Collection of the artist.

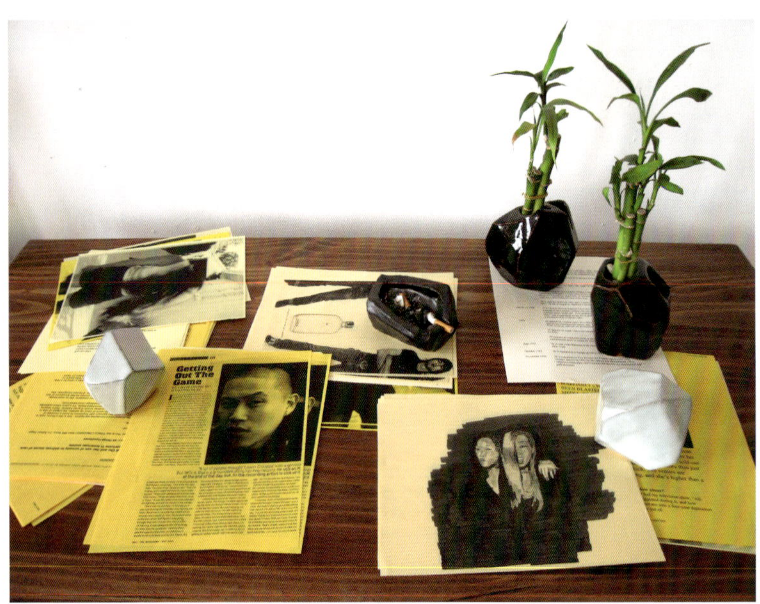

Anna Sew Hoy, *Gettin' Out Tha Game*, 2006. Table, photocopied articles, ceramic pieces, bamboo. Dimensions variable. Collection of the artist.

shirts bought from vintage stores. The project, which blurred the boundaries between printmaking and design, recalls the "art into life" philosophy of Russian Constructivist artists working in the first half of the twentieth century, as well as the multifaceted career of Japanese American sculptor Isamu Noguchi (1904–88), who also designed lamps and furniture. Sew Hoy's varied work suggests a strata of references that cross cultures—from East to West, from high to low, from poetic to prosaic. As Sew Hoy, who describes her background as "Chinatown Chinese" (her family emigrated from China to the United States during the nineteenth-century Gold Rush, then settled in New Zealand), says of her multifaceted approach to artmaking, "My work is about objects . . . and complex layers of identity."[1]

RJ

1. Anna Sew Hoy, conversation with the author, February 21, 2006.

ANNA SEW HOY

Born in 1976, Auckland, New Zealand; Lives and works in Los Angeles, California, and New York, New York

EDUCATION: 2001, Master of Fine Arts program, Hunter College, New York, New York; 1998, Bachelor of Arts, School of Visual Arts, New York, New York; **SOLO EXHIBITIONS:** 2003, "Broken Arm," Peres Projects, Los Angeles, California; 1999, "Koichi-ko," Storefront Project #1, A-Z House by Andrea Zittel, New York, New York; **GROUP EXHIBITIONS:** 2006, "Cosmic Wonder," Yerba Buena Center for the Arts, San Francisco, California; 2004, "Phiiliip: Divided by Lightning," Deitch Projects/John Connelly Presents, New York, New York; 2002, "Unknown Pleasures," Daniel Reich Gallery, New York, New York; **RESIDENCIES:** 2002, Artist in residence of the Space Program, The Marie Walsh Sharpe Art Foundation, New York, New York; 1999, Artist in residence, Taller de Cerámica Contemporánea Suro, Guadalajara, Mexico

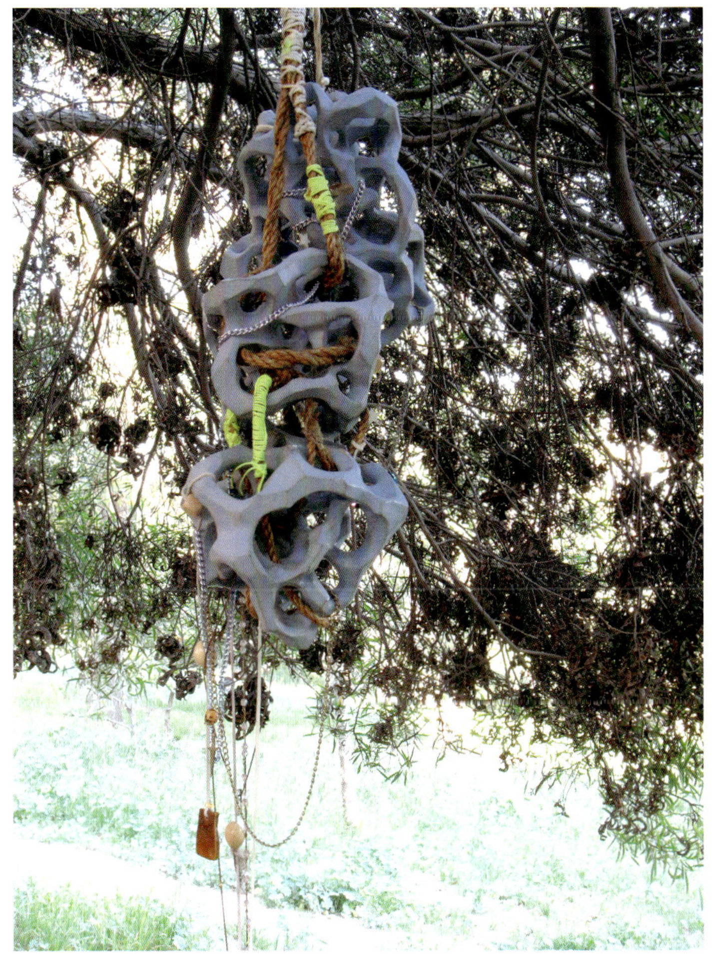

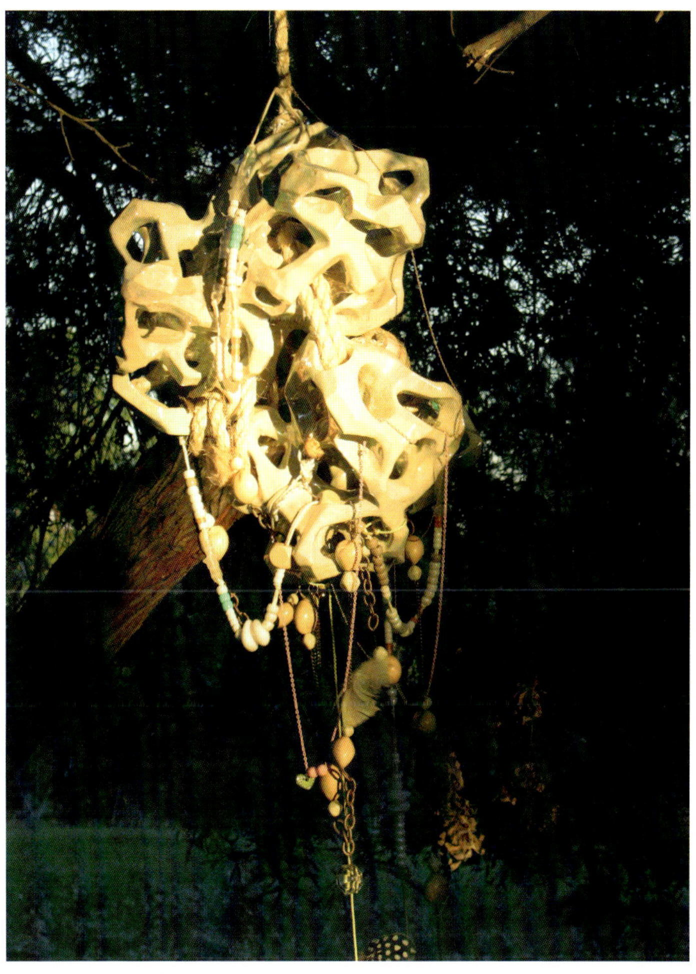

Above: Anna Sew Hoy, *Violet Noir*, 2004. Fired ceramic, rope, beads, charms, chain, charms. Dimensions variable, approx. 14 x 20 x 13 inches (ceramic piece). Collection of the artist. Above right: Anna Sew Hoy, *White Noir*, 2004. Fired ceramic, rope, beads, charms, chain, charms. Dimensions variable, approx. 14 x 20 x 13 inches (ceramic piece). Collection of the artist.

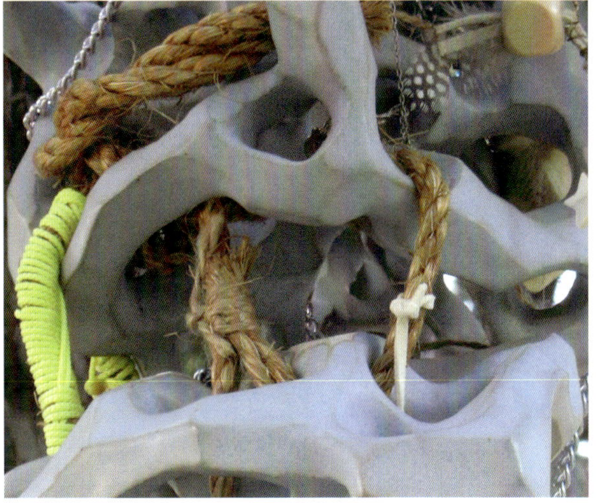

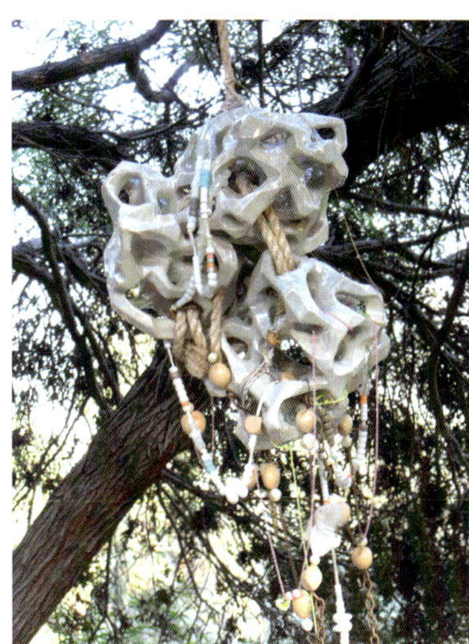

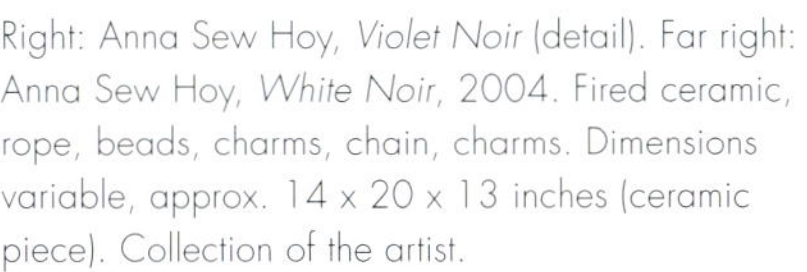

Right: Anna Sew Hoy, *Violet Noir* (detail). Far right: Anna Sew Hoy, *White Noir*, 2004. Fired ceramic, rope, beads, charms, chain, charms. Dimensions variable, approx. 14 x 20 x 13 inches (ceramic piece). Collection of the artist.

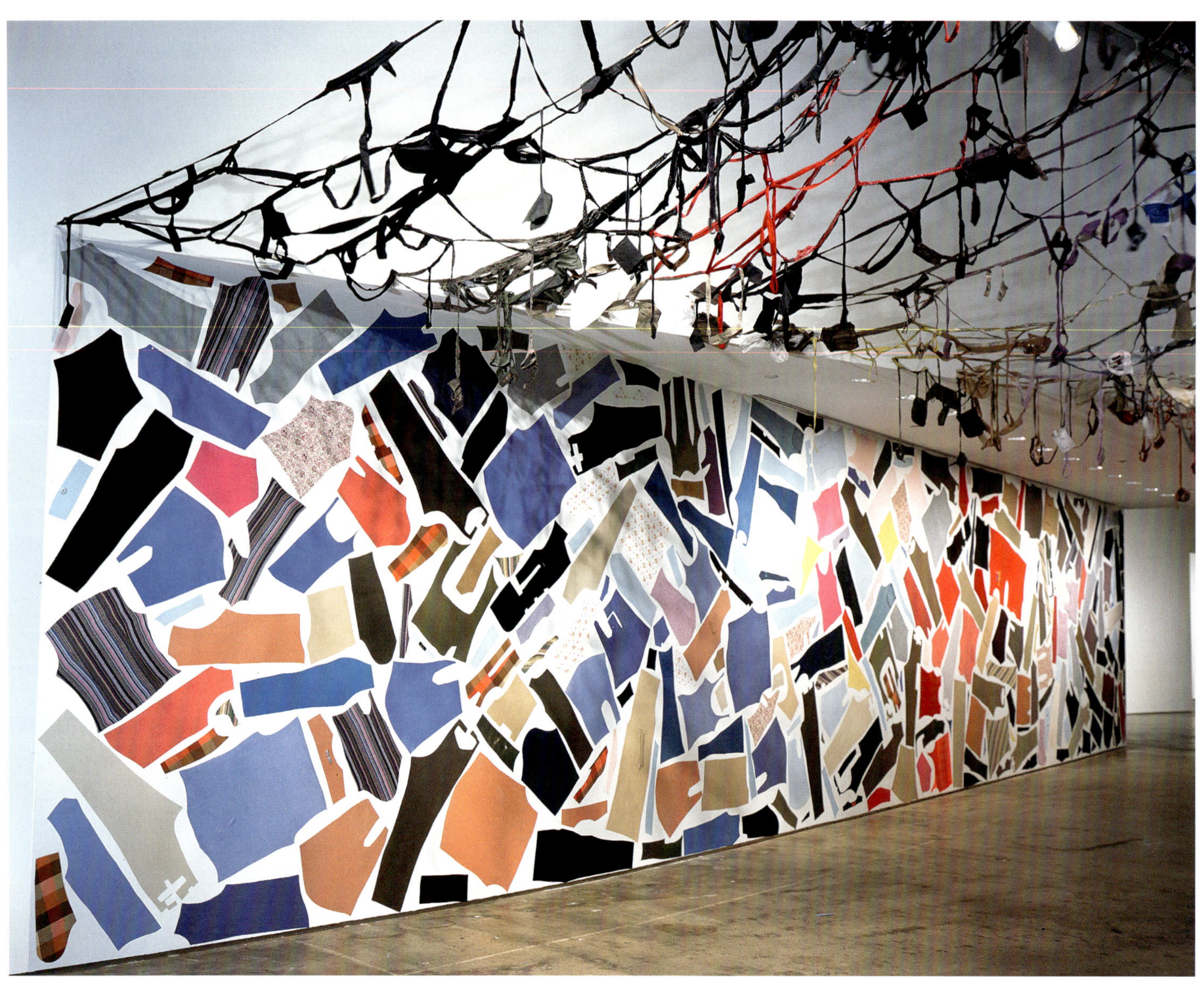

Jean Shin, *Projects 81 (Cut Outs and Suspended Seams)*, 2004. Cut fabric (clothes from MoMA staff), starch, and thread. 624 x 228 x 192 inches. Installation view at The Museum of Modern Art, Queens, New York.

JEAN SHIN

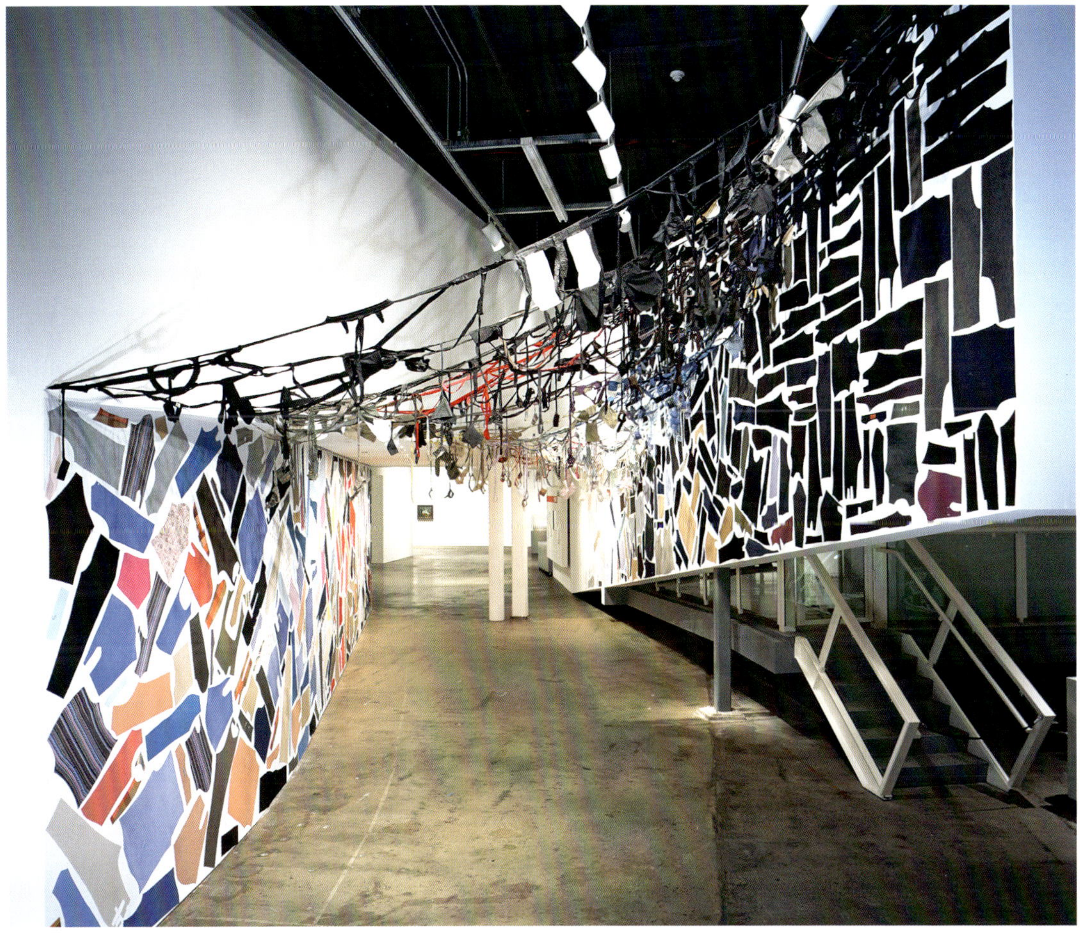

Jean Shin, *Projects 81 (Cut Outs and Suspended Seams)*, 2004. Cut fabric (clothes from MoMA staff), starch, and thread. 624 x 228 x 192 inches. Installation view at The Museum of Modern Art, Queens, New York.

Jean Shin's large scale installations are made of small materials, collected from particular groups of people, places, or communities. Often concentrating on things that would otherwise go unnoticed and discarded, Shin extracts from those small inanimate objects commonalities and differences all at once. Her meticulous process of production with obsessively accumulated materials often results in organic compositions that integrate the nature and context of each display space.

In *Project 81 (Cut Outs and Suspended Seams)*, created in 2004 at the temporary Queens location of The Museum of Modern Art, Shin collected worn work clothes from the museum staff and deconstructed them into patches of colors that resemble a mosaic of Matisse-like cutouts. Starched onto the walls of a passage way to the galleries, various shades of colors, facing each other, silently cohabited the space. The cut fabrics flattened the institutional hierarchy often indicative in work clothes. Seams sewn together and hung over the walls, then, became suspension bridges, connecting the walls physically and the staff figuratively.

In her new installation for the current exhibition, Shin collected used knit sweaters from people who consider themselves a part of the Asian American community. Inspired by Italo Calvino's description of the city Ersilia in his novel *Invisible Cities* (1972), she then unraveled the sweaters and connected loosened yarns to give life to "spider-webs of intricate relationships seeking a form."[1] The initiating point of this networking project was the three curators of this exhibition, who each gave their sweaters to the artist. They then contacted their acquaintances and colleagues, who in turn contacted their circle of friends for their contribution to and participation in the project. The link continued until Shin gathered enough materials to create the present installation. For each traveling venue of the exhibition, Shin plans to continue soliciting sweaters so that the scope of her installation gradually expands with increasing participation from various members of the Asian American community.

In contrast to the community becoming tightly knit through this project, the participants' sweaters were unraveled and loosened; yarn began spreading out of their original form into a larger space. In the form of an intricate three-dimensional line drawing, the deconstructed sweaters were conflated and reconfigured, mapping out varying densities of human connection and veins of association. As a process, *Unraveling* (2006–) shows the cooperative existence of a community that continues to grow and expand. As a material object, the entire installation reflects the flexibility in how identity is determined as each contributor has a particular reason for participating in the project, and thus, identifying with the Asian American community. **MT**

1. Italo Calvino, *Invisible Cities* (New York: Harcourt Brace Jovanovich, 1974), 77.

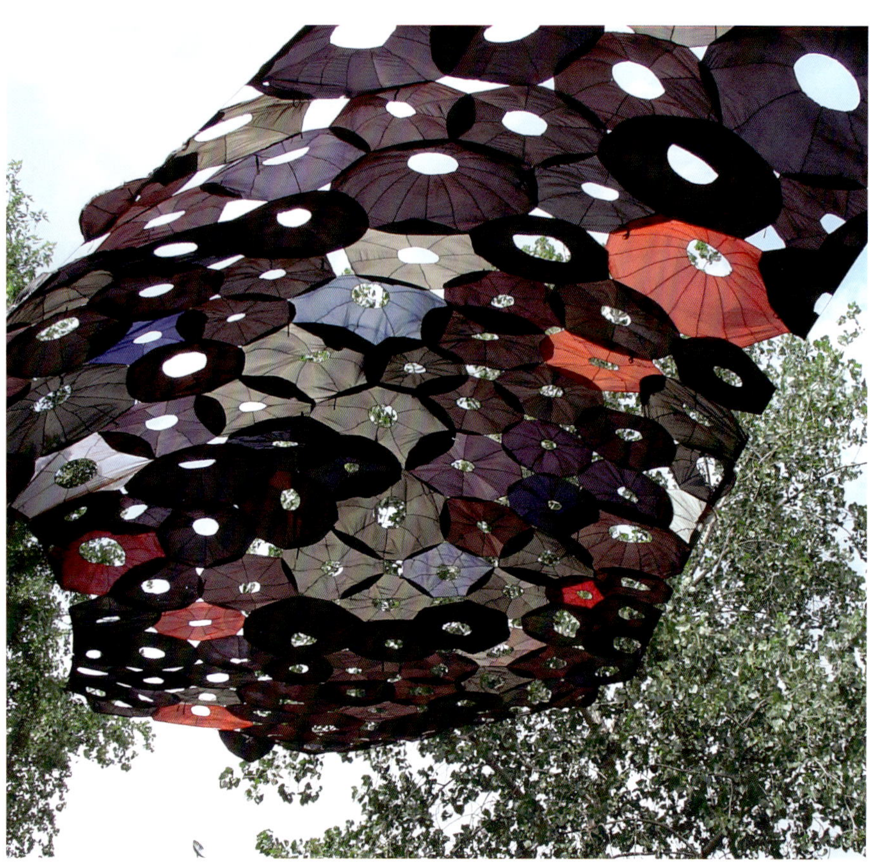

Jean Shin, *Penumbra*, 2003. Fabric (broken umbrellas) and thread. 864 x 540 inches (variable height). Installation view at Socrates Sculpture Park, Long Island City, New York.

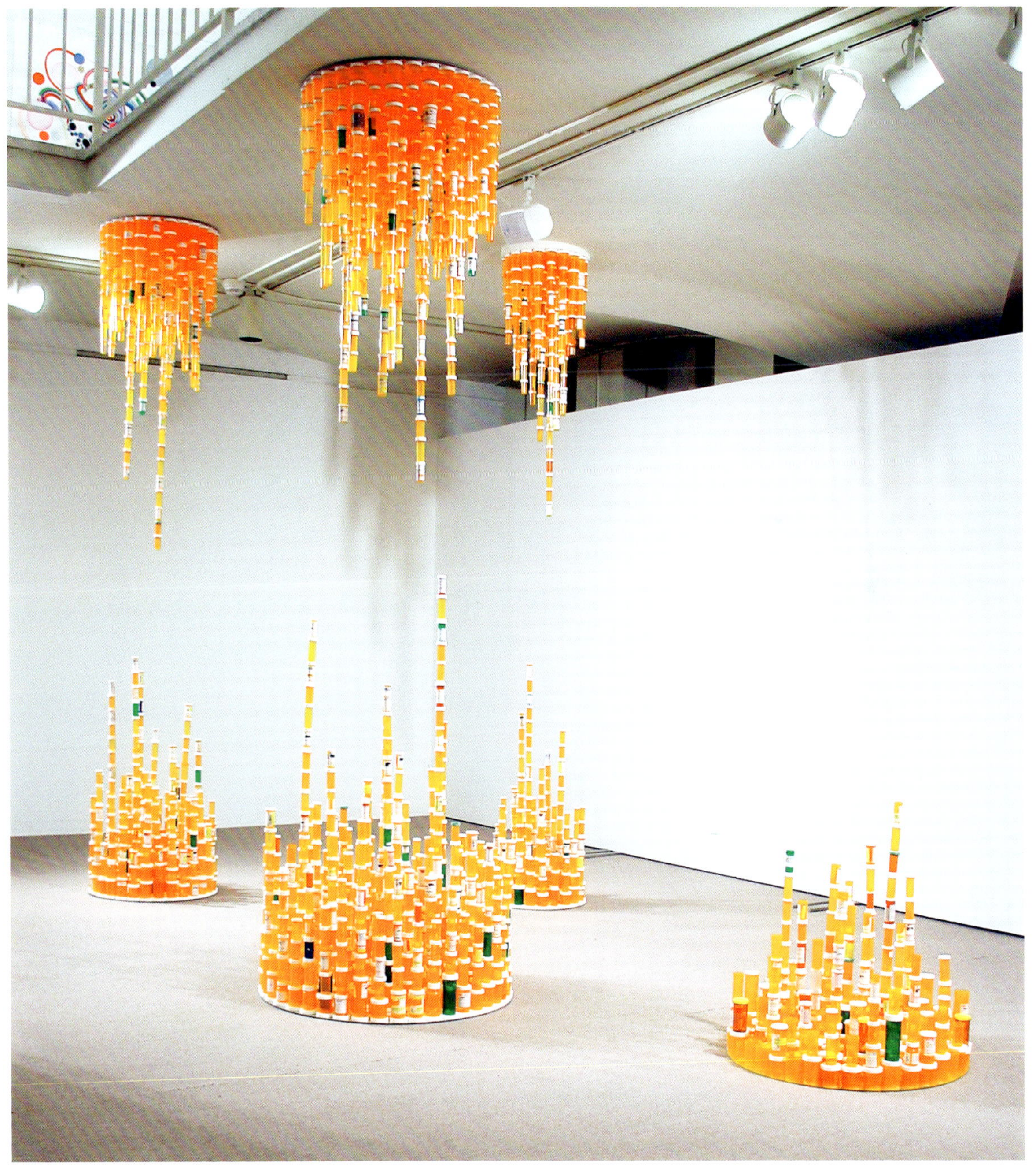

Jean Shin, *Chemical Balance 2*, 2005. Prescription bottles, mirror, and epoxy. Dimensions variable. Installation view at University Art Museum, Albany, New York.

JEAN SHIN

Born in 1971, Seoul, Korea; Lives and works in New York, New York **EDUCATION:** 1999, Skowhegan School of Painting and Sculpture, Maine; 1996, Master of Science, Pratt Institute, New York, New York; 1994, Bachelor of Fine Arts, Pratt Institute, New York, New York; **SOLO EXHIBITIONS:** 2005, "Accumulations," University Art Museum, University at Albany, State University of New York; 2004, "Ulrich Project Series: Jean Shin," Ulrich Museum of Art, Wichita State University, Kansas; 2004, "Projects 81: Jean Shin," The Museum of Modern Art, New York, New York; 1999, "444," Apex Art, New York, New York; **GROUP EXHIBITIONS:** 2005, "Make it Now: New Sculpture in New York," SculptureCenter, New York, New York; 2005, "Chinatown In/Flux," Asian Arts Initiative, Philadelphia, Pennsylvania; 2005, "Harlem Postcards," Studio Museum in Harlem, New York, New York; 2004, "Counter Culture," New Museum of Contemporary Art, New York, New York; 2004, "Open House: Working in Brooklyn," Brooklyn Museum of Art, New York; 2004, "Troy Story," Hosfelt Gallery, San Francisco, California; **AWARDS AND HONORS:** 2004, National Endowment for the Arts in collaboration with The Fabric Workshop and Museum, Philadelphia, Pennsylvania; 2003, Fellowship Award in Sculpture, New York Foundation for the Arts; 2001, The Louis Comfort Tiffany Foundation Biennial Art Award; 2001, Asian Cultural Council Fellowship

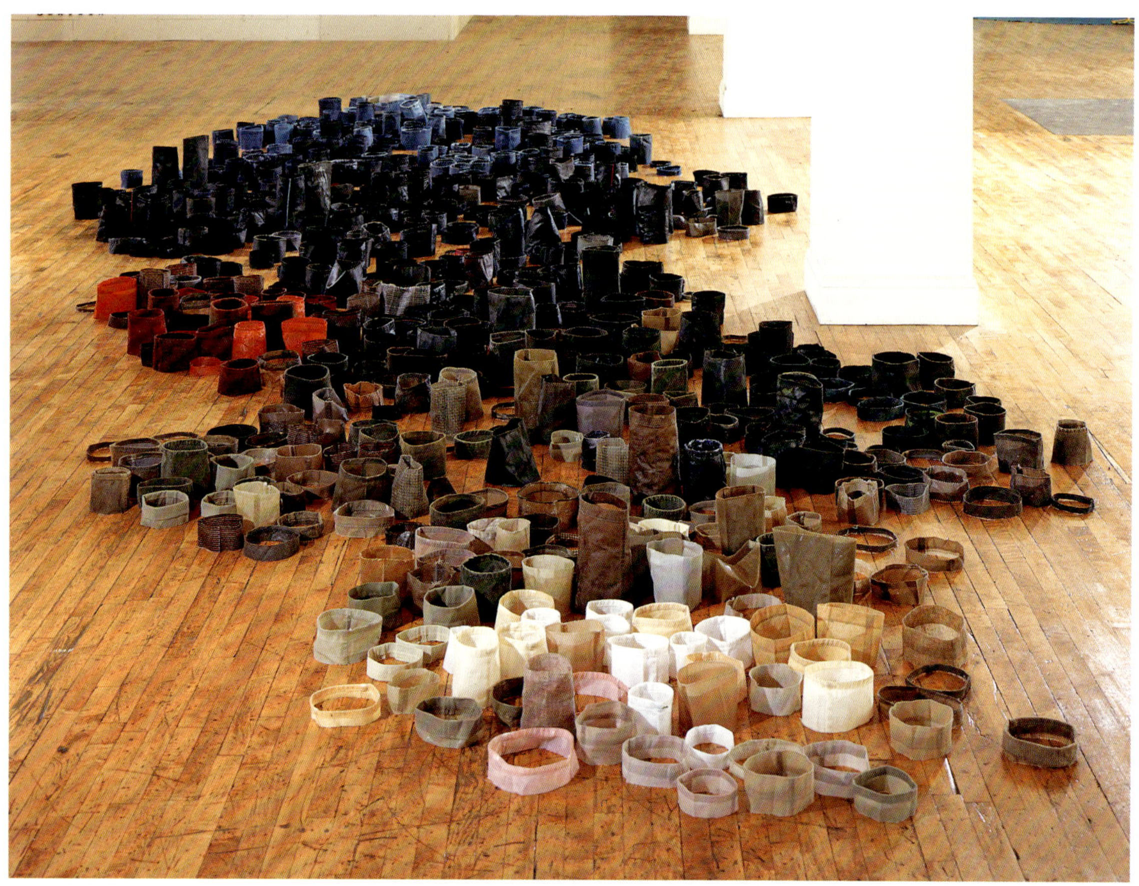

Jean Shin, *Alterations*, 1999. Fabric (pant scraps) and wax. Dimensions variable, approx. 132 x 264 inches. Collection of Peter Norton.

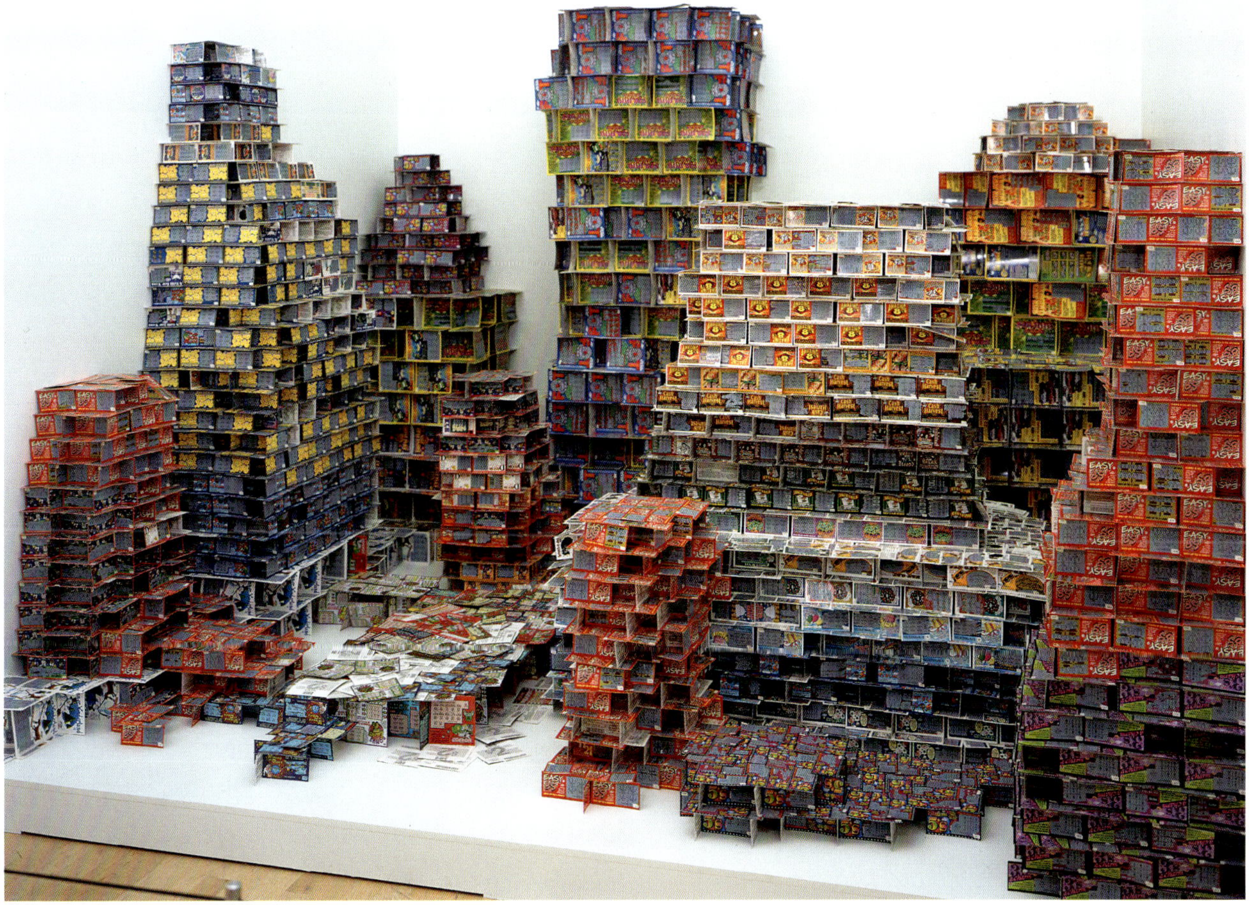

Jean Shin, *Chance City*, 2001–04. $21,496 worth of discarded lottery tickets. 72 x 96 x 96 inches. Installation view at Brooklyn Museum of Art, New York.

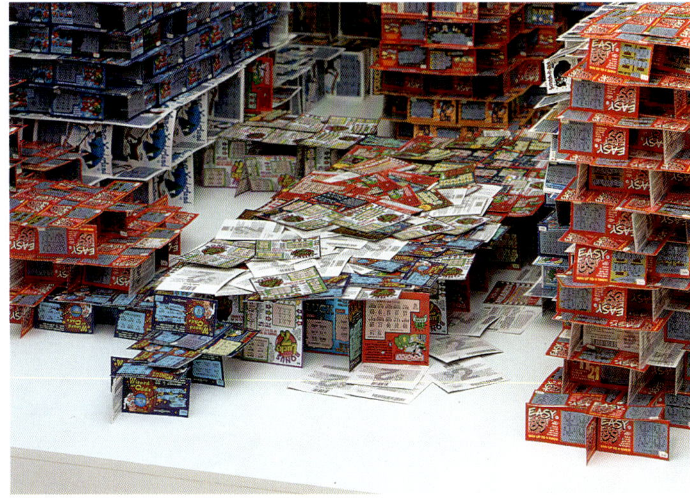

Jean Shin, *Chance City* (detail).

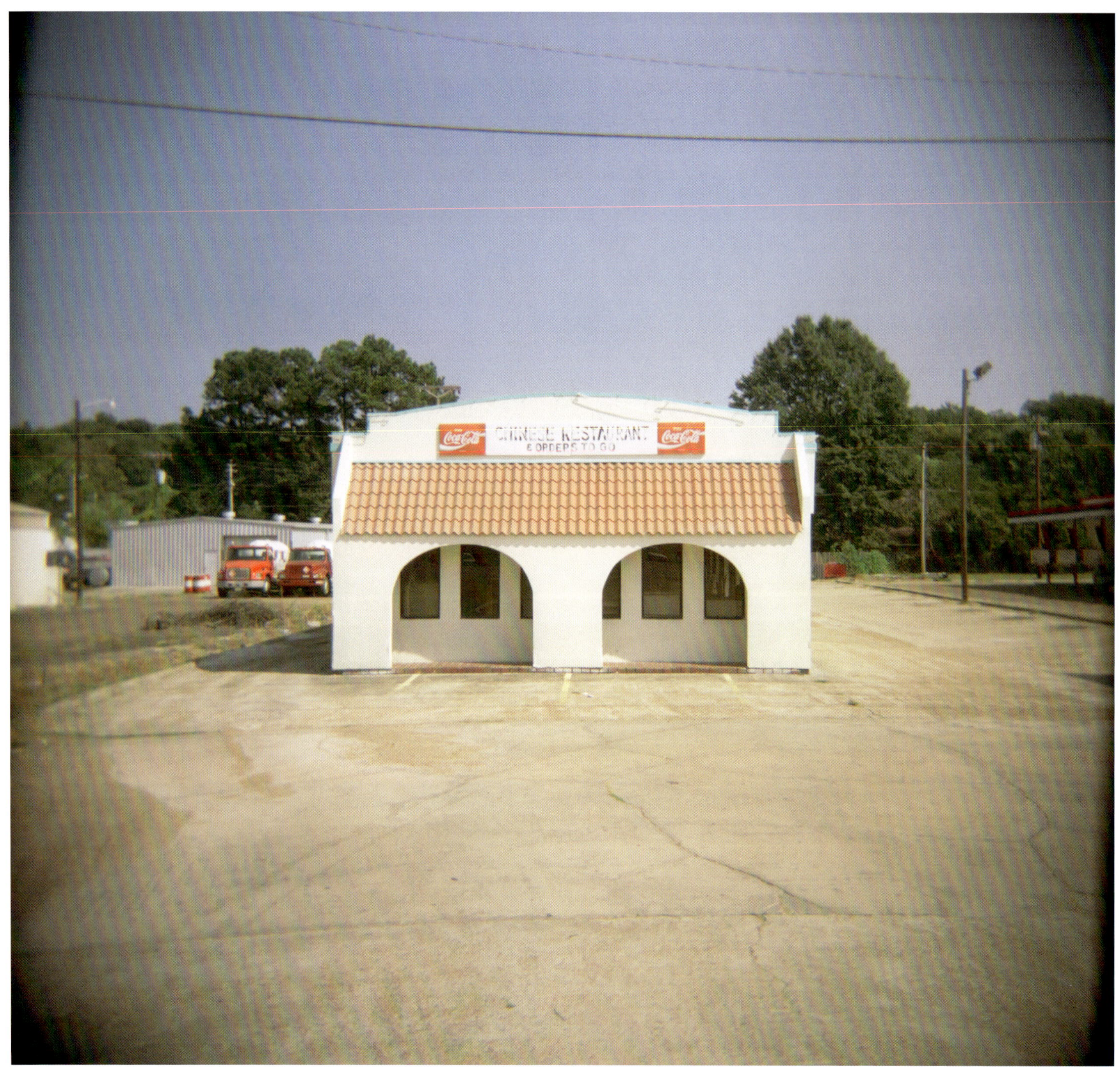

Indigo Som, *China Garden, Yazoo City, Mississippi* (from the series *Mostly Mississippi: Chinese Restaurants of the South*), 2004–05. Digital pigment print. 34 x 34 inches.

INDIGO SOM

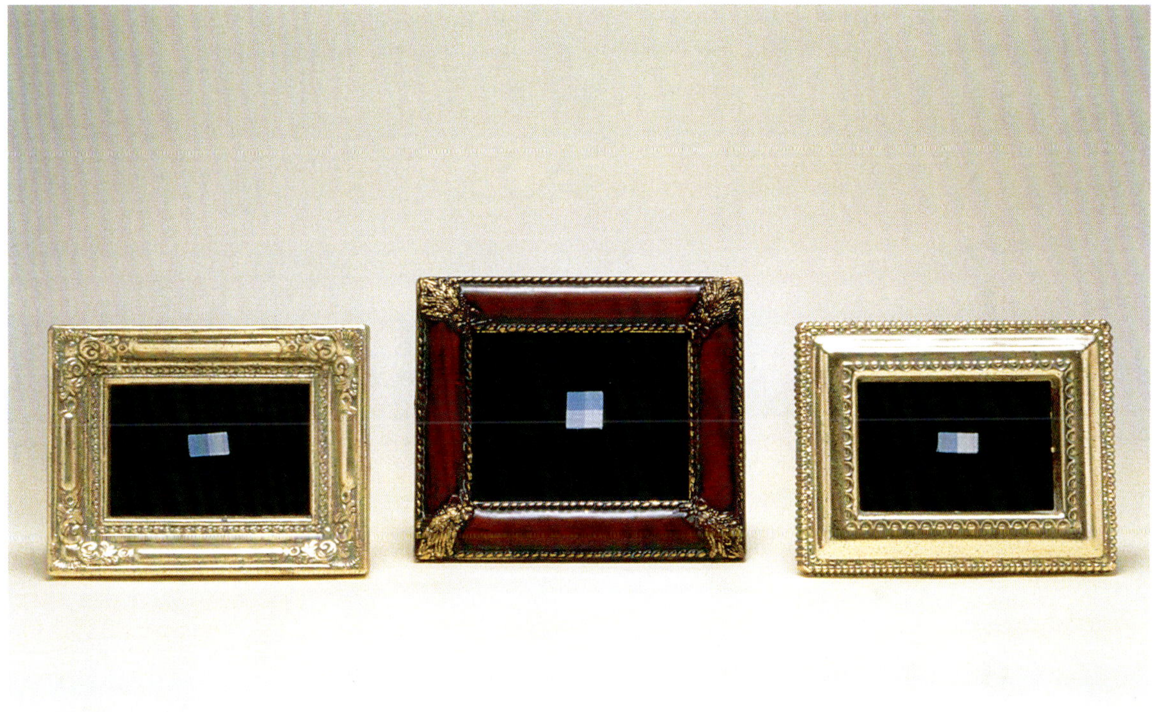

Indigo Som, *Untitled* (from *Gingham Series*), 1998. ¼ inch blue and white checked gingham, pins, khaki, plastic boxes, frames. 4 x 13½ x 3½ inches. Collection of the artist.

Indigo Som spent her adolescent years in a mostly Caucasian neighborhood of Marin, California. Wearing a preppy school uniform in gingham, she felt rather estranged from other students. What made her feel uncomfortable in this cotton fabric?

Growing up in a household where authentic Chinese food was abundant, Som naturally learned that chop suey is an American invention. Why is this item on hundreds and thousands of Chinese restaurant menus?

Issues of identity and authenticity always figure largely in Indigo Som's works. However, instead of searching for an essential origin or original, she explores heterogeneous existences in America that often come dressed up in poetic or humorous attire.

Som's work begins with finding and questioning the forgotten and the invisible in what seem to be mundane facts or everyday occurrences in America. In her *Gingham Series* (1998–1999) she deconstructed the classically American grid-patterned fabric that

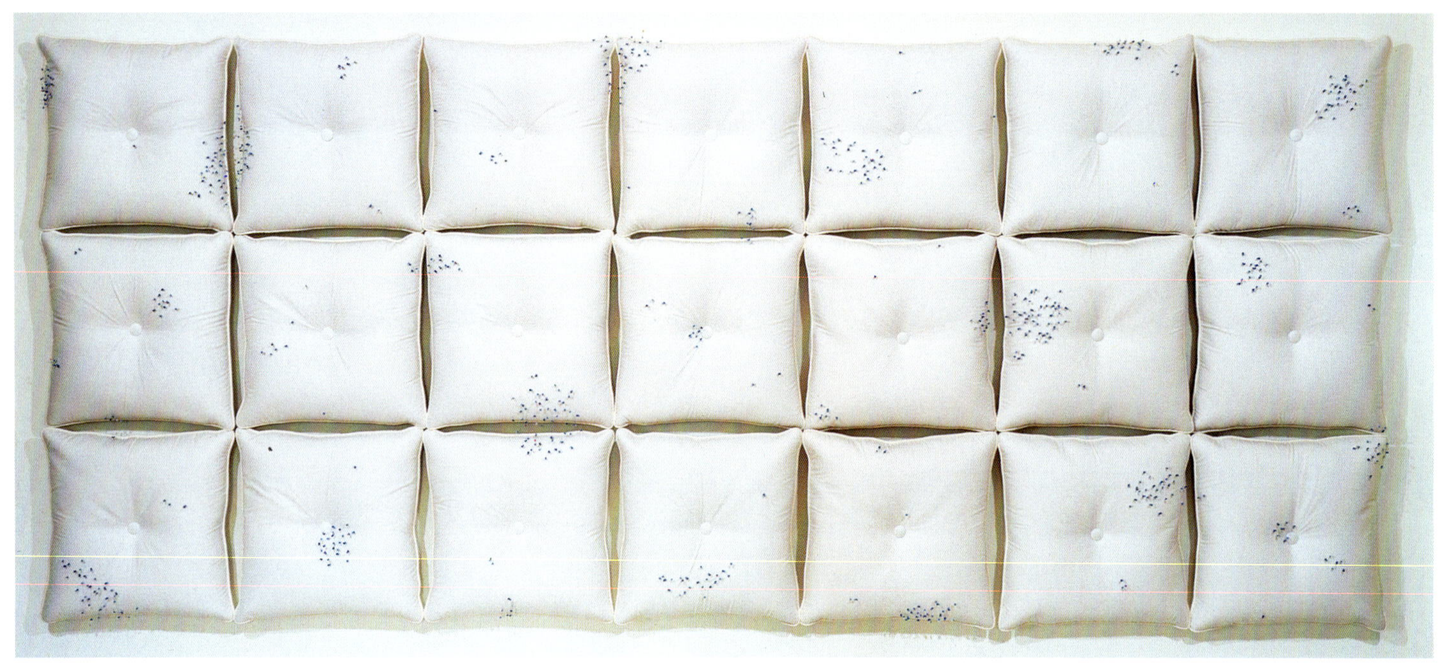

Indigo Som, *Pastel Diaspora*, 1999–2003. Linen pillows, waxed gingham, pins, mixed media. Approx. 84 x 192 x 8 inches (each pillow 27 inches square). Collection of the artist.

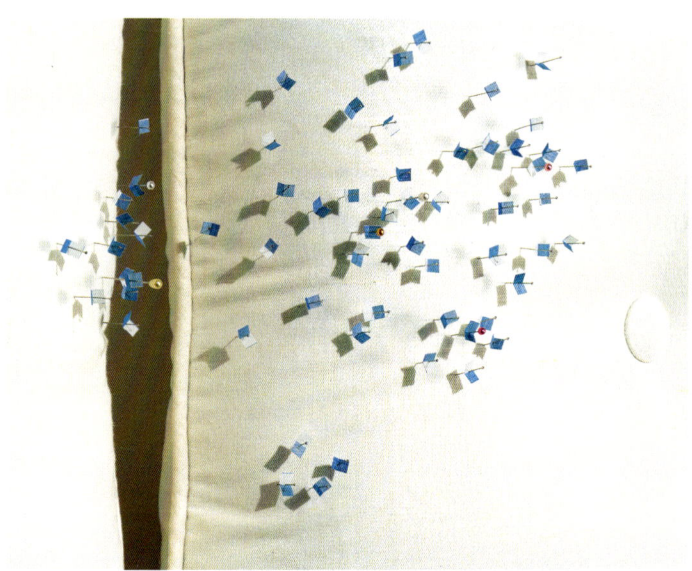

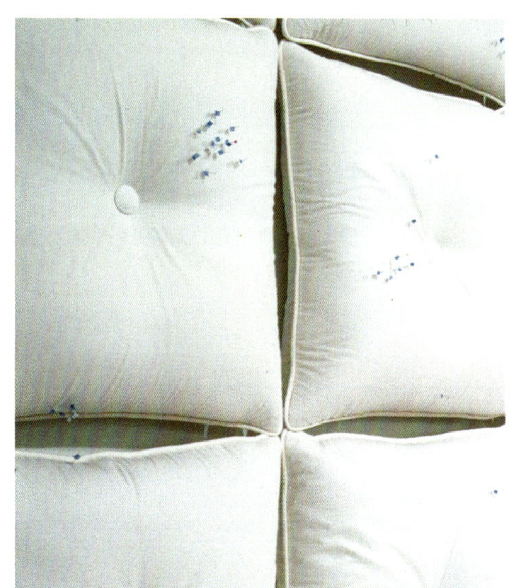

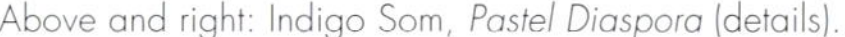

Above and right: Indigo Som, *Pastel Diaspora* (details).

reminded her of her school uniform into monotone squares and stripes. The fragmented pieces conceptually emancipated her unique being, which could not be plainly woven into prep school culture. The series also encompassed numerous patterns and forms into which those fragments could be transformed—perhaps a metaphorical statement about identity that is forever unfixed.

However, in the related installation work, entitled *Pastel Diaspora* (1999–2003), placid fabric squares are mapped out on rows of white pillows, inferring that the emancipated blues are not evenly dispersed but concentrated in some areas. The softly cushioned landscape, then, implies the difficult reality of a racially divided America.

Another characteristic of her works, which often emerges as textual elements, is a more covert, poetic quality reflecting her initial interest in writing. *No One to Call Home/Girl* (1995), for instance, is an accordion-form book with a list of common Chinese American female names—Jade, Harmony, and Cherry—interspersed with a fragmented story about three Chinese American girls. The accumulation of the names itself composes a colorful sting of words and images while simultaneously revealing a certain coding system of one's identity.

Indeed, accumulation has been at the core of Som's creative methodology. Whether in the cut pieces of clothes or in the handmade artist's book, her presence is always viscerally felt through her works. Facing the three large photographs from the series *Mostly Mississippi: Chinese Restaurants of the South* (2004–2005) shown in "One Way or Another," we also sense Som's empathetic eyes focusing on the desolate restaurants as if trying to register the faces of forlorn individuals. The series is a collection of exterior views of restaurants that typically serve Americanized Chinese dishes to clientele in racially divided rural towns in the South. These are the psychic residua of "Chinese-ness" deeply embedded in the quotidian American landscape. As part of the scenic cliché, these roadside eateries would not otherwise catch our attention. Only through the photographic records of Som's accumulated experiences of visiting those locales do they surface as the sight of aesthetic arrest with a hint of irony and humor about one face of the American identity. **MT**

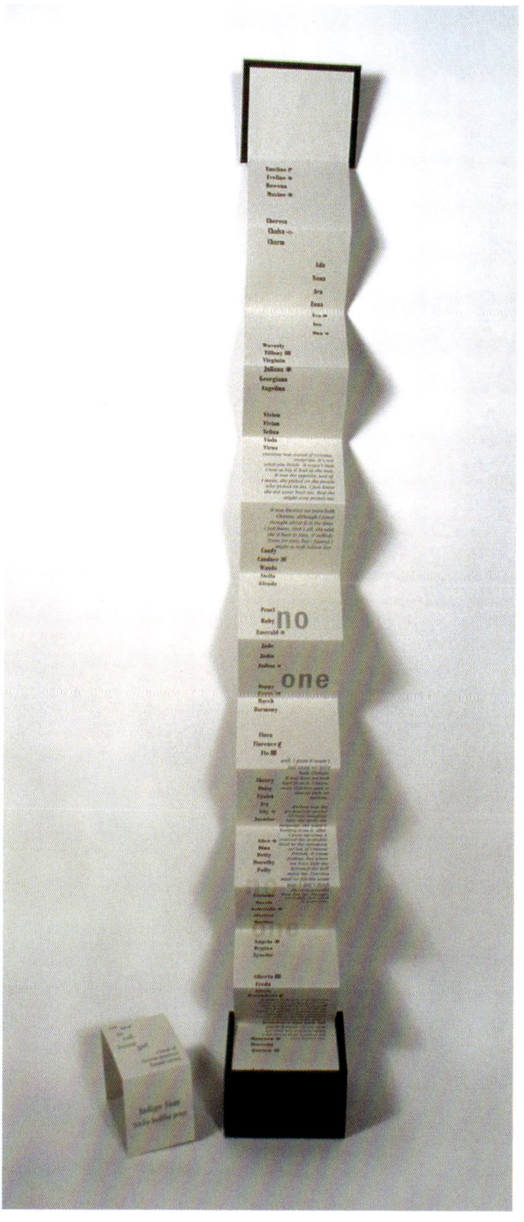

Indigo Som, *No One to Call Home/Girl*, 1995. Handbound letterpress book in box. 2 x 3 x 2⅜ inches closed; height up to 80 inches open. Edition of 37.

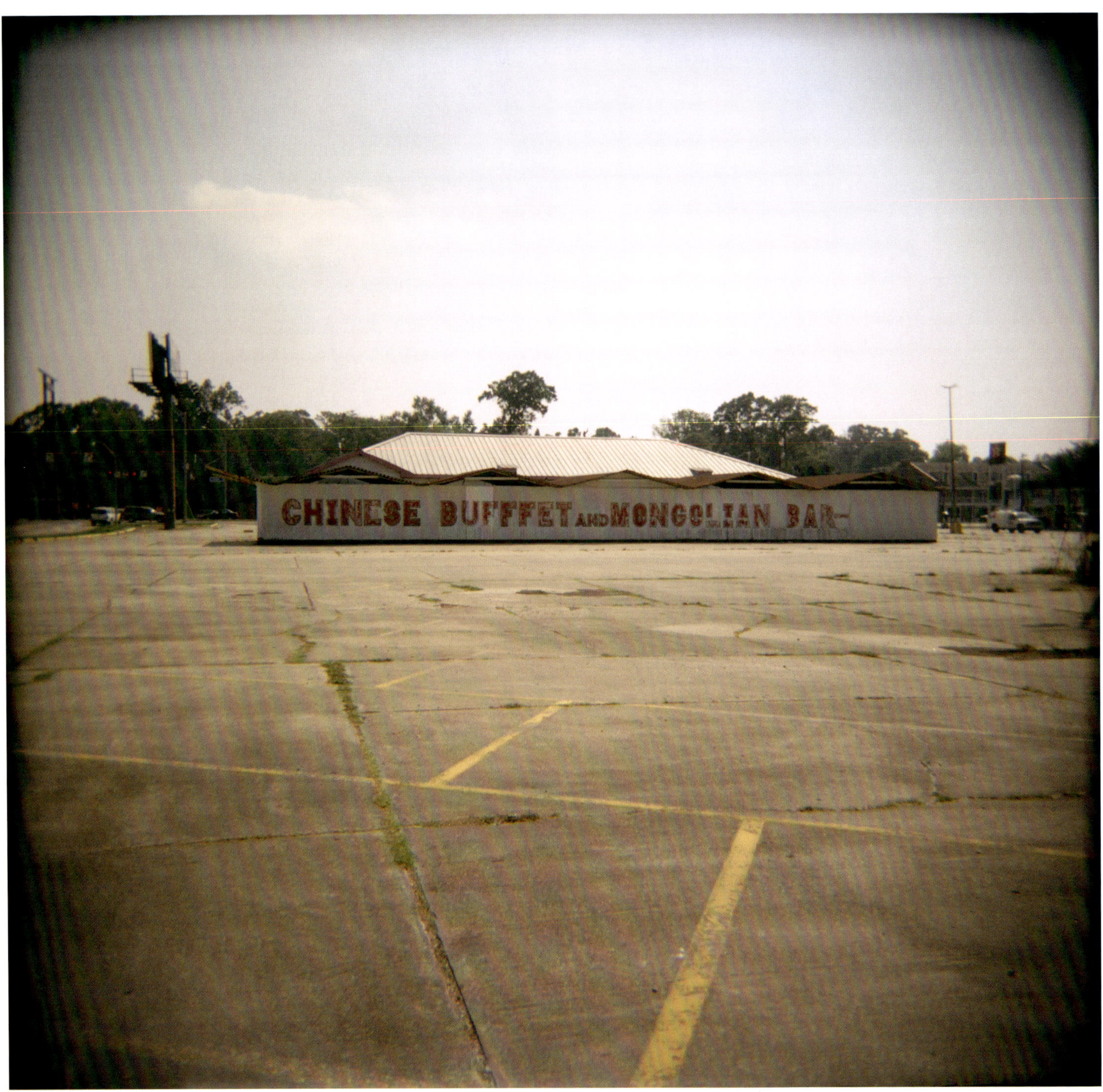

Indigo Som, *Mandarin Seafood & Mongolian BarBQ, Baton Rouge, Louisiana* (from the series *Mostly Mississippi: Chinese Restaurants of the South*), 2004–05. Digital pigment print. 34 x 34 inches.

INDIGO SOM

Born in 1966, San Francisco, California; Lives and works in San Francisco, California

EDUCATION: 1989 Bachelor of Arts, University of California, Berkeley; 1986–87 California College of Arts and Crafts, Oakland, California; 1984–86 Brown University, Providence, Rhode Island; **SOLO EXHIBITIONS:** 2003, "Pastel Diaspora," Ampersand International, San Francisco, California; 2000, "Supply," Sonoma Museum of Visual Art, Santa Rosa, California; 1999, "Introductions," Braunstein/Quay Gallery, San Francisco, California; 1999, "American American," Crucible Steel Gallery at Collectively Explorative Learning Labs (CELLspace), San Francisco, California; **GROUP EXHIBITIONS:** 2004, "Roadside Elixir," Spring Open House, Headlands Center for the Arts, Sausalito, California; 2004, "Ninety from the Nineties: A Decade of Printing," New York Public Library, New York, New York; **GRANTS AND AWARDS:** 2004, Creative Work Fund, Visual Arts Award for collaboration with Chinese Historical Society of America; 2000, Residency Award, Yaddo, Saratoga Springs, New York; 1999, Residency Award, Centrum, Port Townsend, Washington

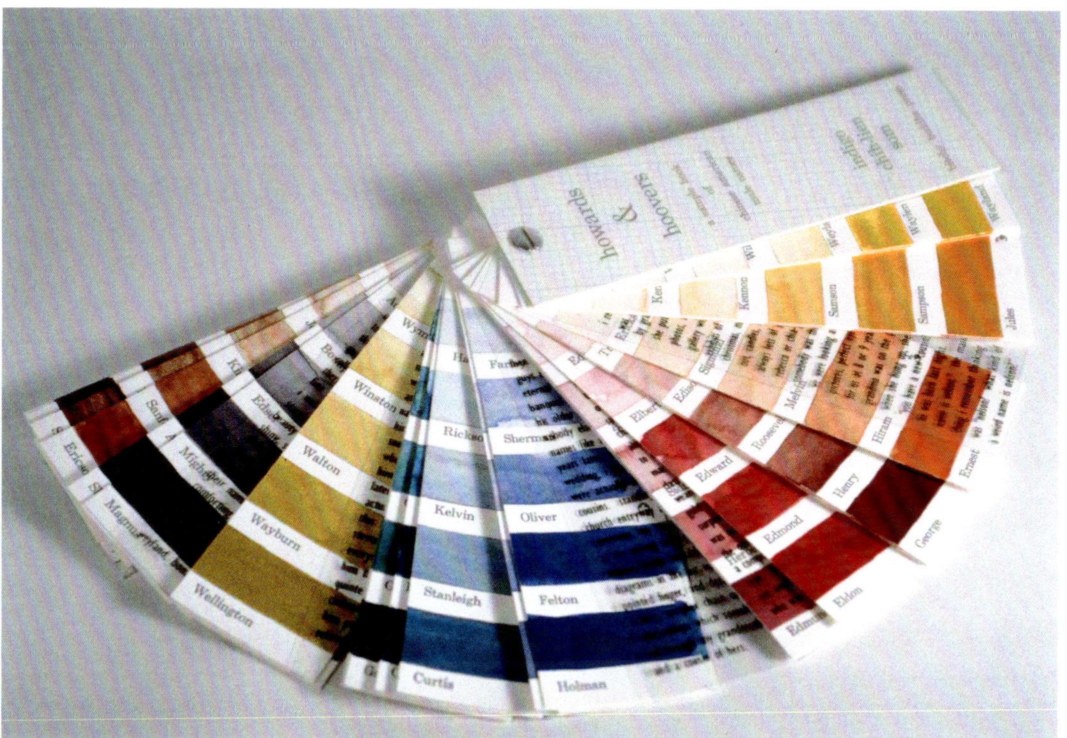

Indigo Som, *Howards & Hoovers: A Sample Book of Chinese American Male Names*, 1994. Letterpress, watercolor, laserprint fan book. 7 x 2 x 1¼ inches. Edition of 9.

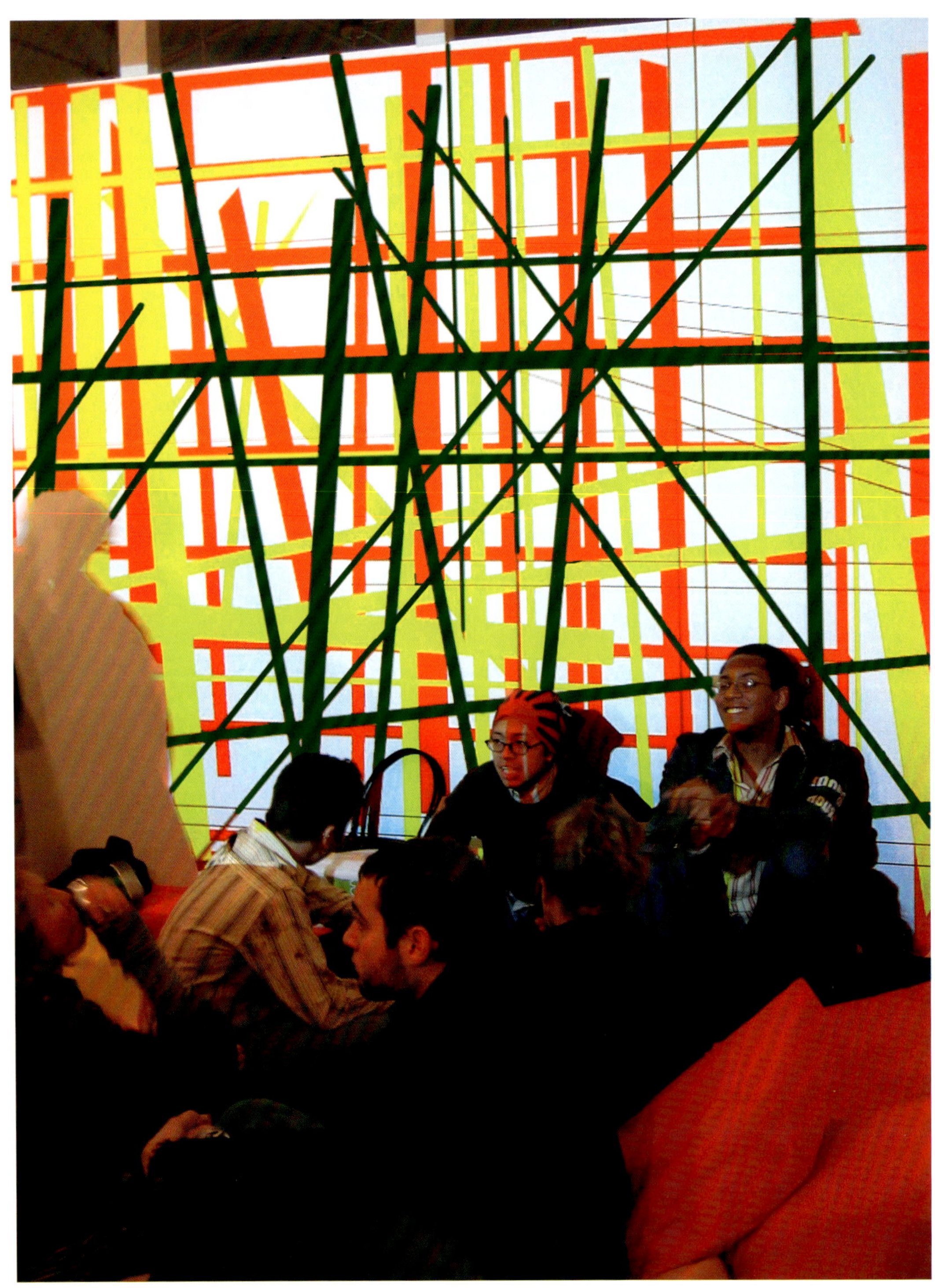

Mika Tajima, *Broken Plaid*, 2003. Foam, fabric, video projection. Dimensions variable. Collection of the artist. Installation view at Rush Arts, New York.

MIKA TAJIMA

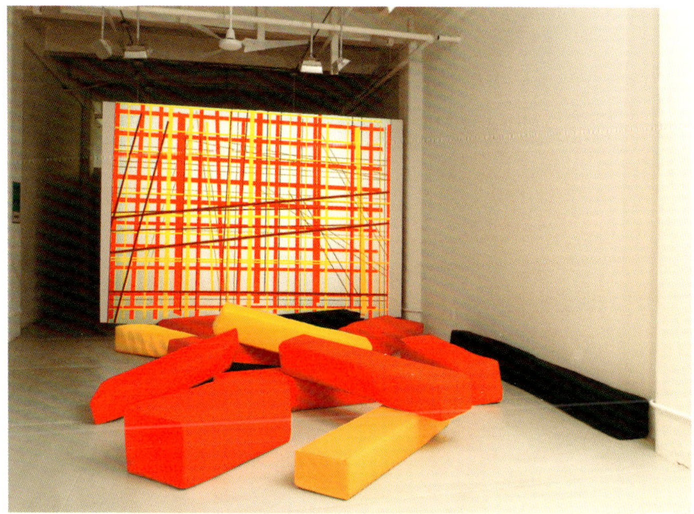

Mika Tajima, *Broken Plaid*, 2003. Foam, fabric, video projection. Dimensions variable. Collection of the artist. Installation view at Rush Arts, New York.

Mika Tajima is interested in the act of destabilizing the original purposes and meanings of objects, images, and art-historical strategies. Her goal: to reveal possibilities within a system of contradictions. In *Extruded Plaid (Suicidal Desires)* (2006), a new work for Asia Society, Tajima begins with a plaid pattern—a familiar unit of design, with its gridded, hatched, and locked form. She strips the pattern to its formal elements and translates the two-dimensional design into a three-dimensional, architectural space. The installation's title refers to "Suicidal Desires," an essay by architectural historian Peter Lang on the work of Superstudio,[1] an Italian avant-garde architectural collective that, in the 1960s and 1970s, challenged the formalist ideals of classic modernism by literally breaking down images and notions of modernist design. Tajima echoes Superstudio's work in her own multifaceted practice.

As in some of her past work, Tajima's installation at Asia Society is also the site of performance. The notion of destabilizing our understanding of installation as a sculptural work of art is amplified, quite literally, by Tajima's decision to perform remixes of pre-recorded samples—which she sees as the audio equivalent of found objects—by Minimalist composers and musicians as an accompaniment to the work. "For me, the addition of music creates a whole sensory environment and an experience through a visual and aural practice," Tajima says.[2] The use of mirrored objects in the installation furthers this sense of reflection, refraction, and repetition—each to be experienced interchangeably as sound, vision, and metaphor.

Tajima draws from the vernacular of American Minimalist and Pop artists of the 1960s and 1970s, leveraging its iconic visual currency and occupying the "empty formalisms they have come to represent," as she says.[3] From the Minimalists, Tajima draws on the now-fetishized geometric formalisms of Sol LeWitt, Donald Judd, Richard Serra, and Agnes Martin. Additionally, she draws upon the Pop sensibilities of Andy Warhol and Claes Oldenburg to inform the graphic, sculptural, and pattern-based components of her installations.

Tajima uses elements of design and architecture in her work to comment on the democratization of the utopian ideas of classic Minimalism and modernism in today's popular culture. Think of the bold lines and elegant silhouettes of mass-market furniture sold at popular outlets like Ikea, which tend to echo the clean geometries of the sculpture—and furniture—created by Judd. The crossover of art and the everyday, for Tajima, is a compelling contradiction—one that points to both Pop and Minimalism's continuous seepage from high culture into low. "In this conflation, the stark oppositional tenets of Minimalism like many other efforts now exist in the complex realm of contradiction. We can't escape from the idea that these two movements mark the ultimate end of the art-historical journey," she says, echoing critic and philosopher Arthur Danto's concept of "the end of art."[4]

Ultimately, however, Tajima would like viewers to draw their own conclusions. "I leave my work open so that there's ambiguity," she explains, "sometimes expectations and intentions don't work out the way we expected and this is what I'm looking for."[5] **RJ**

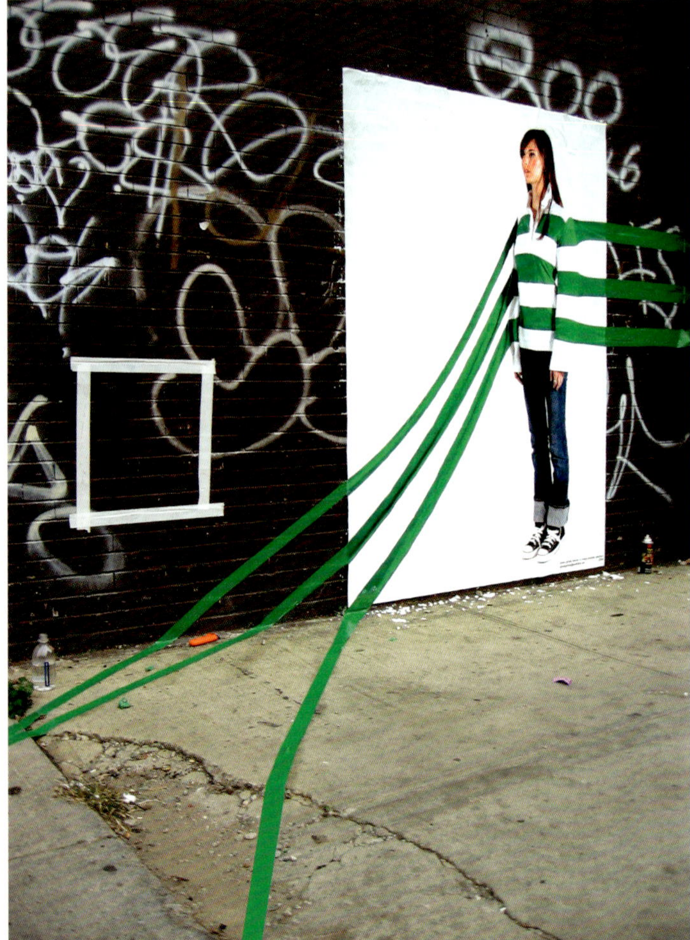

Above: Mika Tajima, *Grass Grows Forever in Every Possible Direction*, 2004. Fabric, photo print, tape, amps, guitars, fluorescent lights, video projection, performance. Dimensions variable. Collection of the artist. Installation view in Bushwick, Brooklyn.

1. Peter Lang and William Menking, *Superstudio: Life Without Objects* (Milan: Skira, 2003).
2. Mika Tajima, conversation with the author, March 5, 2006.
3. Ibid.
4. Ibid.
5. Ibid.

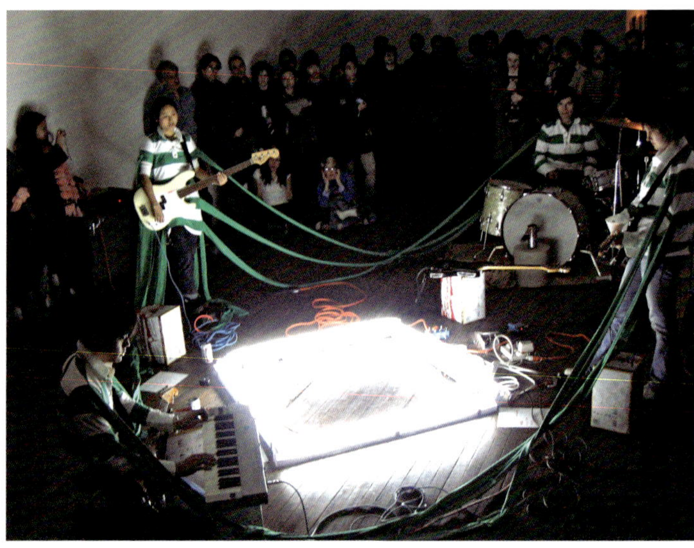

Mika Tajima, *Grass Grows Forever in Every Possible Direction*, 2004. Fabric, photo print, tape, amps, guitars, fluorescent lights, video projection, performance. Dimensions variable. Collection of the artist.

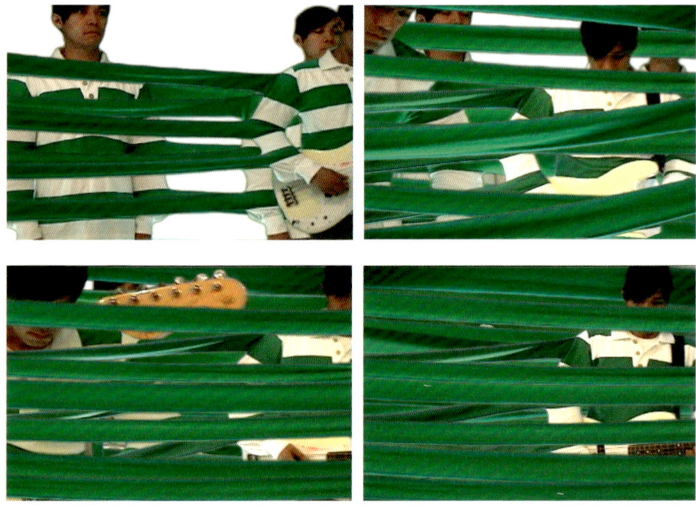

Mika Tajima, *Grass Grows Forever in Every Possible Direction* (video still), 2004. Fabric, photo print, tape, amps, guitars, fluorescent lights, video projection, performance. Dimensions variable. Collection of the artist.

MIKA TAJIMA

Born in 1975, Los Angeles, California; Lives and works in New York, New York **EDUCATION:** 2003, Master of Fine Arts, Columbia University, New York, New York; 1997, Bachelor of Arts, Bryn Mawr College, Pennsylvania; 1997, Post-Graduate Apprentice, The Fabric Workshop and Museum Apprentice Training Program, Philadelphia, Pennsylvania; **EXHIBITIONS AND PERFORMANCES:** 2005, "Interface in Your Face," Swiss Institute - Contemporary Art, New York, New York; 2005, "Videos in Person," Rhode Island School of Design Museum, Providence, Rhode Island; 2005, "Musica Video Musica," Museo Nacional Centro de Arte Reina Sofía, Madrid, Spain; 2005, "Cosmic Microwave Background or the Problem with Interstellar Communication Breakdown," New Humans with Matt Suib, PS1 Contemporary Art Center, Long Island City, New York; 2005, "Grass Grows Forever in Every Possible Direction," Walker Art Center, Minneapolis, Minnesota; 2004, "Solo Project," United Bamboo Daikanyama, Tokyo, Japan; 2004, "I'd Rather Jack," S1 Artspace, Sheffield, England; 2003, "New Humans Collective," Sculpture-Center, Long Island City, New York; 2003, "25 Hrs," The Video Art Foundation, Barcelona, Spain; 2002, "Get Out," Paley Gallery at Moore College of Art, Philadelphia, Pennsylvania; 2000, "Foreign Body," White Columns, New York, New York; **AWARDS:** 2004, Independent Project Grant, Artists Space, New York, New York; 2002, World Studio Foundation Scholarship, New York, New York

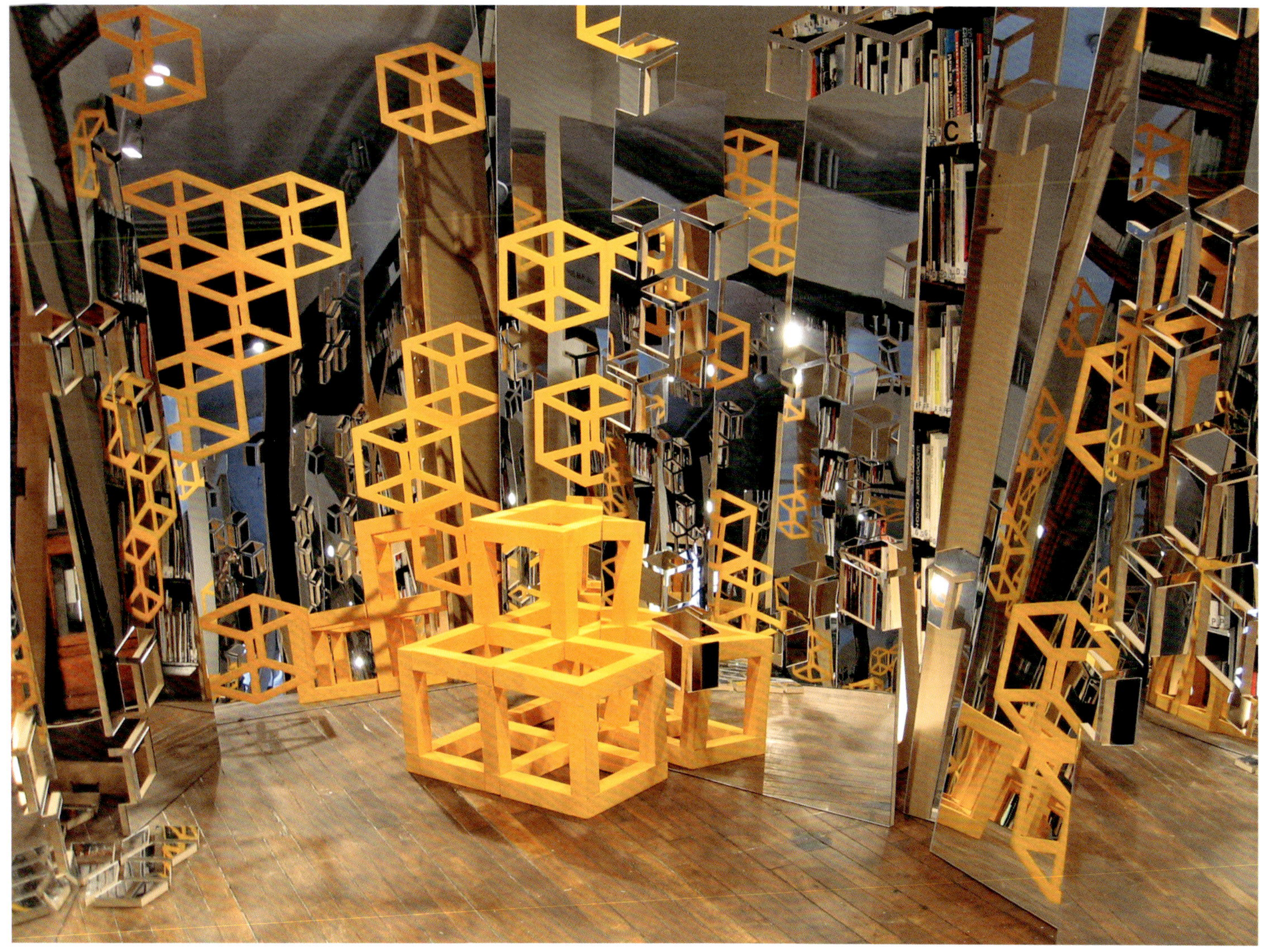

Mika Tajima, *Echoplex*, 2005. CNC-cut mirror plexiglass, MDF, silkscreen, lights, wood, 5.1 sound. Dimensions variable. Collection of Galleri S.E. (Sjur Nedreaas), Norway. Installation view at Swiss Institute - Contemporary Art, New York.

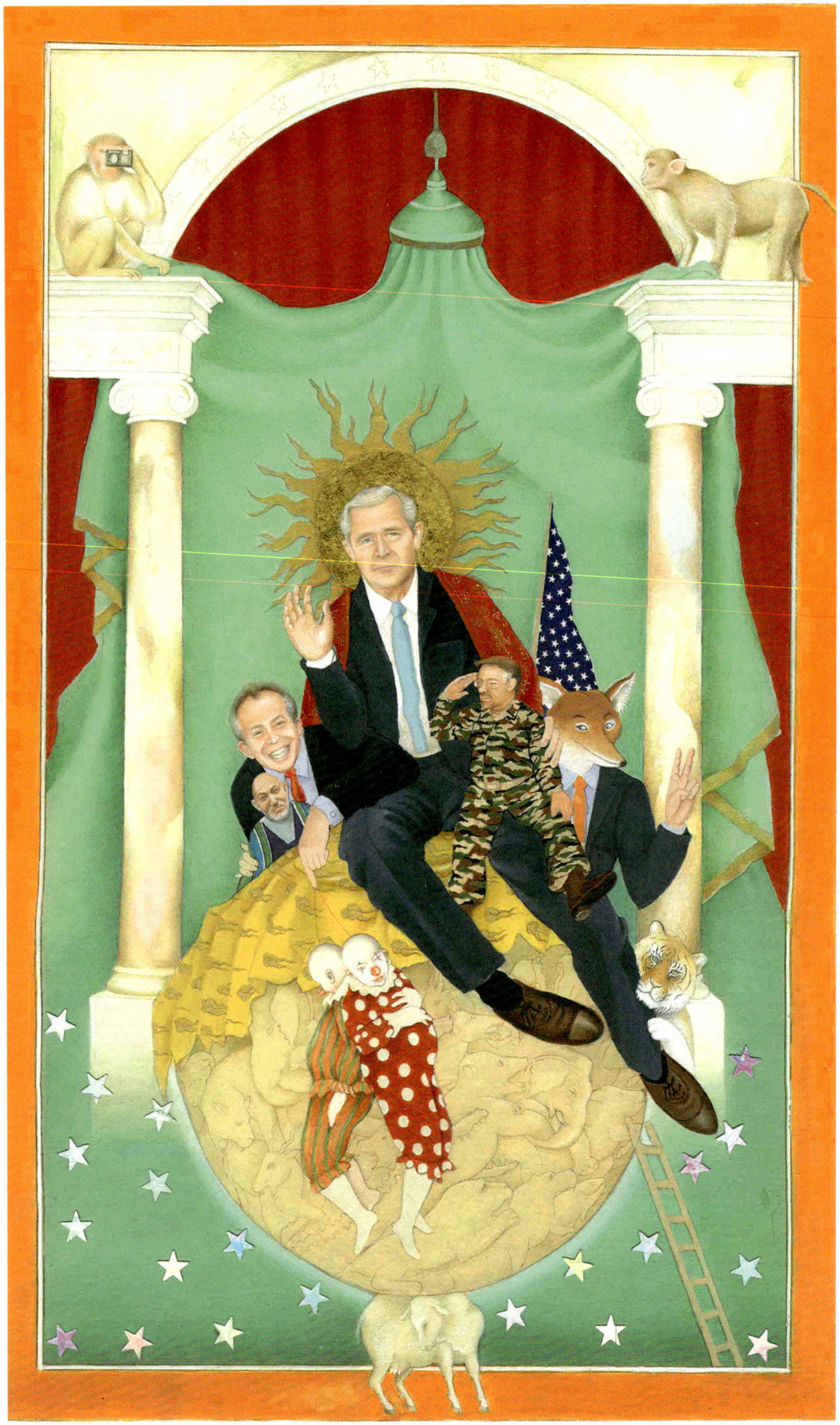

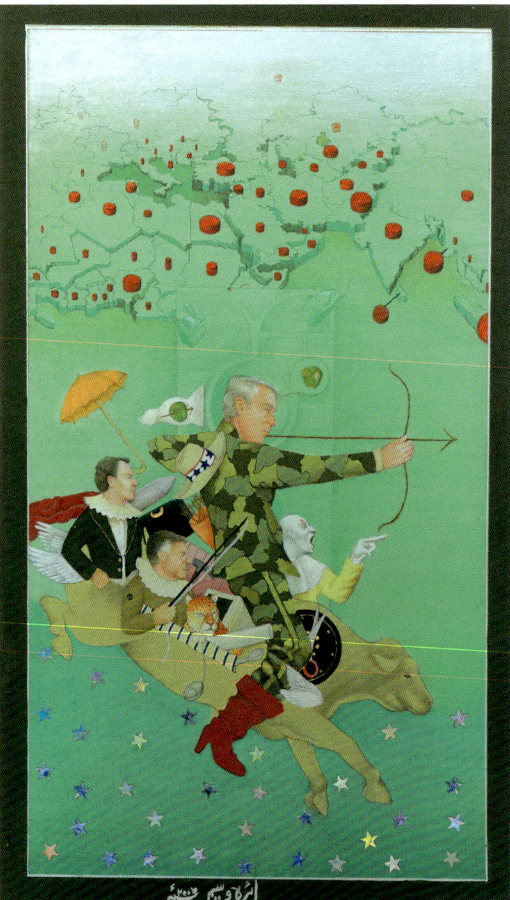

Saira Wasim, *Mission Accomplished*, 2004. Gouache, ink, and wasli. 11¾ x 6½ inches.

Saira Wasim, *New World Order*, 2006. Gouache and gold on wasli paper. 6¼ x 10¼ inches. Private Collection.

SAIRA WASIM

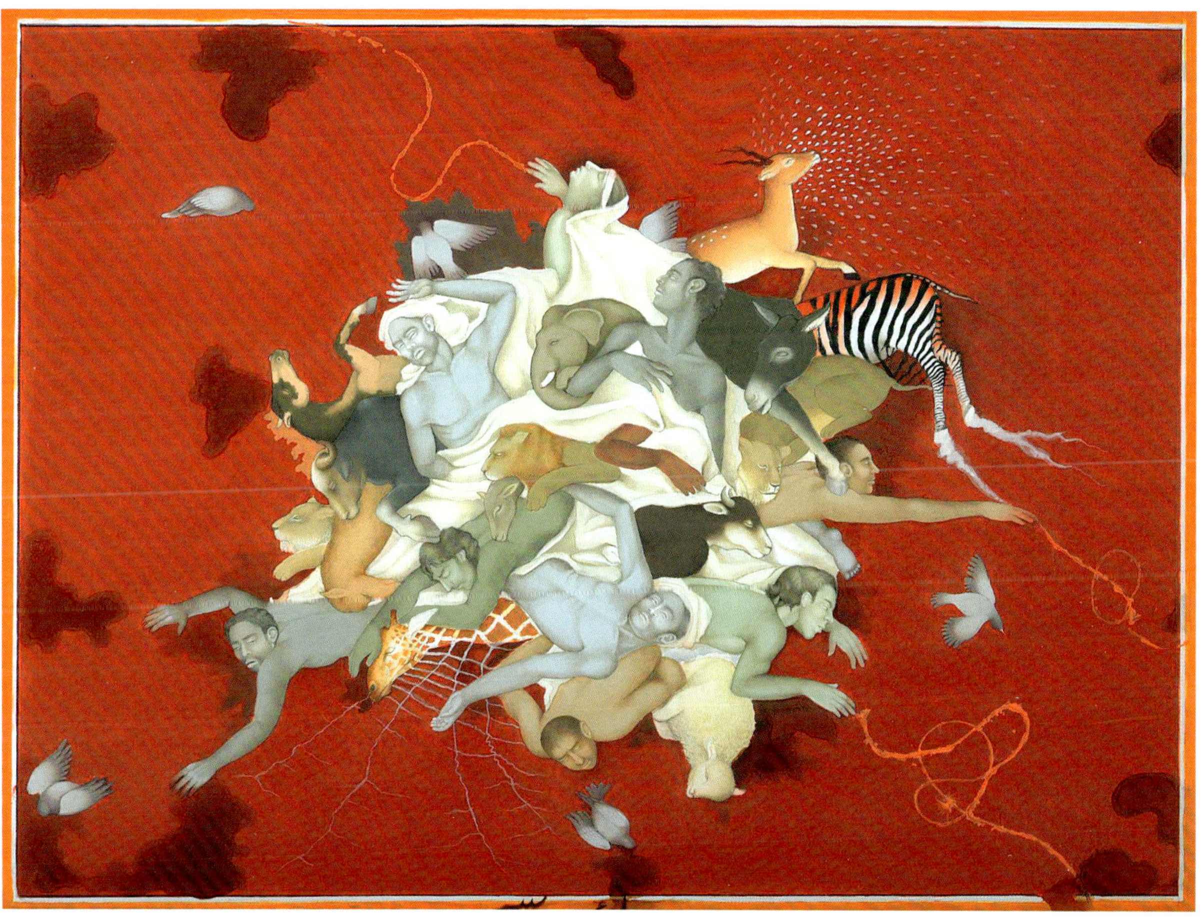

Saira Wasim, *Lamentation of Innocence, Genocide*, 2005. Gouache on illustration board. 11¾ x 7 inches. Collection of Queensland Art Gallery and Museum, Australia.

Saira Wasim is a new American. Born in Pakistan, she moved to the United States in 2003. At that time, she participated in "The American Effect," an exhibition at the Whitney Museum of American Art. Her paintings humorously pictured the serious relationship between the United States and Pakistan. Since then, the artist has light-heartedly yet poignantly offered both insider and outsider perspectives to the consequences of American foreign policy around the world.

Her latest works present a roster of international leaders including Tony Blair and Hamid Karzai, in addition to George Bush and Pervez Musharraf who have made previous appearances. Their portraits are precisely drawn, making these figures easily recognizable. Yet they do not appear in a context that would be familiar to most. Instead the images reveal how Wasim pictures these leaders and their actions. Bush looks like a holy being—the direct messenger of God that he believes himself to be. Meanwhile, Musharraf

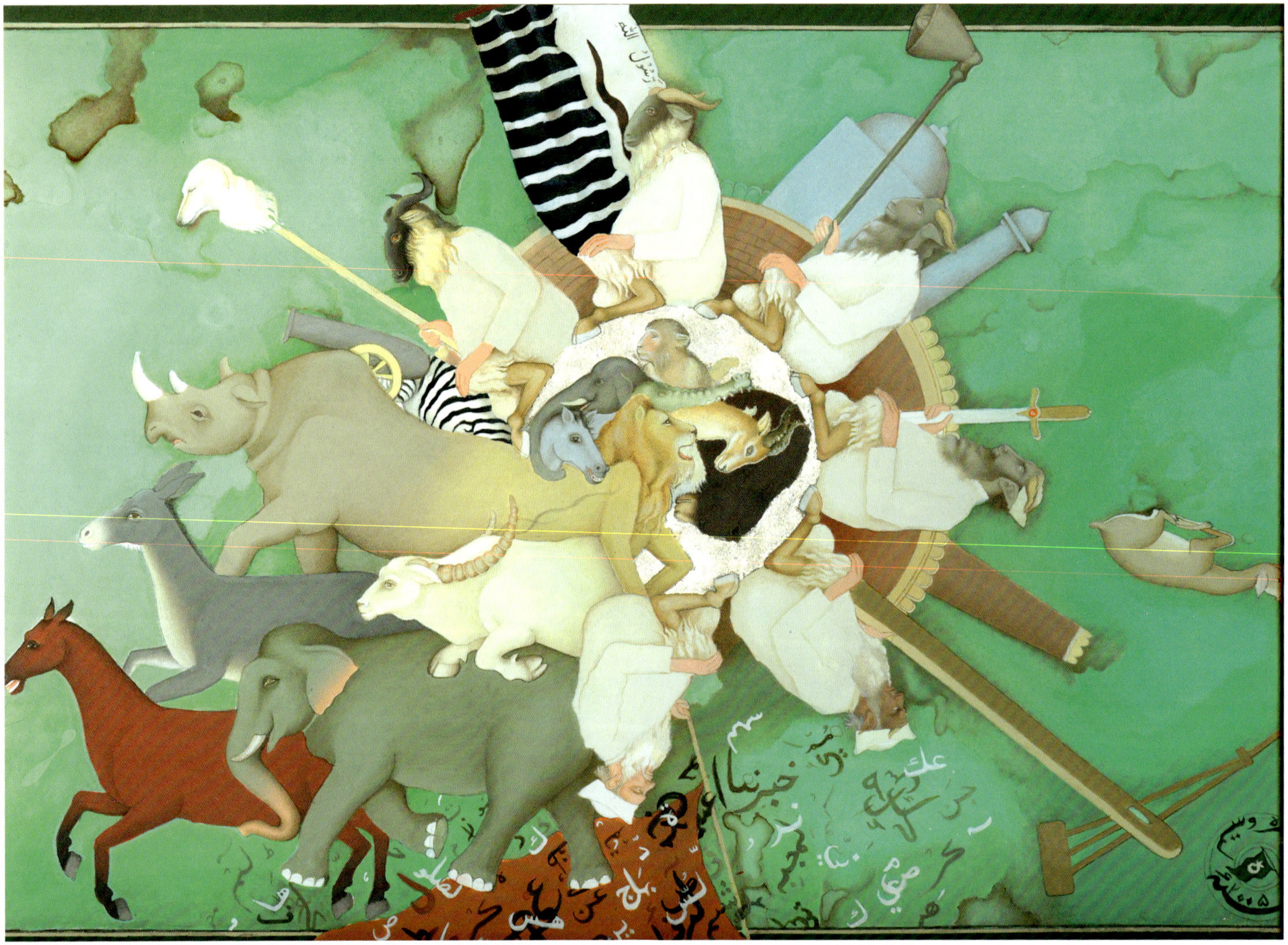

Saira Wasim, *Holy Matrix*, 2005. Gouache, tea wash, and silver leaf on illustration board. 13 x 9½ inches. Collection of Queensland Art Gallery and Museum, Australia.

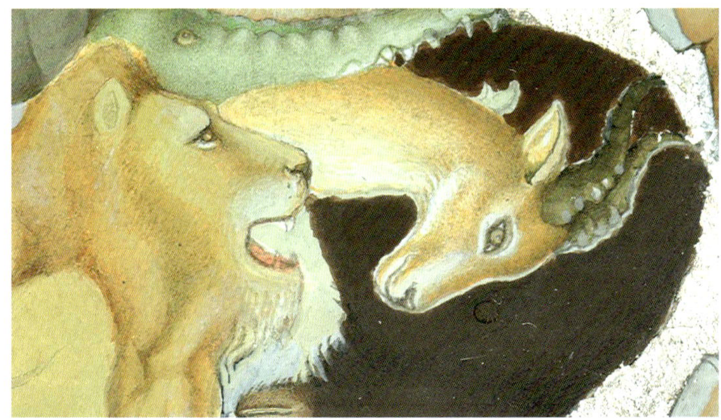

Saira Wasim, *Holy Matrix* (detail).

appears childlike in the lap of the U.S. president. He is a toy with body parts that the owner can twist and turn.

These works are about Wasim's observations. In fact she has always presented her views on the socio-political climate wherever she may be. Exhibiting sensitivity to her surroundings, the artist keys into these circumstances and explores them symbolically in her art. In her earlier work, for example, flowers symbolized women—for her the beautiful and delicate parts of nature. Using flowers, she metaphorically described a serious offense committed against women in Pakistan—murders in the name of honor. The resulting imagery is both exquisite and disturbing—water lilies that turn into bloody veils.

All of this is expressed in miniature paintings—small-scale works on handmade paper colored with water-based paint. The tiny, yet fully articulated images beg viewers to take a closer look at all that is going on in the world she has depicted. From famous personae to familiar flowers, everything is carefully rendered in her dazzling works. She learned this technique in her native Pakistan at the National College of Arts—the oldest, most prestigious art school in the country.

The miniature painting department at the college has steadily produced graduates in the field since it became a major course offering in 1985. With a foundation in the basics of the technique, Wasim and several other artists have taken to experimenting with miniature painting in the manner of artists working for emperors of the Mughal dynasty (1526–1857). Instead of appropriating elements from European prints as her predecessors did, Wasim uses images shown in mass media today.

These pictures, as seen on the nightly news, are ingrained into the American psyche. For example, the artist used the potent sight of Saddam Hussein's statue being pulled down by Iraqi civilians and U.S. troops after the initial American victory in 2003. In her painting, this action is quickly followed by the raising of another icon—a statue with George Bush's face on the Roman Emperor Augustus's body. Like the Roman rulers, American presidents use propaganda to their advantage. Saira Wasim sees beyond these appearances and exposes what she thinks is really going on. **AA**

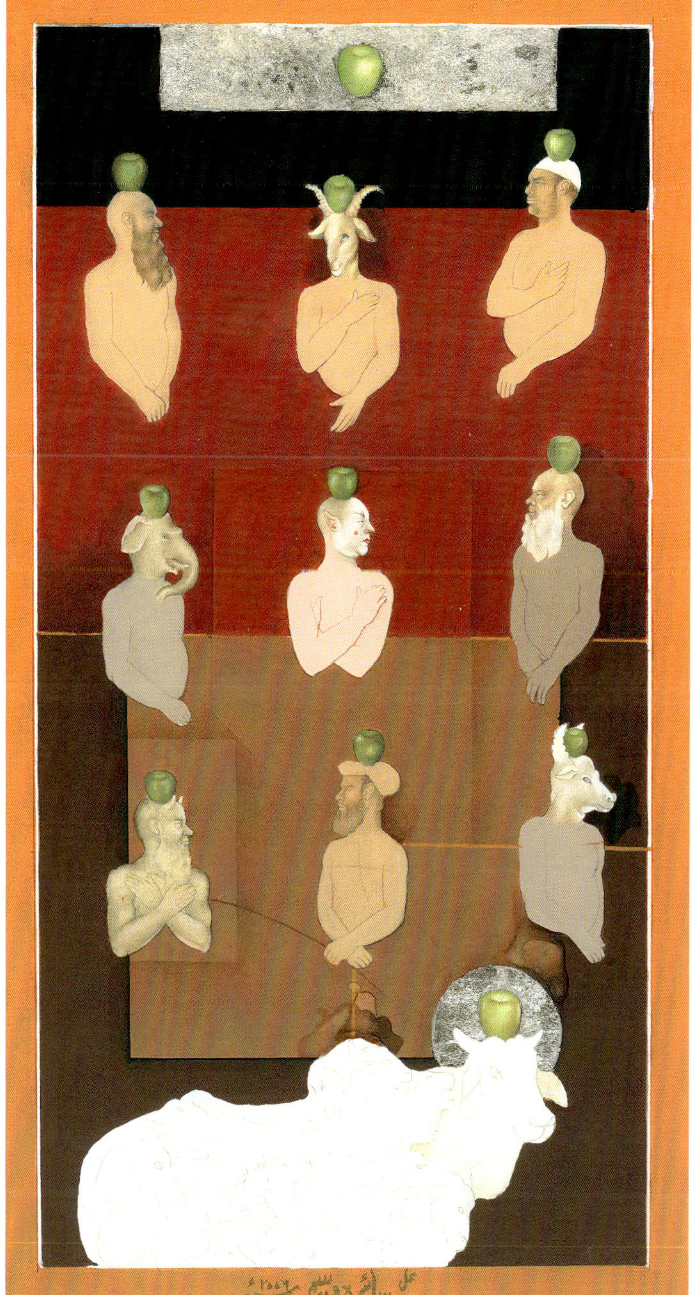

Saira Wasim, *Few Bad Apples*, 2004. Gouache, ink, and silver leaf on wasli. 11¾ x 6½ inches.

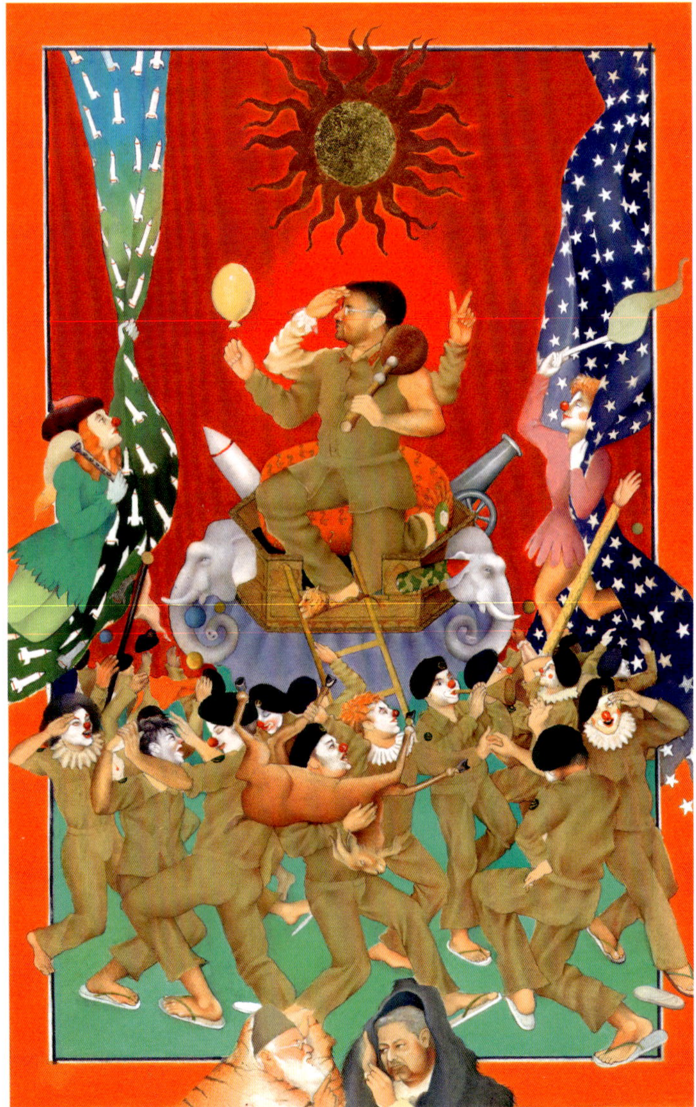

Saira Wasim, *Buzkashi*, 2004. Gouache on wasli. 10 x 6½ inches. Collection of Smith College Museum, Massachusetts.

SAIRA WASIM

Born in 1975, Lahore, Pakistan; Lives and works in Chicago, Illinois **EDUCATION:** 1999, Bachelor of Fine Arts, National College of Arts Lahore, Pakistan ; **SOLO EXHIBITION:** 2005, "Political Carousel: Miniature Paintings," Alma Thomas Fine Arts Center, Southwestern University, Georgetown, Texas; **GROUP EXHIBITIONS:** 2005, "Karkhana: A Contemporary Collaboration," Aldrich Contemporary Art Museum, Ridgefield, Connecticut; 2003, "The American Effect," Whitney Museum of American Art, New York, New York; 2003, "Playing with a Loaded Gun," Apex Art, New York, New York; 2002, "Exotic Bodies," Harris Museum and Art Gallery, Preston, England; 2001, "Maneuvering Miniatures," India International Centre, New Delhi and Sakshi Gallery, Mumbai, India; **RESIDENCY:** 2003, Vermont Studio Center, Johnson, Vermont

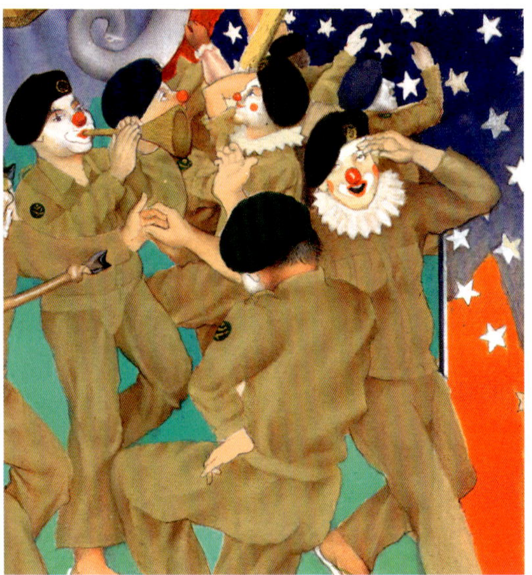

Saira Wasim, *Buzkashi* (detail).

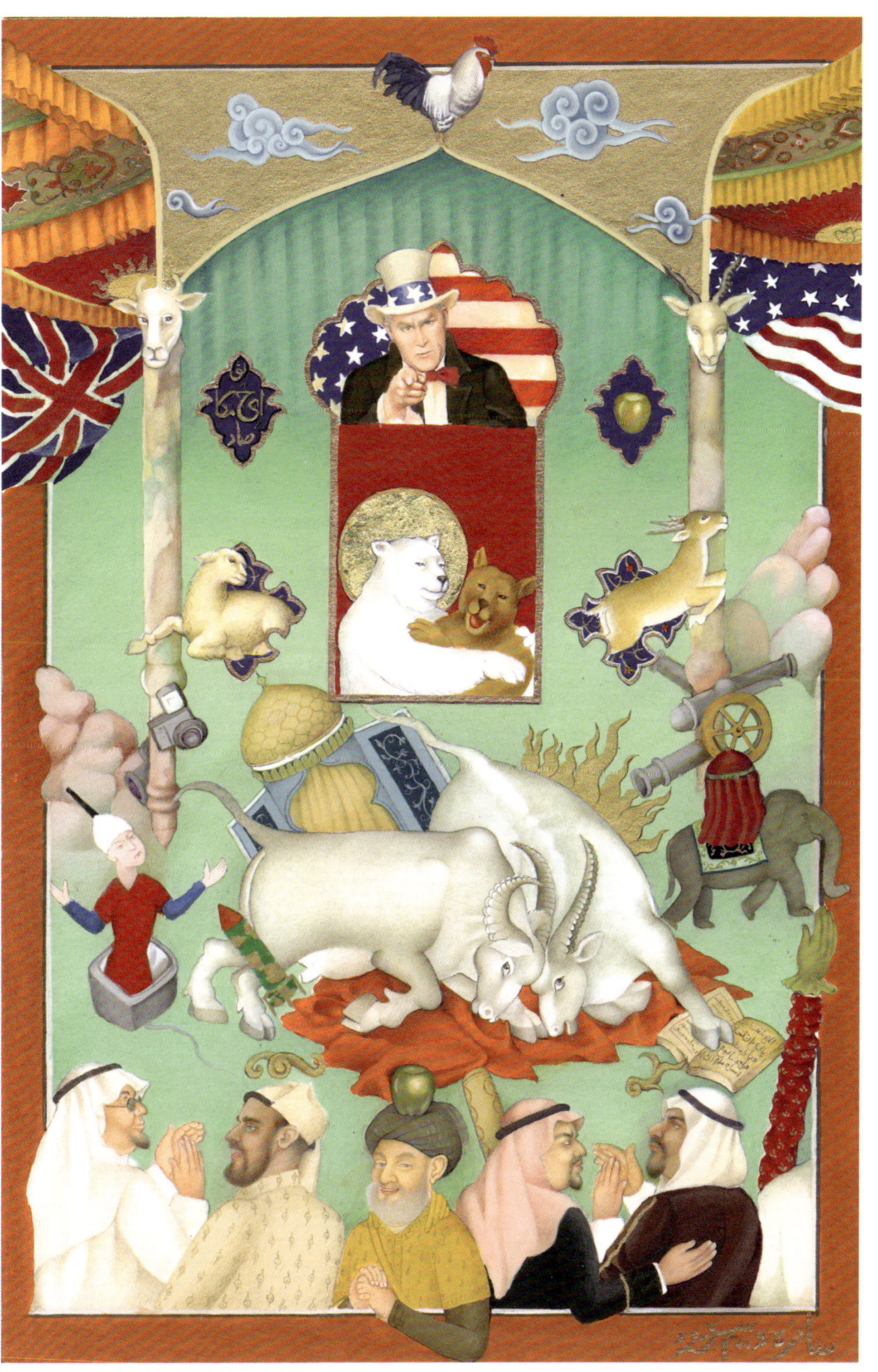

Saira Wasim, *The Battle for Hearts and Minds*, 2004. Gouache and gold on wasli. 9½ x 6¼ inches. Collection of Mr. and Mrs. Indar Pasricha, London.

SELECT BIBLIOGRAPHY

Asia/America: Identities in Contemporary Asian American Art. New York: The Asia Society Galleries and New Press, 1994.

Asian Traditions/Modern Expressions: Asian American Artists and Abstraction 1945–1970. Edited by Jeffrey Wechsler. New York: Harry N. Abrams, 1997.

Chuh, Kandice. *Imagine Otherwise: On Asian Americanist Critique.* Durham, NC: Duke UP, 2003.

Kim, Elaine H., Margo Machida, and Sharon Mizota. *Fresh Talk, Daring Gazes: Conversations on Asian American Art.* With a foreword by Lisa Lowe. Berkeley: University of California Press, 2003.

Liu, Eric. *The Accidental Asian: Notes of a Native Speaker.* New York: Vintage Books, 1999.

Picturing Asia America: Communities, Culture, Difference. Houston, TX: Houston Center for Photography, 1994.

Poon, Irene. *Leading the Way: Asian American Artists of the Older Generation.* With a foreword by Nanying Stella Wong and historical essay by Lorraine Dong. Wenham, MA: Gordon College, 2001.

Shifting Perceptions: Contemporary L.A. Visions. Pasadena, CA: Pacific Asia Museum, 2000.

Site of Asia, Site of Body: Contemporary Asian Women Artists. New York: Taipei Gallery, 1998.

They Painted From Their Hearts: Pioneer Asian American Artists. Edited by Mayumi Tsutakawa. Seattle, WA: University of Washington Press, 1994.

Uncommon Traits: Re/Locating Asia, Parts I–III. Buffalo, NY: CEPA Gallery, 1997–98 (Part I. September 13–October 31, 1997; Part II. December 6, 1997–January 23, 1998; Part III. February 14–March 28, 1998).

With New Eyes: Toward an Asian American Art History in the West. San Francisco: San Francisco State University, 1995.

Yang, Alice. *Why Asia?: Contemporary Asian and Asian American Art.* New York: New York UP, 1998.

Yellow Light: The Flowering of Asian American Arts. Edited by Amy Ling. Philadelphia: Temple UP, 1999.

Zia, Helen. *Asian American Dreams: The Emergence of an American People.* New York: Farrar, Straus and Giroux, 2000.

PHOTOGRAPHY CREDITS

Frontispiece, pp. 62–65: photograph by Robert Wedemeyer, courtesy of Karyn Lovegrove Gallery, New York; fig. 1: courtesy of Saichi Kawahara and the UCLA Asian American Library, Special Collections; fig. 2: courtesy of Filmakers Library, New York; fig. 3: courtesy of Asia Society, New York; fig. 4: courtesy of Allan deSouza and Talwar Gallery, New York; fig. 5: courtesy of Paul Pfeiffer and The Project, New York; fig. 6: photograph by Tom Finkelpearl, courtesy of Tom Finkelpearl; fig. 7: courtesy of Carol Sun; figs. 8, 9: photograph by Nina Kuo, courtesy of Nina Kuo; fig. 10, pp. 90–95: photograph by Laurel Nakadate, courtesy of Danziger Projects, New York; fig. 11, pp. 55–56: photograph by Patty Chang and David Kelley, courtesy of the artist and Kustera Tilton Gallery, New York; figs. 12, 13: photograph by Leah Tepper-Byrne; fig. 14, pp. 110, 113–115: photograph by Indigo Som, courtesy of the artist; figs. 15, 16: photograph by Frank Oudeman, courtesy of Sarah Sze and Marianne Boesky Gallery, New York; fig. 17: courtesy of Max Protetch Gallery, New York; fig. 18: photograph by Bari Ziperstein, courtesy of Rosamund Felsen Gallery, Santa Monica, California; fig. 19, pp. 96–99: photograph by Douglas M. Parker, courtesy of Rosamund Felsen Gallery, Santa Monica, California; fig. 20: courtesy of Murray Guy, New York; fig. 21: photograph by Anna Sew Hoy, courtesy of the artist; pp. 44–45: photograph by Pablo Mason, courtesy of Heather Marx Gallery, San Francisco; pp. 46–47: photograph by John White, courtesy of Heather Marx Gallery, San Francisco; pp. 48–49: photograph by Josh White, courtesy of the artist and Taxter & Spengemann, New York; pp. 50 (top), 51–53: photograph by Nancy de Holl, courtesy of the artist and Taxter & Spengemann, New York; p. 50 (bottom left, bottom right): courtesy of the artist and Taxter & Spengemann, New York; p. 54: courtesy of the artist and Kustera Tilton Gallery, New York; p. 57: courtesy of Art in General and Kustera Tilton Gallery, New York, © Patty Chang; pp. 58–61: photograph by Binh Danh, courtesy of the artist and Haines Gallery, San Francisco; pp. 66 (left), 67: photograph by Jay Jones, courtesy of the artist; p. 66 (top right, bottom right): photograph by Scott Chernis, courtesy of the artist; pp. 68–69: photograph by Ala Ebtekar, courtesy of the artist; pp. 70–71, 72 (left, bottom right), 73–75: photograph by Chitra Ganesh, courtesy of the artist; p. 72 (top right): photograph by Ka-Man Tse, courtesy of the artist; pp. 76–78: photograph by The Project, courtesy of the artist and The Project, New York; p. 79: photograph by SJK, courtesy of The Project, New York; pp. 80–83: photograph by Geraldine Lau, courtesy of the artist; pp. 84–85: photograph by Bart Kasden, courtesy of Curator's Office, D.C.; pp. 86 (top left), 87 (top, bottom left), 88: photograph by Jiha Moon, courtesy of the artist; pp. 86 (bottom left), 87 (bottom right): photograph by Jiha Moon, courtesy of Curator's Office, D.C.; p. 89: photograph by Troy Bennett, courtesy of Curator's Office, D.C.; pp. 100–103: photograph by Anna Sew Hoy, courtesy of the artist; pp. 104–105, 109: photograph by Masahiro Noguchi, courtesy of the artist and Frederieke Taylor Gallery, New York; p. 106: courtesy of the artist and Frederieke Taylor Gallery, New York; p. 107: photograph by Ford Bailey, courtesy of the artist and Frederieke Taylor Gallery, New York; p. 108: photograph by Steven Tucker, courtesy of the artist and Frederieke Taylor Gallery, New York; pp. 111, 112 (bottom right): photograph by Sibila Savage, courtesy of the artist; p. 112 (top, bottom left): photograph by Frank Ross, courtesy of the artist; pp. 116, 118 (left, bottom right): photograph by Mika Tajima, courtesy of the artist; p. 117: photograph by Rush Arts, New York, courtesy of the artist; p. 118 (top right): photograph courtesy of Swiss Institute - Contemporary Art, New York; p. 119: photograph by Mika Tajima, courtesy of Galleri S.E. and Swiss Institute - Contemporary Art, New York; pp. 120–125: photograph by Haroon Chaudhry, courtesy of the artist